HEROIN
Myths and reality

JARA KRIVANEK

Sydney
ALLEN & UNWIN
Wellington London Boston

© J. Krivanek 1988

This book is copyright under the Berne Convention. No reproduction without permission. All rights reserved.

First published in 1988
Allen & Unwin Australia Pty Ltd
An Unwin Hyman company
8 Napier Street, North Sydney, NSW 2060 Australia

Allen & Unwin New Zealand Limited
60 Cambridge Terrace, Wellington, New Zealand

Unwin Hyman Limited
37–39 Queen Elizabeth Street, London SE1 2QB England

Allen & Unwin Inc.
8 Winchester Place, Winchester, Mass 01890 USA

National Library of Australia
Cataloguing-in-Publication entry:

Krivanek, Jara A.
  Heroin, myths and reality.

  Bibliography.
  Includes index.
  ISBN 0 04 302006 2.

  1. Heroin habit. 2. Heroin habit — Treatment.
  3. Heroin. 4. Narcotics, Control of. I. Title.

362.2'93

Library of Congress Catalog Card Number: 87-25264

Quotation on p. vii from *The Ramayana*
A. Menen (ed.) Chas. Scribner's Sons, 1954

Set in 10/11pt Plantin, Linotron 202 by Setrite Typesetters Ltd, Hong Kong
Produced by SRM Production Services Sdn Bhd, Malaysia.

Contents

Preface *vii*

1 Images of heroin *1*
    1984—that was the year when ... *2*
    Heroin and the media *25*

2 Heroin in history: a tale of two countries *30*
    Opiates in Britain *33*
    Opiates in America *51*

3 Heroin the drug *68*
    The positive side: uses of heroin *69*
    Mechanisms of action *76*
    Inherent problems: tolerance and physical dependence *81*
    The negative side: harm and the question of recognition *93*

4 Heroin the commodity *103*
    The international heroin market *105*
    The domestic market *114*

5 Controlling the heroin market *130*
    International heroin controls *135*
    Domestic heroin controls *138*

6 How much heroin? *149*
    'Known' statistics and doing the best we can *152*
    'Declared' statistics and vested interests *168*

7 Heroin users and heroin addicts *180*
    Mythology of drug use *181*
    Why heroin? *191*
    Making addicts out of users *195*

8 The war on heroin: what are our chances? *216*
    Managing the addict *217*
    Managing the drug *222*
    Managing the system *236*

References *248*

Index *257*

For W. E. F.
who understands word processors,
and without whom Chapter 3
might have looked quite different

Preface

The best way to avoid confusion in thinking about the ways of human beings is to remember that the number of ideas that have really moved mankind is very small and most of this small number of ideas is very simple. The difficulty is that you and I have room in our heads for only one or two of these simple ideas at the same time.

The Ramayana, pp. 13−14

That, unfortunately, puts it in a nutshell, and the world moved at a more decorous pace when those words were written. Today, while individual bits of heroin lore may be simple enough, the totality of relevant information is overwhelming. It is indeed impossible to keep all this together in individual heads, but that is a very different matter from behaving as if what is in individual heads, however eminent, is the whole story. And we do behave in this way. We proceed as if heroin use was a moral, or medical, or legal, or economic, or any one of a number of other problems, and within each of these areas particular moral medical, legal and other positions have passionate and uncompromising adherents. All of these positions are probably partly valid; equally, all probably contain fundamental errors.

The above is by way of explaining that no one will be pleased with this book. All experts will find their particular fields inadequately represented. The merely inquiring will find the endless exploration of intellectual positions tiresome. Those personally involved with heroin use—the users, their families, friends, therapists and adversaries—will find the practical information given insufficient. And everyone will doubtless be irritated by the failure to provide simple, final solutions. There is something objectionable for everyone.

I can only add that I feel the same frustration. At the same time, looking back over the past few years, I find that my own position on a number of drug-related issues has changed, sometimes dramatically. There is no reason to believe that this process will stop. One needs to remind oneself constantly that the way an issue is perceived describes only the immediate state of one's knowledge, not some ultimate truth about things or persons. So I offer this discussion not as truth, or even as a 'modest proposal', but rather as the way I see things now, and as a stimulus for further thought.

Jara Krivanek
Sydney, 1987

1
Images of heroin

There has been no conspiracy of silence. If anything, there has been far too much shooting from the lip. Everyone is so busy talking that no-one is listening and thinking. A little more silence would be most welcome.
Matthew Goode, 1985, p. 223

Florid reporting, pointing out the evils of drugs in the liveliest fashion, is justified by popular commentators on the grounds that it acts as a deterrent. But it is likely that such a picture acts instead as an attraction to just the unbalanced people who are likely to become drug dependent ... Everyone's interests would be better served by a more sober and rational attitude. The drug addict's presentation of himself as an infernal circus is part of his malady; we should know better than to collaborate with him.
Peter Laurie, 1971, p. 64

Early in 1985, Matthew Goode spoke at a conference entitled 'Drugs and Alcohol—a Conspiracy of Silence'. He expressed his 'utter amazement' that there had been any such conspiracy.

> There has hardly been a day in at least the last ten years when the public has not been subjected to the high profile of drug and alcohol issues in Australian society. We have had the Sackville Royal Commission, the Woodward Royal Commission, the Williams Royal Commission, the Costigan Royal Commision, we have had sensational accusations that the South Australian Police have been involved in illicit drug trade, ... we have had a Senate Standing Committee Report, we have had a New South Wales joint parliamentary inquiry, we have had an endless series of seminars on various issues, we have had the investigative journalism of Mr Bottom, we have had ever increasingly harsh laws with ever increasing penalties, we now have a Drug Summit, or more properly a national campaign against drug abuse ...
> There was no paucity of publicity ... no conspiracy of silence. And what was the result? People got upset about something they did not understand ... And as a result, there is a very fair chance

that legislation will result which will create different and probably worse problems. (1985, p. 222)

Goode was addressing a largely professional audience. For the general public, information about drug-related issues comes mainly from media sources. The average person, therefore, tends to think about drug 'problems' in the language the press uses, and the words and images of the media professionals inevitably become accepted as common sense about drugs and drug users. The Australian Press Council and the Australian Journalists' Association state clearly that news must be reported factually, objectively and accurately. But is it? Does the press provide comprehensive and accurate information about drug use, or are these issues presented in ways that mislead, mystify and generally perpetuate ignorance?

To help decide the issue, the reader is invited to scan excerpts from a year's heroin-related happenings, seen through the eyes of metropolitan Sydney's major daily newspapers. The year 1984 was chosen primarily because formal analyses of reporting trends are available for this period. In general, the newspapers had a lot to say about drugs in 1984. According to *Connexions* (1985), a total of 2 468 press items and 702 television items on drugs were presented to the Sydney public—an average of seven news reports and two televised drug stories each day. Not all dealt with heroin, but without a doubt in 1984 heroin was *the* illicit drug.

1984—that was the year when ...

On 12 January, customs officers at Sydney Airport seized a large shipment of heroin on a flight from Thailand. As one of those who broke the news on 3 February, the *Daily Mirror* had this to say:

POLICE STAKE-OUT ON RICHEST HEROIN HAUL

The drug seized has been identified by police as Grade A Number 4 heroin, the purest and most valuable form of the drug known. Conservative estimates have put the street value of the 23 kg cache at around $24 million but one police officer involved in the operation said it could be worth well in excess of $100 million.

'It's the highest grade uncut heroin ever seized in Australia and virtually impossible to value', he said.

In March, the *Sydney Morning Herald* reported that experts could offer little hope for the drug trade battle:

Dr Grant Wardlaw of the Australian Institute of Criminology [said] 'It seems that the first fact we have to face is that drug enforcement is in a mess ... Drug squads are increasing in size and resources. More and more money, time and expertise is being poured into drug enforcement ... Yet, even with such successes, with such resources, and with increased police powers, the evidence is overwhelming that a law enforcement approach to drug use control has not succeeded in effectively diminishing the availability and use of illicit drugs.

'Drugs continue to flow into the country in increasing amounts and there is no evidence of a diminution of a demand for them. Given the huge cost of drug enforcement and its demonstrated inability to curb illicit drug use—why does society insist that because what we are doing is failing, we should do more of it?'

Sydney Morning Herald, 26 March 1984

The drugs–crime link was topical in April. A policeman had been shot, and the Police Minister announced a neighbourhood 'crime watch' scheme to help stem the epidemic of drug-related crime. The *Sun-Herald* was not sanguine about its effectiveness:

Amanda ... shares a flat with her addict boyfriend, Geoff, and the two work as a team breaking into houses and 'doing over' shops ... Amanda says that junkies have two methods of making money to support their habit. One is crime and the other is prostitution. 'I used to be a pro but I gave up cracking it when my little girl looks fell off ... No one wants a rake for a working girl so Geoff and me started as a team doing B and E (break and enters) and we haven't looked back. It's only the dumb street junkies that get caught'...

Amanda and Geoff are two of the thousands of drug addicts in NSW who survive by a life of crime. In their occupation, they are smart, well-versed and quick off the mark.

They represent the vast majority of heroin users who will probably never even try to give up their habit. This core drug-using population is responsible for an estimated 50 per cent of all property crimes in NSW and is costing the community between $50 million and $100 million a year ...

Mike Dowding, like many of his fellow drug rehabilitation workers, is sceptical about the neighbourhood crime watch scheme recently announced by Police Minister Anderson ...

'If junkies can't get their money from house thefts then they obviously turn to crimes like armed robbery or extortion'.

Sun–Herald, 15 April 1984

May saw two spectacular drug hauls. The *Sun* (1 May 1984) reported that five people, including the daughter of a 'leading Sydney businessman' had been arrested and charged with the importation of '28 kilos of heroin with a street value of $28 million dollars'. One week later, a woman carrying heroin worth $2.4 million was arrested at Sydney airport.

The pace began to pick up in June. Several decisions were reached in the courts:

HEROIN ADDICT GETS LIFE FOR KILLING NEWSAGENT

'If evidence was ever required of the appalling consequences to society of the trade in heroin, this case provides it', a Supreme Court judge said yesterday. At the Central Criminal Court Justice Wood sentenced Gary James Boreland, 28, to life imprisonment for the murder of an East Ryde newsagent, Ernest William Heatley, 64, on July 4 last year ... Sentencing Boreland, Justice Wood said he had stolen about $31 400 altogether ... None of the money had been recovered and Boreland had used most of it to support his heroin habit.

Sydney Morning Herald, 1 June 1984

The shooting of an undercover drug squad detective was alleged to be an assassination attempt.

'GANG REVENGE' ON DETECTIVE

Undercover drug squad detective Michael Drury is believed to have been the victim of a carefully planned assassination attempt by two notorious Melbourne painters and dockers involved in interstate heroin dealing. Detectives investigating the shooting believe that Drury was shot in a bid to silence him from giving evidence in a Melbourne drug case ... Detectives believe that the two painters and dockers are trying to eliminate all witnesses ... Drury, who is still fighting for his life in hospital, was shot twice at point blank range through the kitchen window of his Chatswood home in the presence of his young family last week ... A detective who knew Detective Drury at the police training college said ... 'His shooting was unprecedented—it's like throwing down the gauntlet to the whole police force. No one can remember a shooting where a criminal has had the audacity to actually hide outside a detective's home and gun him down in cold blood'.

Sun–Herald, 10 June 1984

At about the same time, the NSW Opposition Leader argued that heroin addicts should be given free drugs by their local general practitioners.

Mr Nick Greiner ... said: 'Too much time is wasted looking for the "Mastermind" behind Sydney's horrible drug scene. Finding the top man in the drug world may be important but it is unlikely to be the complete solution ...

'A very large part of criminal activity in NSW—be it bashing up old ladies or burglary—is drug-related. If we can bring these drug-addicted people away from having to commit crime to get the money to pay their pusher—that would mean a drop in crime. As a first result that must be useful. If we can wean them off the drugs in a controlled system then we are winning. And if the demand is not there the drug bosses have no one to supply to'.

Mr Greiner said that he expected some hostility to the idea from the medical community.

Sun—Herald, 10 June 1984

Whatever the medical community may have thought, some of the media themselves were unimpressed by the idea of prescription heroin. The *Sun* had this to say:

HEROIN: NO QUICK FIX

By advocating Britain's legal heroin program for addicts, the Opposition Leader, Mr Greiner, is not so much suggesting a solution as a cause to take up ... The case for making heroin to some degree available to addicts has been put on economic grounds. It would break the drug's link with organized crime, lower the rate of burglaries committed by addicts, reduce jail and hospital costs. The case is attractive but flawed. The TAB was supposed to kill off SP betting and take gangsters out of gambling. Neither has happened. In fact, SP flourishes.

Legalised heroin will seem to many people too much like a pact with the Devil to be useful or honourable ...

26 June 1984

About mid-June, the *Sydney Morning Herald* prepared an extensive series, 'Hooked on Heroin'. The series described user lifestyles—and their deaths.

A WORLD DOMINATED BY HAMMER AND TICKLE

Early in April, a 35-year-old Liverpool mother walked into her loungeroom after getting the train home from a City office job. Her 15-year-old son, who she believed had gone to school that day, lay on the sofa with the television on. On the floor beside him was a hypodermic syringe. When she tried to wake him she found he was dead from a heroin overdose. Her son had been using heroin for a year ...

Despite a fourfold increase in the size of the NSW Drug Squad and seizure by Federal agents of more than 100 kg of high-grade heroin this year, police still admit the streets of Sydney are awash with heroin ...

When heroin is bought, usually at $50 a syringeful, a hardened addict will inject as soon as possible. 'I'd use it anywhere', said

Michelle, an 18-year-old Melbourne user hooked since she was 16. She is now in Sydney attempting a cure. 'Service station toilets and friends' cars—anywhere to get that rush'. Her 22-year-old friend, who is also trying to rehabilitate, said he'd grabbed bloodied syringes straight from friends and injected with them. 'I've sucked water out of toilets to mix a hit'.
Sydney Morning Herald, 18 June 1984

'Hooked on Heroin' commented on the cost of the problem and particularly on its relation to crime. The series also described the treatment options:

GETTING USERS OFF THE HOOK

To get off the hook, a NSW addict can try to quit by doing drugless therapy in a country boarding house, part-time group discussion with fellow abusers, taking the heroin substitute, methadone, or trying a cure in a rigorous institution.

The Drug and Alcohol Authority says the divergence of treatments gives addicts a choice. An ex-addict and rehabilitation worker of 16 years says it is because nobody really knows what they are doing.

Treating addicts is not cheap. The authority says it costs $5 500 to keep a heroin addict in the WHOS treatment for a year. But this is less than half the cost of a year in jail and one eleventh of the cost of a bed in a public hospital. A year's course in a State clinic, which uses no volunteer staff, costs $26 000. An addict left on the street is estimated to cost the community $18 000.
Sydney Morning Herald, 19 June 1984

Despite the high cost of treatment, the results were felt to be unimpressive:

While some claim rates as high as 80 per cent, these figures generally apply only to those addicts who complete their programs and not those who drop out or are expelled ...
According to one counsellor: 'Treatment is actually not very effective, although it depends what your criteria of success are. If it's total abstinence (after treatment) then a 5 to 10 per cent success rate would be considered good'.
Sydney Morning Herald, 20 June 1984

At the end of the 'Hooked on Heroin' series, the *Sydney Morning Herald* expressed its concern about the issue in the following editorial:

The *Herald*'s disturbing series on heroin is making it clear to the community what the drug world has always known, that heroin kills people and has the potential to poison societies ... While heroin addicts remained in their dark, unsavoury world, the community could (and did) comfortably ignore them. This is no longer possible. Three-quarters of armed robberies in NSW are now committed to raise money for heroin. It costs $85.5 million a year to treat and police the State's estimated 10 000 addicts. Last year 87 people died from heroin overdosing, some of them found with needles still in their arms. The NSW hospitals treat about 500 morphine and heroin addicts a year for their addiction, and so on. Statistics like these finally become frighteningly vivid when, as is happening with increasing frequency these days, people find their houses ransacked by addicts frantically trying to find something to sell to get money for another 'hit'.

Sydney Morning Herald, 20 June 1984

The month of August brought a spate of criminal activity:

A man running a drug courier organization had bought heroin in lots of $100 000 from a supplier who probably imported it, police told the Magistrate's Court here yesterday ...

Vance had made in that time two or three $100 000 purchases of heroin which was to be distributed. He had been operating a drug ring from eight addresses. Potential customers would telephone their orders to hired staff, and a time and drop-off point would be organized. A beeper would be used to contact Vance or someone else, who would ring in to get the order.

Sydney Morning Herald, 17 August 1984

2 SHOT BY DRUG FRENZY GUNMAN

Two Sydney businessmen were shot when a gunman demanding heroin burst into their motel room early this morning ... Detectives believe the men were mistaken for drug dealers. They are in a satisfactory condition after undergoing surgery.

Sun, 22 August 1984

September was another busy month. Drug-related crime dominated the news for the first three weeks, but the real news came on 24 September, when the Prime Minister's wife, Mrs Hazel Hawke, went on national television to explain that her husband's tearful breakdown during a press conference the previous week had been motivated by personal tragedy. She revealed that her younger daughter and son-in-law were both heroin addicts. The hard-headed saw the affair as a strategic political move. Peter Robinson of the *Sun—Herald* had this to say:

BOB: A WARNING IN THE TEARS ...

In taking the calculated risk of exposing an intimate family tragedy last week, Prime Minister Bob Hawke not only provided evidence of the toll politics can take on family relationships but also demonstrated how family life itself becomes a hostage to political strategies ... His exposure of daughter Rosslyn's drug problem last week was not only intended to underline his own hatred of the drug trade, but was also a political warning to Labour, particularly in NSW, that he could not be expected to support any cover-up for reasons of party loyalty ...

These days, it is doubtful whether any lucrative area of underworld activity can be disentangled from drugs so that links that were once regarded as relatively innocent are now direct ties to the big-time corruption of international drug trafficking ...

There can be no doubt that Mrs Hawke's performance on television was moving, dignified, and politically invaluable.

As a prominent Labour politician said alter: 'Hawkie's tears had hurt us, but Hazel turned it around. Her performance had a spell-binding effect. She was great. She won us thousands of votes'.

Sunday Telegraph, 30 September 1984

A few of the readers were critical of the way the affair was managed:

Sir: I realise that this is bound to offend some people, but I really don't think I can take much more of the Hawke family tragedy.

True, anyone on drugs has a real problem, but is it always someone else's fault? Are addicts forcibly held down and injected? I'm not suggesting that this was the case with Rosslyn (Hawke) Dillon, but the dramatic disclosure by her mother certainly came at a propitious time—after all, things were looking a little sticky for the Prime Minister ...

Although I can feel sympathy for anyone in Mr and Mrs Hawke's position, I would have felt more if the whole sorry affair hadn't been handled in such a maudlin and tasteless manner. I sincerely hope all our public figures are not going to feel the need to reveal all the family skeletons. (P.P., Wahroonga)

Sydney Morning Herald, 29 September 1984

The majority, however, were fulsome in their sympathy, and many hastened to offer explanations.

The Hawke family would have been through 'absolute hell' facing the problem of their daughter's addiction, according to the Reverend Ted Noffs of the Wayside Chapel. He said life with an addict meant a family never knew from one day to another whether they had a child or a corpse ...

'Mr Hawke must be given credit that he has been able to run the country while coping with the problem ... Heroin addiction in most cases belongs to the up-and-outs, not the down-and-outs', he said . . . 'the addict tends to come from well-to-do families in respected areas . . .'

Rev Noffs said many people believed the threat of nuclear war was the world's biggest problem, but he put drug abuse above that. The head of the heroin treatment centre at St Vincent's Hospital, Dr David Bell, said heroin addiction could start with a child having a cigarette in primary school before the age of 12.

Daily Mirror, 25 September 1984

Mr Unsworth, the NSW Minister for Transport, is an avid anti-drugs campaigner. His son, Anthony, 20, died of a heroin overdose in Malaysia on Christmas Eve, 1977. Mr Unsworth said he was able to offer support and understanding to Mr Hawke . . .

Mr Unsworth said that many children whose parents are in the public eye 'feel they have to live up to the image their parents have created, and some young people in that situation tend to react against the pattern of life established by their parents, whether it be politics, sport or business. Some feel they are placed in an impossible situation and turn to narcotic abuse'.

Sydney Morning Herald, 26 September 1984

The media carried advice on what to do 'when the horror hits home', and helping groups offered their wares:

HEROIN: WHEN THE HORROR HITS HOME

Drugs and their evil consequences always tear other people apart—never you. So the sudden shock and horror of finding a child who has a serious drug problem can be as emotionally devastating for parents as it is physically terrifying for the addict.

The tragic case involving the family of our Prime Minister, and the brave face of Mrs Hazel Hawke talking on national television of her daughter Rosslyn's heroin habit surely touched every Australian heart. It also underlined the need for parents to understand and support a child who comes under the deadly hammer of heroin or any other addiction. A number of drug rehabilitation groups in Sydney are now offering parent and family support services—as well as helping those who are hooked . . .

Anthony Stanfield, WHOS adviser and consultant to the organisation's board . . . said that it was important that support was sought quickly from those who knew what they were doing—and this could mean parents who had already worked through the problem with their own teenagers . . . [He] repeatedly stressed the need for families to recover as well. 'Parents have to feel they are individuals too . . . They need to have a pride and purpose in their lives as well. With the support we offer we make them understand that' . . .

HOW TO READ THE EMOTIONAL DISTRESS SIGNALS

How do parents tell if their children are becoming drug addicted? It is not something that happens overnight, without warning. There are a number of telltale indicators for parents to watch for, according to WHOS, the drug rehabilitation group. They are:

- Physical changes. Steady loss of weight, no interest in food.
- Mood chages. Erratic behavior, with tantrums, preceded by amiable manner.
- Keeping odd hours. Sleeping through the day, then going out late at night. Little or no interest in work.
- Secretive attitude about one's movements and friends.
- Shortage of money when in normal circumstances bank balance should be healthy.
- Sudden disappearances from house of jewellery, sporting equipment and household wares.

Daily Telegraph, 26 September 1984

And newspaper editorials urged the mobilisation of forces to deal with the menace in the strongest terms:

We also hope [Mrs Hawke's revelations] will awaken the national consciousness to the enormous problem hard drugs like heroin and cocaine have become. Every year thousands of young Australians are maimed and killed—and all for the enrichment of a corrupt, ruthless few.

People who deal in drugs, who profit from death and suffering, are lower than vermin. *They should be stamped out, wherever they exist and wherever they are found.*

Daily Mirror, 25 September 1984

Mrs Hawke's startling revelations—to explain her husband's tears—brought their private life into politics. We hope the explanation will be accepted by the electorate and the family will be allowed to close its ranks to protect and support Rosslyn and Matt Dillon, as they fight their problem.

The heartbreak of the Hawke family brings home in a dramatic way the insidious nature of the drug trade. No family is safe. The trade is not restricted to grubby backstreet urchins, weak-willed youngsters and no-hopers. Its tentacles are able to crawl into the most caring and respected homes and cause destruction.

We now know the Prime Minister has very personal reasons for leading the war on the vermin involved in the drugs trade. It is to be hoped his faith in the National Crimes Authority proves justified and it can identify and destroy the drug czars.

Daily Telegraph, 26 September 1984

Heroin addiction today is a situation a little like divorce or illegitimate children 30 or 40 years ago—everyone knew they existed but they were not 'nice' to talk about ...

All children in Australia are now probably aware of illegal drugs by the time they leave primary school. Newspapers, radio and television are constantly running articles or programs on the dangers associated with illegal drug use but the number of addicts shows no sign of diminishing. Obviously there is something radically wrong with drug education programs or with the emotional help available to our young ...

Mrs Hawke may have been trying to explain—and ease the possible electoral damage of—the Prime Minister's emotional outbursts of last week. But she did Australia a greater service by forcing public debate on an unpleasant subject.

Australian, 26 September 1984

Meanwhile, there were other reasons for outrage beside the Hawke affair:

BLOOD MONEY FOR DRUGS ... BRUTAL MURDERERS PREYED ON PENSIONERS

Heroin was at the bottom of the brutal slaying of three defenseless Sydney pensioners. A gang of four young unemployed men waged a terror campaign in the inner suburbs, leaving three dead and 15 others injured—to feed their drug habits ... The irony of their killing spree was that they got only a few dollars from each victim—not enough to buy even one 'deal'. They killed one man for a dollar and another for about $2 ...

Their rapid graduation from street hoodlums to multiple murderers is a chilling reminder of the perils of drug addiction.

Daily Mirror, 26 September 1984

On 27 September, Drug Squad detectives also seized $276 000 worth of heroin, and the public was titillated by a report of international panty girdle smugglers:

MODELS 'HID DRUGS IN UNDERWEAR'

A group of models suspected of smuggling heroin and cocaine around the world in their underwear was arrested yesterday at London's Heathrow Airport. While the models were detained at the airport a model agency suspected of fronting a $45 million drugs syndicate was raided ... No drugs were recovered yesterday and the women are not suspected of smuggling them into Britain. But they could still face prosecution because of international agreements on drug trafficking.

Daily Telegraph, 27 September 1984

In October, a Melbourne radio announcer attempted to involve the family of yet another public figure in the heroin issue. The action was roundly denounced.

> Allegations that the 22-year-old son of Mr Frank Costigan QC was a heroin addict and had been charged with loitering for the purposes of prostitution led to a rare and terse public statement from the royal commissioner yesterday . . .
> 'This morning the radio station 3AW saw fit to discuss publicly the problems besetting my son Timothy. Timothy has had problems and has received treatment. I hope it is successful but by this publication it may suffer. I have not heard any suggestion that any aspect of this matter is of interest to the public other than that Timothy happens to be my son. It is of great regret to me that such circumstances may make his recovery more difficult. I have nothing else to say about this matter' . . . .
> Hinch . . . defended his broadcast, saying: 'It was a news story in the same category as the Hawke story . . . I am not a callous person and I feel sorry for both him and his dad, but it was a news story'.
>
> *Australian*, 4 October 1984

> Melbourne radio announcer Derryn Hinch last night denied it was his ego and desire for publicity which prompted him to name the son of Mr Frank Costigan, QC, as a heroin addict . . .
> 'I know Timothy Costigan will be hurt by this but I did it to show the extent of drug addiction in this country', he said last night.
> Journalist Mungo McCallum . . . said Hinch had broken the journalists' code of ethics by airing the story. He said members of the Canberra press gallery had known about Timothy Costigan's plight for some time, and about the drug addiction of the Prime Minister's daughter, but had refrained from publishing either because they did not consider them to be in the public interest.
>
> *Australian*, 5 October 1984

Nevertheless, concern about heroin continued. The *Daily Mirror* printed 'names, addresses and numbers that could ultimately save your child or friend's life. If you are worried about someone close to you using drugs, ring them for advice'. The same issue also carried a report that 'every family should read' on the first signs of heroin use:

HEROIN: THE FIRST SIGNS

> It is often hard for parents or friends to pick the early signs of heroin use. And very often, when they do, parents refuse to accept the terrifying fact, according to Brian Stewart, director of the Drug and Alcohol Authority . . .
>
> ● 'The best thing is to try and stay in touch with your kids, and

try to observe changes in behavior.
- 'There might be deterioration in school work, or a change in general attitude around the house—a loss of interest in sporting or recreational activities.
- 'They often become lethargic. There might be a loss of appetite. Their circle of friends might change radically.
- 'You might also notice a disinclination to participate in normal family activities. They become more withdrawn.
- 'You don't get physical changes, in skin for example, in the early stages unless there is chronic use' . . .

Heroin use produces some characteristics that other drugs do not, such as mood swings. 'A high then a low. Very marked swings. Heroin is an extremely euphoric drug. That's why it's so attractive, but once the effect wears off the mood changes radically.

'The first thing is to confront in a gentle and non-threatening way. Sit down and talk to them. It's very unlikely that kids will at first admit they are using but if the parents are vigilant they quite often do. At this stage the parents will naturally become very distraught and very emotional and they should seek help'.

The same article also supplied some 'facts' about heroin:

About 400 young Australians will die from heroin this year. Their average age will be 24. And heroin use is on the increase, starting with kids as young as 12 and 14. Hazel Hawke called it the white plague . . .

Heroin use has always been regarded as a dirty, sleazy habit, confined to Kings Cross dropouts who live in bare, dingy one-bedroom flats—stoned 24 hours a day. But the Prime Minister's wife revealed that their daughter and son-in-law are heroin addicts, proving once again that heroin users come from all walks of life. They include the children of some of our top politicians, businessmen, lawyers and doctors. The legal, medical and social consequences are horrific . . .

About 15 000 young Australians are addicted to heroin today. One in four heroin users will die prematurely, most in their 20s. Almost all heroin users die or quit the habit painfully before the age of 35. The majority of heroin users started taking the drug in their teens . . .

About 60 per cent of burglaries, thefts and robberies are to support a drug habit, including heroin . . . Almost all heroin users resort to crime to support their habit. It is estimated half the women addicts take up prostitution at some stage.

And there was a statement by the Reverend Ted Noffs:

'I have buried 159 young people from heroin overdoses. This is a war, there is no other word for it . . . It is as deadly a war as we have fought—World War II, Korea, Vietnam—it is a war without honor, not like the boys who were wiped out with napalm in Vietnam. It happens quietly and subtly, year by year, and we are not organised to handle it . . .

'Tens of thousands of people march against a nuclear war that *might* happen but this *is* happening. Family fortunes are being lost as a result. Husbands are leaving wives, wives leaving husbands. It is no longer something that can be ignored . . .

'It is common to hear of families losing $20 000 or $50 000 or even $100 000 to pay for their children's habits. The kids keep promising their parents that they have given up the habit and all they need is $10 000, and the parents believe them because they don't want to believe anything else', Rev Noffs said.

Daily Mirror, 3 October 1984

But by far the biggest news for October was the allegation that NSW police officers were involved in drug trafficking. An editorial of 3 October attests to the *Sun*'s outrage:

THE SLOW DRUG PROBE

Slow justice can be diluted justice, and processing of the latest allegations to be made public against NSW police has been drawn out indeed . . . On Saturday, a former associate of the Mr Asia drug syndicate, Mr Stephen Bazeley, claimed seven NSW Drug Squad officers had been involved in heroin trafficking; that he provided the Federal Police with this information in April last year, and that the officers were still serving.

The Police Minister, Mr Anderson, now says the Federal Police passed the information to the then NSW Police Commissioner, Mr Abbott, in June last year. An investigation was started which had not yet finished.

If Mr Bazeley's timetable is correct, the Federal Police took two whole months to inform Mr Abbott. Mr Abbott seems to have been remarkably relaxed in not telling his minister about charges so obviously capable of being political dynamite.

Mr Anderson says he learned of the allegations last Wednesday. He, too, seems remarkably relaxed about being left in the dark for so long.

The public will not share these easy-going attitudes. And until the charges are acted on or rejected outright the police force will stay under a cloud.

Sun, 3 October 1984

The Police Commissioner defended the inaction:

'We would stand down police officers if we had any substantial allegations which might lead to criminal charges but without substance or corroboration we would lay ourselves open to the opportunity for any criminal who was charged with any sort of offence to make an allegation. If we suspended police under those circumstances we would leave this city unprotected' ...

The Leader of the NSW Opposition, Mr Greiner, yesterday said: 'I am beyond amazement. I would have thought the people of NSW would wonder what sort of State we live in, what sort of police force we have. It defies comprehension to believe that there has been no attempt to interview the seven officers involved, no attempt to keep them under surveillance, indeed no serious action at all to investigate this matter'.

Sydney Morning Herald, 4 October 1984

Mr Hatton, Independent MP for the South Coast, was even more forthright:

'What we have here is a situation where certain corrupt officers are so well entrenched they can dictate whether such allegations are looked into or not ... It seems fairly obvious that certain people within the force did not want the allegations checked'.

Mr Hatton said there was no more serious crime than officers responsible for suppressing the drug trade being involved directly in the distribution of drugs.

Sun, 4 October 1984

Questions began to be asked in parliament:

The Leader of the Opposition, Mr Peacock, earlier in the House asked whether Federal police had expressed concern that co-operation in investigations of drug trafficking were complicated by the fact that NSW police were allegedly corrupt. His question was directed to the Special Minister for State, Mr Young, who replied that the Federal Government was not responsible for the conduct of the NSW Police Force.

Sydney Morning Herald, 6 October 1984

On October 20, the NSW Premier Mr Wran launched a massive blitz against drug traffickers.

'UNTOUCHABLES' OUT TO SMASH HEROIN MENACE

Only 'untouchables' will be allowed into the powerful new police squad formed to smash the heroin trade in NSW. The Premier, Mr Wran, said yesterday the Government was waging not just an attack but all-out war against heroin traffickers.

'We want to build up a bureau of untouchables who will unleash an onslaught on the drug trade in NSW the likes of which has never been seen before', he said.

Nearly 50 extra police officers along with undercover agents, computer experts, legal officers and existing Drug Squad detectives will make up the new Drug Law Enforcement Bureau. Mr Wran said hot-lines would be set up to enable people to 'dob in' heroin trafficking in hotels and other public places and police would be stationed in suburban areas where heroin was being sold to try to smash drug rings.

Mr Wran said all officers put up for appointment to the new bureau would be fully screened to ensure they were incorruptible.

Daily Telegraph, 22 October 1984

Mr Wran launched his $1.5 million a year war with a 'guarantee that the new bureau will be backed by every ounce of Government muscle in its primary charter—to identify and crush heroin dealings and pushers wherever they exist' (The *Sun*, 21 October 1984). According to the Leader of the Opposition, however, 'What Mr Wran probably should have said was that it was the biggest and most comprehensive attack against his failing popularity and that of his Government' (The *Australian*, 22 October 1984).

November began with a $9 million dollar heroin seizure at Sydney's Mascot Airport, and the publication of the *Costigan Report* on organised crime. The report concluded that methods of importing heroin into Australia were as varied as they were bizzare, that federal customs were fighting a losing battle, and that 'the best that can be done is to carry out random and intuitive checks of passengers, save where the couriers are either on some kind of alert system or come from a suspect departure point' (The *Australian*, 2 November 1984).

The undercover agent who was a victim of an apparent assassination attempt in May recovered, and on 11 November the *Sun—Herald* carried the news that he had been offered a $30 000 bribe by a prominent Sydney detective to cover up evidence of drug trafficking.

> The undercover detective, Michael Drury, who was investigating the main sources of supply of heroin, had uncovered evidence that the Sydney detective was one of the suppliers. The Sydney detective visited the undercover detective to offer him the bribe, which was rejected. The shooting occurred at Drury's home three days later...
>
> A handful of top officers at Police Headquarters in Sydney has been told that the same Sydney detective named by Drury approached a contact in the Drug Squad and made the same offer of $30 000 if Drury could be stopped ... The detective named by Drury has been linked to one of Australia's most colourful criminals.
>
> *Sun—Herald*, 11 November 1984

On 13 November, the *Sun* heralded Operation Noah with front page headlines to 'Name The Dealers! And Save Our Kids From

Drugs'. On 15 November, the same paper reported that 1 902 calls had been received on the police hotline. Considerable success was claimed:

AND NOW FOR THE BIG FISH!

Police say they have begun closing in on the 'big fish' of the heroin trade in the wake of the outstanding success of Operation Noah. Already eighteen arrests have been made in relation to other drugs ...

In fact, the majority of the arrests were for cannabis-related offences, as the *Sun* duly recorded. At the same time, many of the calls seem to have revealed more about the callers than about heroin dealers:

One father rang because his schoolboy son had told him of other children at school buying heroin and amphetamines ...

Const Michael Velo said he received a call from a woman whose daughter was hooked on heroin and had already tried to commit suicide twice, by slashing her wrists and taking an overdose ...

Another constable said: 'One terribly concerned woman rang about her daughter, a reformed drug addict, claiming her former pusher was hassling her daughter over the phone'.

A school principal from the northern beaches called to give details of a milk bar he believed was supplying kids with marijuana and amphetamines. Other teachers called because they had either caught students or heard them talking about getting 'speed' from within the school.

A Katoomba woman rang because she knew an addict so hopelessly hooked that her baby girl was kept in grubby nappies and left in a cot all day.

Nevertheless, the dealers did react—or so the *Telegraph* implied in reporting on the death of a young addict on 14 November.

DEATH RIDDLE OF SOCIALITE'S SON
MUM SAYS HER SON WAS MURDERED

Police this weekend renewed their investigations into the bizzare death of a young man from one of Australia's wealthiest and best known families following claims that he was murdered ... because he allegedly kept a secret diary which listed the names of Sydney heroin pushers ...

Daily Telegraph, 25 November 1984

Operation Noah was a test run for a full-time phone-in operation. The *Telegraph* described its launch in early December in an impassioned editorial:

PLEASE SUPPORT CRIME FIGHT

Anyone unfortunate enough to have seen a heroin addict will know—and remember for a long time—the hideousness of it . . .

That there are those who will stoop to make money from this foul trade and, in the process, destroy thousands of largely young lives, is a blot of heinous proportions on so called civilised man . . .

The time has come, indeed it is probably long past, for Australians to set aside their traditional aversion to 'dobbing someone in'. The drug trafficker, through his evil trade, has disqualified himself from any such sentiment . . .

Operation Crime-Stop gives each and everyone of us in the community the chance to help police find, charge and jail these menaces to society. All that is needed is a phone call . . .

The *Sunday Telegraph* strongly urges its readers to get behind Operation Crime-Stop. The time is now, the need is urgent, the responsibility is yours.

The *Daily Mirror*, on the other hand, urged its young readers with drug problems to seek help:

DO YOU WANT TO DIE AT 24?

About 400 young people will die this year, their lives laid waste by the ravages of heroin addiction. Their average age will be 24. Why do young people allow heroin to grab them by the throat and turn them into shadows of human beings? How do they get on the roller-coaster ride to hard drugs and death? . . .

Drug addiction is a fatal price to pay for a few hours escape. For many junkies life is a triangle of heroin, methadone and going cold turkey . . . The tragedy is that it can happen to anyone in our society . . .

If you feel unable to cope, need help and can't confide in your parents, try [list of resources given] . . . At first it may seem difficult, but believe me—after death there are no second chances.

Daily Mirror, 10 December 1984

The great Kings Cross exposé began on 17 December, in the wake of a wave of overdoses on 14 December. The *Sun* spoke of 'Sydney's Shame', and described the incidents as 'Murder Bids':

The wave of Sydney heroin overdoses in which 20 addicts collapsed may have been a deliberate attempt by pushers to murder those who knew too much.

The Rev Ted Noffs said dealers may have fed bad heroin onto the streets to eliminate users with too great a knowledge of the $1 billion trade. He said he believed they feared the police program to 'dob in' a pusher, Operation Noah . . .

'The attitude of the big dealers is that they can eliminate people who have too much knowledge about drug suppliers and pick-up points. The introduction of murder by overdose is almost unthinkable—but for these people it is easy'.
On a normal night ambulance officers treat between two and four for heroin overdose.

Sun, 17 December 1984

On 18 December, the *Australian* carried a photograph of junkies shooting up in Kings Cross' Hope Lane. David Hirst reported:

THE END OF THE ROAD IS A SYRINGE IN HOPE LANE

Three boys—they could have been anyone's sons in their shorts, T-shirts and sneakers—sitting in the sun on a Monday morning, shooting up ... the youths barely bothered to look up as they pumped their arms. Beside them were the upturned soft drink cans on which they had mixed their heroin base. Using fresh needles and sterile water bought in tiny ampules from a nearby chemist, they were injecting what appeared to be highly refined Thai 'white powder'. Two of them were 17, the other 18. Their habit costs them $7 000 − $8 000 a week ...

Along with 'hundreds of their mates', they follow a strict daily routine. 'We meet in the streets about 10.30 (am). Then we steal a car and head for the rich suburbs like Rose Bay and Double Bay, do (grab) a couple of handbags and head here. We usually get at least $100 from a handbag ... The cops are miles behind. They have no hope in the world' ...

At CIB headquarters, a spokesman admits forlornly that 'we are running around in circles. They are like mice,' he says ...

Mr Noffs says the extent of the problem is terrifying and if the pattern of blatant use gets out of the Cross and into the suburbs and other cities, the situation will be 'genocidal'.

'The fact is that no one will believe the truth of what you have just seen ... No one is ashamed, no one is ducking for cover. No one has the slightest fear of reprisals. Once heroin use was analysed in terms of rebellion. Now it's like ice cream.'

Australian, 18 December 1984

On 19 December, the story continued:

BOSS OF THE CROSS FLAUNTS HIS HEROIN DEALING

Sydney Drug Squad detectives yesterday arrested the three youths of Kings Cross' Hope Lane pictured, after 'shooting up' on the front page of the *Australian* yesterday ... The arrests were not made in the course of normal police work but only after the *Australian* sought reaction from the NSW Drug Squad to the situation exposed yesterday ...

I saw not one police officer in four hours yesterday in the country's notorious drug capital. In that time I found, with a little help from a few locals and a social worker in the area, the place reputed to be the scene of the main heroin deals in the Kings Cross market. It was a seedy amusement arcade. A social worker . . . asked that it not be identified as it 'will only boost their trade'.

The NSW Drug Squad confirmed that the police have a good idea of who the major distributors are, but pointed out the frustration of arresting offenders only to see them immediately back on the streets on bail . . . [A spokesman] said dealers used the court system and that some of the offenders were at present out on bail after two or three arrests. But others in the Cross claim that the police 'rarely if ever' go near the known supply point . . .

Back in the hopelessness of Hope Lane, a sole addict, in an advanced stage of withdrawal, cowered shaking and sweating in a corner hoping that someone might turn up and give him a 'taste'. After attacking the Government, the doctors, the police and the jails where he claimed he had spent five years for armed robbery, he turned and cried:

'Why don't they just shoot us?'.

Australian, 19 December 1984

The *Australian* expressed its extreme concern in an editorial:

BRINGING HOPE BACK INTO HOPE LANE

That such a scene can be played out on a sunny summer morning in the middle of Sydney with no interest from the police is more than a disgrace, it is a national scandal . . .

Our police forces appear powerless or unwilling to stop the flood of drugs. And we must now reluctantly accept that all our police forces, both state and federal, and presumably also our customs forces, have been corrupted to some extent by the drug peddlers' dollars. How else could the steady flow of heroin reach the addicts? . . .

Young people are the human resources of this country. They are our future. But today it is far easier for them to get a hit of heroin than it is to get a job. We must not let our future die in a grubby back-street to make a sleazy criminal rich.

Australian 19 December 1984

On 20 December the public read of the tragic death of Mrs Bubbins:

HEROIN WIFE DIES 8 DAYS FROM FREEDOM

Mary Bubbins was eight days off shaking free from the grip of the city's drug scene. Today she lies on a slab in the Sydney City

Morgue, dead from an overdose of a new, high-grade heroin which is flooding the nation. Mrs Bubbins, with her husband and two children, was to have left Sydney yesterday to begin a new life in the Northern Territory . . .

Mr Bubbins, a former Navy petty officer who resigned 10 weeks ago and who himself was a junkie until his wife's death, told yesterday of his final days with his wife. The two had been 'scoring' from what Mr Bubbins described as a rare, reliable dealer who a few weeks ago decided to quit. They then began to buy in the Cross. 'She went up to the Village to shop and came back with a good-sized deal, excellent by Village standards . . . When she brought it home we decided to save it till 5 o'clock that night as we weren't sick (withdrawing). After she had her hit she went to stand up but collapsed' . . .

Mr Bubbins has a lot of hate, most of it directed at dealers in the Cross.'It was only eight days to go to freedom. Had she not scored in the Cross, we would have been driving together to the Northern Territory'.

Australian, 20 December 1984

On 21 December, there was the charging of three men with possessing and supplying heroin valued at more than $500 000, and the *Daily Mirror's* evocative picture of life at the Cross:

I OF THE NEEDLE

Kings Cross, 7.50 am: A young woman sits stupefied in Darlinghurst Rd then slowly tilts. Two uniformed police, unaware a *Daily Mirror* team is watching, interrogate her for five minutes.

In a back lane doorway behind the Wayside Chapel a spent syringe and spoon lie on newspaper. A fresh needle is hidden in the chapel's brickwork.

On a pillar facing the scene are droplets of sprayed blood shaped like a question mark.

A metre away on a wall are instructions on how to 'shoot up' heroin . . .

Daily Mirror, 21 December 1984

Both items, however, paled before the revelation that the heroin trade was very much alive in the state prison system:

ONLY THE BEST FOR PRISONERS

A huge heroin trade is flourishing in the jail system and is aided by prison officers . . . Jails offer not only one of the most reliable supply centres for addicts, but also supply the highest grade of the drug in the country . . .

[A former prisoner said] 'The smack (heroin) you get there is always the best, because if you give me bad stuff I will know where to find you—you're not going anywhere ... What you have to realise is that police have arrested importers, dealers, the whole lot and put them in one place—then have thrown the drug user in with them ... A person who was selling ounces of heroin when he was on the street doesn't lose his accessibility to ounces just because all of a sudden you find him in jail'.

A spokesman for the NSW Corrective Services Department acknowledged that the department knew the trade was going on ...

Australian, 21 December 1984

It was perhaps as well that on the same day the Acting Prime Minister called on all State Premiers to attend a drug summit in early 1985 to set up a National Campaign Against Drug Abuse. The campaign was to be a matter of highest priority for the government. It was to address problems being encountered in the fight, with emphasis on educating youth about the danger of drugs and on rehabilitating drug users. The *Australian* felt the action was timely:

HELL ON EARTH ...

At last, the Federal Government has stirred itself to take concrete action on the drugs menace ... We have had all the royal commissions; we have had a Prime Minister in tears over the addiction of his daughter and son-in-law; but as we showed this week, on the streets nothing much has changed.

To the victims and their relatives, the verbose commission reports, the indignation over civil liberties, the personality fights, is something happening in the stratosphere. What is happening on the ground is hell on earth.

Probably millions have been spent on talking about drugs. Now we want action.

Australian, 21 December 1984

Over the following weekend, the *Australian* carried a serious and balanced assessment of the situation:

DRUGS FIGHT: WE HAVE TO LOOK AT OURSELVES

Yesterday we carried an astonishing article on a huge heroin trade flourishing within the NSW jail system, allegedly aided by some prison officials ... This situation is plainly ludicrous. If the trafficking and use of heroin cannot be controlled within a closed system like a jail, what hope is there for the rest of our society? ...

While all Australians will welcome the move by the Acting Prime Minister, Mr Bowen, to hold a national drugs summit, we must ask if it will generate any real answers to Australia's drug problem ...

We must face reality. Unless a great deal of money is spent improving coastal surveillance, waterfront and airport procedures and law enforcement agencies, heroin will continue to flood into Australia because of the huge profits to be made by those who deal in its lethal trade ... The way the heroin trade has flourished over the past five years prevents any conclusion other than that a significant number of those in power—from politicians through to law enforcement officers—have been persuaded to turn a blind eye to the business ...

We need immediate action that extends from the very top to the bottom of our society ... But the ultimate question we will still face after all the talking is: what is so wrong with our society that our young people seek to escape it through the end of a needle?

And here we must look at ourselves—you and me. The situation is an indictment of us. It is an indictment of the 1984 family—as the parents of those youngsters who get hooked on heroin are often the last to recognise their offspring's drug dependency. How many parents can honestly say they are aware of the real risks and dangers their children face each day? Do we always know where our children are? Or, what is more pertinent, do we care where our children are?

We don't know why children get hooked. No rational person, no matter how young or immature they might be, would willingly volunteer to become one of the 'zonked-out' teenage wrecks one can see prostituting themselves on the streets of Kings Cross or St Kilda. But thousands of young Australians willingly experiment with heroin every week.

As the drug shows no social barriers, the sons and daughters of the rich and influential are at no less or greater threat than the sons and daughters of less socially advantaged Australians. If we were more caring of, and interested in, our own children, we might not be in such a sad situation as many Australian families are this Christmas.

The drug problem involves us all. It will not go away or be defeated unless we are all prepared to fight. There is a New Year's resolution we should all make: to cleanse this country of this dreadful destroyer.

Australian, 22–23 December 1984

But the *Daily Telegraph* was not to be outdone:

PREGNANT MUM HAD DRUGS SECRETED

A doctor had to extract 15 packets of heroin from a pregnant drug pusher so he could deliver her baby, the Rev Ted Noffs said yesterday ... 'The women are hiding the drugs in their bodies,

not their underclothes, to evade detection by police when
arrested', he said ... 'Buyers meet the women in shops and
pinball parlours, hand over the money, and the women simply
reach into their bodies to deliver', he said.
Daily Telegraph, 22 December 1984

And still more was to come:

CURIOUS CASE OF HEROIN DEALER SET FREE BY CANBERRA

The NSW police just can't win! Subject to criticism for not
catching enough heroin dealers, they found this week that one of
their prize catches, the Mr Asia king-pin, Peter Fulcher, had
been set free by the Federal Government ...
Weekend Australian, 29–30 December 1984

Fulcher, a senior member of the Mr Asia drug syndicate, had been found guilty of conspiring to import heroin worth $1.5 million in 1982. He was sentenced to eighteen years' hard labour, with a non-parole period of nine years. On 24 December he was reported to have been released, after serving three years and three months of his sentence. According to the *Telegraph*, his mother was upset:

MUM DISOWNS DRUG SON

'We don't want him to come back', Mrs Fulcher said in
Auckland. 'All this latest news has shocked me. It has made
things very unpleasant for the family—we had hoped we had
heard the last of him several years ago. He has made our lives a
misery'.

Mrs Fulcher said her son had 'once been a good person' but
had changed for the worse. She said she would find it hard,
probably impossible, to take him back under any circumstances ...
Daily Telegraph, 30 December 1984

The *Telegraph* was also upset. 'Free the Facts, Not Criminals!' it thundered:

It is 24 days since heroin pedlar, stand-over man and associate of
murderers, Peter Fulcher, was let out of jail. And still no one—at
least no one outside official circles—has been told why ...

Decent people have little regard for informers and if, by being
one, this dealer in death has placed his own life in danger, so be
it. And if this constitutes the 'exceptional circumstances' given by
the Attorney-General, Mr Bowen, as reasons for Fulcher's
release, then not many people will accept it.

Fulcher, with a long history of thuggery in New Zealand, was
sentenced in NSW to 18 years jail for importing heroin He was

given a nine year non-parole period. He was back on the streets after just four years. Exceptional indeed. But nowhere near as exceptional as the fact that there was not one condition attached to his release on license. He didn't have to report to a probationary officer or to the police. Or to anyone else, for that matter. He was as free as any law-abiding citizen ...
Again the question: why? The public deserves some answers.

Sunday Telegraph, 30 December 1984

Heroin and the media

What can we conclude? For one thing, it is obviously misleading to speak of 'the media' in any general way. Our sample of news stories concentrated on heroin and so cannot provide data on relative emphasis, but different papers in fact give very different prominence to drug stories. According to a survey conducted by Sydney's Centre for Information on Drugs and Alcohol (White, 1985), drugs formed 21.8 per cent of the *Australian's* total press for 1984. The *Sydney Morning Herald* came second with 18.8 per cent, with the *Daily Telegraph*, the *Sun*, and the *Daily Mirror* showing 15.4 per cent, 7.5 per cent, and 6.2 per cent respectively. The sample does show, though, that the different papers tend to concentrate on different themes, and their reporting style is clearly very different.

Whether the media reflect society's concerns about drug problems or actually create them is a moot point. Probably the earliest demonstration that the press can 'launch a nationwide drug menace' was provided by Brecher (1972). He attributed the genesis of American glue sniffing to two enterprising reporters from the *Denver Post* who wrote a story about the effects of inhaling glue vapour. The headline ran: 'Some Glues are Dangerous, Heavy Inhalation Can Cause Anemia or Brain Damage.' Denver, at the time, showed no evidence of sniffing activity. However, the scare headline, together with what amounted to a detailed description (with photographs) of how to sniff glue to get high began a vogue for sniffing that spread through Denver and eventually over the nation. Each local paper in turn used the same tactics and further popularised the activity.

The Australian media did not create heroin use as such, but they were very much part of the process whereby it became a *problem*. Until the mid−1930s, Australians did not see heroin as inherently evil, and they gave it no special powers. It was a legal drug, known to be addictive but not considered particularly dangerous. It had a recognised place in medicine, primarily as a cough suppressant. Even the report by the League of Nations in 1936 that Australia had the highest per capita consumption of narcotics in the world did not cause particular concern. The steps that led to its prohibition in 1953 have been traced by Davies (1986), and the motivation for this action was largely political. Australian society, as a whole, was generally unworried.

Nevertheless, what Davies calls the 'seeds of plague' were already there. The media were beginning to deal with heroin-related issues in terms like 'sinister', 'menace', 'alarm' and 'danger'. By the time heroin officially reappeared as a black market street drug in the mid–1960s, it had a completely new image. It *was* sinister, malevolent, uncontrollable and contagious—words which the media have recycled for decades for each succeeding problem substance. As Plant (1986) points out, society as a whole seems to prefer to acknowledge only one drug problem at a time. Heroin is 'it' at the moment (though it may soon lose out to cocaine), just as cocaine was 'it' in the 1920s and opium in the late 1800s. 'The same words and images [have] traversed eighty years of journalism' (Davies, 1986, p. 59), and they are as effective as ever.

The thesis that the media are part of the drug problem is rather common among drug addiction specialists, but formal studies of the relationship have begun to appear only relatively recently. Their results, however, are disturbing. In 1981, Cowling reported that press coverage of drug issues was generally simplistic and that alarmist stories actually encouraged, provoked or challenged people to experiment with drugs. She also felt that the news items were not presented objectively; rather, journalists selected and interpreted events to fit pre-existing concepts and ideologies.

The NSW Drug and Alcohol Services had somewhat different concerns. In 1982, they argued that conventional media reporting of drug material reinforced current drug stereotypes, and that while this was not necessarily a bad thing, it did tend to prevent significant positive changes in addressing drug problems. Bell, whose systematic studies of media representations of drug issues are discussed below, reached a similar conclusion. The media, he feels, 'educate their audiences to a resigned, alienated passivity' (1985, p. 235).

Perhaps the biggest problem with media coverage of drug issues is that it is so selective. The situation is like an incomplete jigsaw puzzle. The general idea may be there, but the total picture must be inferred from the pieces actually available. All too often, the general public does not realise just how many pieces are missing. Thus, the media generally ignore the historical, political and economic aspects of drug production and marketing. The problem is seen simply as the consumption of illicit substances. Moreover, eradication of this problem is presented as a simple matter of medical treatment, educational reform and legal controls—again without regard to the political and economic costs of such moves. Nor, for that matter, is much attention given to the actual extent of the problem and to the track record, if any, of the proposed control measures in solving it. The reality is that the media reporting of heroin addiction is way out of proportion to its actual occurrence in the community. As we shall see, estimates of heroin use in Australia are exceedingly unreliable, although we can safely say that use is considerable. By no stretch of the imagination, though, is it widespread enough to merit 21.8 per cent of the *Australian*'s total press.

But then, as Windshuttle (1978) pointed out, the media almost have to highlight the unusual, the surprising and the abnormal. Nothing is as stale as yesterday's news, and in their own highly competitive sphere the media must focus on items which are newsworthy. The aberrations allegedly resulting from heroin use are the very stuff of news copy, and the media's use of them has become remarkably sophisticated. Thus, very few news items today involve grossly stereotypical portraits of crazed drug fiends committing heinous crimes. Instead, they play on widespread social discontent and insecurity by emphasising the implicit *moral* content of their coverage of drug issues. The ability to shock and titillate is only part of the perennial appeal of media drug stories. An equally important aspect is the provision of scapegoats that can be condemned with a clear conscience.

In their general form, media drug stories resemble classic morality tales within an adventure story framework. Nemesis, in the form of powerful drugs and vicious pushers, follows the culpable—the weak, amoral users and their incompetent parents—who can thus be seen as partly responsible for their own predicament. According to Bell (1985), the proper staging of such a plot requires an equally rhetorical representation of pro-social agents. Experienced professional heroes and helpers are needed, the former to fight against the villains, the latter to allay the victims' sufferings. Police, doctors and drug workers typically fill these roles, as do researchers. But 'even representatives of the bureaucracy may be represented as knights in shining armour who fight by means of knowledge and words ... [and] governments themselves can be construed as antagonists in the battle, with their spokespersons seen as the embodiment of a will to win the war with "drug chiefs"' (p. 238). The prevalent metaphor is one of war-like conflict, in which a wide range of heroic actors 'fight', 'save', 'win' and 'raid' on society's behalf. The reader is invited to review some of the above news extracts from this perspective.

It is grand 'infotainment', as *Connexions* (1985) called it, but what are its effects on the public's conception of drug-related matters?

First, illicit drug use generally, but the use of heroin in particular, is seen as a *problem*.

Second, it is a problem for one or more of the following reasons.

Heroin has an intrinsic capacity to possess people who use it, to enslave and eventually destroy them. Its mere presence breeds corruption, crime, prostitution, sickness and death. It is highly contagious, and a single user will infect all acquaintances with the plague on contact. The whole evil scenario is controlled and manipulated by depraved pushers who deliberately set out to destroy the very fabric of society.

And finally, the media have connived with the public by largely exonerating them from any responsibility for either causing or solving this problem.

> Press stories are always about 'someone else' yet they imply a concerned (even personally threatened) reader who shares their values ... Drug stories in the press seem to deny the reader the very knowledge that they promise (or assume). Not only do they see drug problems as almost exclusively concerned with *consumption by individuals* (not production in a specific context), they also posit heroes and helpers acting on behalf of the administrative arm of society in just the right proportion to allay any excessive threat that the villainy of racketeers and the weakness of victims might arouse. Perhaps the most likely reaction ... is one of fatalistic alienation tinged with hope that one's own friends and family will not arbitrarily succumb to the threat that 'drugs' pose. Newspapers educate their readers to resigned passivity. (Bell, 1985, p. 238)

Can we do better? In some ways we *are* doing better. In his analysis of trends in media reporting of drug issues, White (1985) noted that between 1982 and 1984, emphasis shifted from a narrow focus on the drugs–crime link to a more measured, wider ranging view of drug use. The press was also using increasingly varied sources of information, and a greater variety of perspectives. It seems, therefore, that the coverage of what is really happening in the field as a whole is becoming more comprehensive.

However, the search for professional saviours continues. Currently, the media are focusing public attention on solutions through governmental action and research. Fully one third of the drug stories published in 1984 dealt with what heroes and helpers from these areas could do to save the day. A more appropriate emphasis would be on what individuals and communities can do to save themselves, but so far there has been little enough action on that front. Unfortunately, until this issue is tackled, the continuing and increasing engagement of the media with drug problems can only be counterproductive. No new solutions will be proposed and public anxiety will continue to rise.

Earle Hackett commented much along these lines when reviewing his experiences at the Drug Workshop that was convened to advise the 1985 summit meeting of state premiers:

Attending the Drug Workshop in Canberra gave me a feeling of *deja vu*, for nine years ago I was a member of the Sackville Royal Commission. That had involved me for almost two years in hearing all the reiterated positions regarding drugs, accompanied by the shrill chorus kept up by the media. I remember that at that time I had written privately to a very experienced medical acquaintance who had spent his whole professional career advising the Home Office in London on the Drug Problem. I asked him to distil all his experience for me. He replied promptly. 'What the Drug Problem needs', he said wearily, 'is a good dose of boredom.' (1986, p. 270)

Active, creative boredom with the drug problem is not likely to impress either politicians or the public as a constructive solution—and yet it may be the only realistic one.

2
Heroin in history: a tale of two countries

HEROIN ADDICT NEEDLES COURT

LONDON: *Police watched in amazement as a man, 22, injected himself in the buttocks with heroin as he waited in a court-room dock for sentencing on drug charges.*

The syringe was passed to him from the public gallery by his 21-year-old girlfriend during a lull in the proceedings.

Daily Mirror, 17 April 1984

ONLY IN AMERICA ...

A man, alone in a bathroom with heroin swirling down the toilet cannot be considered 'in control' of the drug, a state appeals court ruled.

Harold Johnson, who had been accused of possession of heroin, and of flushing the drugs down the toilet to foil police, had been sentenced to 15 years' jail after a jury decided that the drug was 'under his control'. Johnson appealed, saying he did not have the heroin under his control at the time of his arrest. The appeals court agreed.

Australian, 31 January 1984

Opium, the parent of heroin, is perhaps the oldest drug known. The ancient Sumerians grew it at least as early as 6000 B.C., and it was widely used both in medicine and for recreational purposes throughout the ancient world. By 1000 A.D., opium was well established in both India and China. Knowledge of its effects declined in Europe during the Middle Ages, but it was reintroduced into Western medicine early in the sixteenth century by Paracelsus, who also seems to have been the originator of a secret potion called 'laudanum'. It is not clear whether his version contained opium, but two centuries later opium was undoubtedly the principal active ingredient of laudanum as prepared by Dr Thomas Sydenham. Ray (1978) gives Dr Sydenham's recipe as 2 oz strained opium, 1 oz saffron, a drachm each of cinnamon and cloves, dissolved in 1 pint of Canary wine and taken in small quantities. 'Without opium', wrote Dr Sydenham, 'the healing art would cease to exist' and he was correct. For several centuries, opium preparations were very nearly the only medicines that genuinely worked.

In Dr Sydenham's time, medicinal opium was taken as an infusion, and the process was referred to as *opium eating*. *Opium smoking* was always a predominantly recreational activity, and it actually developed from tobacco smoking. The tobacco habit had been brought to Europe in the 1400s from the Caribbean and the Spaniards then exported it to the Philippines. From there, it spread to China and Formosa, where its use became so offensive that it was forbidden by Imperial edict in 1644. It was this restriction that led to the combination of opium with tobacco for smoking. Initially, the opium was used to disguise the smell of the tobacco. However, the tobacco was soon omitted from the mixture and, while opium eating had never been especially attractive to the Chinese, the practice of its smoking spread rapidly. In a sense, tobacco led directly to the first international drug laws: these were intended to control opium smoking in China and elsewhere.

In Europe, non-medical use of opium began to gain notoriety in the early part of the nineteenth century. In Britain, it came to be associated with several famous authors including De Quincey and Elizabeth Barrett Browning. Their careers aroused considerable and slightly shocked public interest, and the image that all opiates have today—part angel of mercy, part vilest of all evils—began to emerge. Opium also became the focus of Britain's long, controversial and highly publicised Opium Wars with China.

The early years of the nineteenth century also saw the isolation of opium's chief active principle. *Morphine* was discovered in 1806 and it slowly began to replace opium in medicine. The ability of opium to produce physical dependence had been known and described since at least the 1500s, and the same problem was quickly demonstrated with morphine. But its positive effects on pain and bowel complaints far outweighed this slight disadvantage. Still, thoughtful physicians emphasised caution in its use, and much of the subsequent research on the opium alkaloids was undertaken in the hope that some of these compounds would be free from morphine's habit-forming properties, or could actually cure the morphine habit. The semisynthetic *heroin* was prepared in 1890 and introduced commercially in 1898.

The United States waged no opium wars, but it did perfect the hypodermic syringe, and it seems to have been the first country to have large-scale problems with morphine. The first hypodermic injection of morphine occurred in the United States in 1856, and the first needle addict may well have been Mrs Alexander Wood, whose husband was prominent in the development of modern injection techniques. Initially, injected morphine was thought to be less habit-forming, and from 1861 to 1865 the Civil War provided America with ample opportunity to use it. The Prusso—Austrian War (1866) and the Franco—Prussian War (1870) offered similar venues in Europe. Morphine worked rapidly and well in two major battlefield problems, pain and dysentery. After the wars thousands of ex-soldiers continued to use the drug for these purposes, and they recommended it to friends and relatives. The United States Pension Bureau had difficulties with large numbers of veterans suffering from the 'army disease', as morphine addiction came to be called, until well into the twentieth century.

Today, discussion of drug problems as unique geographic phenomena is rather artificial, at least for the more developed countries. Strategies for dealing with them—and, some would argue, the problems themselves—are increasingly the result of attempts to comply with international drug laws. Nevertheless, perceptions of the opiates as a problem differed considerably in English-speaking countries in the early part of the twentieth century, and they gave rise to distinct prevention and treatment policies. Thus, Britain early developed an official policy of regarding opiate dependence as a disease requiring treatment, while the United States generally viewed it as a moral issue and relied heavily on control through criminal law. Both countries use an essentially similar mixture of controls to deal with opiates today, but this is not generally appreciated. For many people, the 'British' and 'American' systems have come to stand for support and punishment of the user respectively, and the basic policy choice relating to official methods of drug control is still often assumed to be between these two approaches. It is therefore useful to examine the history of early drug policy in these two key countries separately, with special attention to the critical period between the mid—1800s to approximately the end of World War II.

Australia's own involvement with opiate misuse is necessarily briefer and less complex than that of the two older nations. Its drug laws were shaped by theirs in its earliest days and, in due course, it became signatory to the same international treaties. In the last two decades, it has experienced much the same pressures, and if these have been less in an absolute sense, their relative effects have been as great and perhaps greater. In almost every sense, Australia has led a very sheltered existence, and its confrontation with twentieth century problems has been sudden and painful. For reasons of space, therefore, we will not consider Australia's drug history, although Australian statistics will be used in the discussion of heroin-related problems in Chapter 6.

Opiates in Britain

The first nation to become concerned about the consequences of opiate use was imperial China. Opium for non-medical purposes was outlawed in 1729, but a large and highly profitable smuggling system developed with India under the auspices of the British East India Company. The rationale was purely commercial—England needed the profits from the opium trade to offset the cost of the tea, silk and other luxuries coming from China. Similar commercial concerns motivated China to attempt to block the opium smuggling. While opium smoking was regarded as a vice, public health was not a major consideration; China was worried primarily about the drain on its foreign exchange. The complexities of the resulting Opium Wars are beyond the scope of this discussion, but their impact on Britain's own perception of domestic opium use was considerable.

Anti-opium organisations of various kinds existed in Britain before the Opium Wars, and on the medical front a distinction was developing between legitimate medical and other, non-medical uses of the drug. Early anti-opium initiatives were generally short-lived and had little public support. The year 1874, however, saw the foundation of the Society for the Suppression of Opium Trade. It began with a group of Quaker anti-opium campaigners, and its main aim was abolition of the government monopoly on opium in India as well as withdrawal of pressure on the Chinese government to admit Indian opium. The Society continued to press the anti-opium cause with varying political success for the next twenty years, though after 1885 the originally coherent anti-opium platform splintered into a number of separate camps. Several rival anti-opium organisations came into being, and this considerably weakened the cause.

The Society had its own journal, *The Friend of China*, and most of the other anti-opium organisations also published various tracts. From these, the controversy spilled over into the public journals. Among other things, this drew attention to the expanding Chinese community in London, and helped form the largely mythical image of the mysterious and threatening opium 'dens' in the back streets of the East End. This remained very much a popular stereotype and it had considerable influence on the moral campaign.

Many of the issues in the anti-opium campaign had little relevance to opiate use in England. There were endless arguments, for example, whether Britain had in fact forced opium on China, and whether the Chinese were sincere in their efforts to suppress the drug. There were also many confusions. Thus, opium was smoked in China, but 'eaten' in England, and debate often became tangled when evidence relating to one form of use was introduced into discussions of the other.

And there were some notable setbacks, at least from the anti-opium standpoint. After 1885, emphasis shifted from China to India, where opium was not only produced but also eaten, and the anti-opiumists succeeded in getting a Royal Commission established to investigate the situation. Its 1895 report was in many ways a whitewash; the Indian sittings of the commission had been carefully stage-managed by the Indian government. Nevertheless, anti-opium testimony proved hard to find: the opium-besotted addict of the anti-opium tracts seemed very rare in practice, and the realities of the Indian experience were clearly not entirely congruent with the anti-opium cause. Still, much was made of the need to bring the Indian system of sale into line with the British one. Lax though they were, the restrictions on opium availability imposed by the *Pharmacy Act* of 1869 in Britain were an improvement on the open availability of the drug in India. The end result of all this was an emphasis on increased restrictions at home as well.

Probably the most influential aspect of the anti-opium campaign, however, was the character of the campaigners themselves. From the beginning, the clergy figured prominently. Active missionaries formed a strong contingent among the campaign's leaders, and public support for the cause came largely from the membership of non-conformist congregations. Still more important were the medical representatives. The anti-opium movement had many doctors in its ranks, and many of these were 'addiction specialists'. Existing concepts of addiction had been worked out for alcohol. They included the temperance view that certain substances were inherently addicting and could take over the will. They also included the idea that this condition was a disease, total abstinence being the only cure. Most important, since the proponents of these concepts were doctors, they naturally promoted the view that addiction was a medical issue. Both the moral campaigners and the addiction specialists agreed that moderate use was impossible. Dosage always increased, addiction was inevitable, and it always produced moral debasement as well as physical deterioration. The existence of moderate users, if accepted, would have undermined both the case for ending the cultivation of the poppy and the medical argument that all regular users of opium were the proper concern of the profession.

The anti-opium movement as such essentially disintegrated with the report of the Royal Commission on Opium in 1895. Its views, however, continued to be expressed by the elite of medical addiction specialists. Not all addicts accepted the new medical definition of their condition. Those who refused to conform to the model of disease and treatment were a continual source of official anxiety. Berridge and Edwards (1981) cite the case of one addict, the son of a leading South Wales physician. This 'drug-inebriate' was refusing to go to any sort of retreat. 'He is not a drunkard', mourned the family solicitor, ' . . . and he cannot be certified insane . . . After the effects of the drug are over he is mentally well. If he were insane he could of course be taken to an Asylum . . . but not being a drunkard nor insane and refusing voluntarily to go to any "Home", the problem is what to do with him . . .' (p. 228).

But most agreed that addicts were sick rather than deviant, and by and large non-medical use of drugs was not a major legal concern at this time. At the official professional level, however, contemporary civil servants and the medical profession were in general agreement on the disease concept of addiction. When Britain ratified the Hague Convention of 1912, this consensus became the basis of the formal policy on opiates.

Signatories to the Hague Convention resolved to bring about the gradual suppression of the abuse of drugs. 'Abuse' essentially meant non-medical use, and the drugs in question were opium, morphine and cocaine. Signatory countries were to enact national laws to limit the manufacture, sale and use of drugs to medical and legitimate research purposes, and illegal possession was to be considered a penal offence. America's *Harrison Act* of 1914 was passed to meet these requirements. In England, World War I intervened and legal action on the matter was deferred until after the Versailles Peace Treaty which, incidentally, required signature of the Hague Convention by both the victors and the vanquished.

England's eventual response to these agreements was the passage, in 1920, of the first *Dangerous Drugs Act*. This established a series of controls over the import and export of opium, morphine and cocaine, and it restricted their handling to authorised persons—doctors, veterinarians, dentists and pharmacists. Any of these professionals could be in possession of and supply the drugs covered by the Act 'so far as is necessary for the practice of his profession'.

As in the case of the essentially similar *Harrison Act* in the United States, the question arose as to whether this allowed prescription of the drugs to addicts. In 1924, the Departmental Committee on Morphine and Heroin Addiction (subsequently known as the Rolleston Committee after its chairman) was set up to consider the matter. In the United States, the issue had been resolved by the Supreme Court and the conclusion was that administration of opiates to addicts was not part of legitimate medical treatment. However, the members of the Rolleston Committee were all medically trained and they came to the opposite conclusion.

Briefly, the Committee heard evidence that addiction was rare and seemed to be declining. They noted that addicts came mainly from the great urban centres, and that they were either in occupations which entailed great nervous strain or which permitted ready access to the drugs. Among the predisposing factors listed were environment, physical distress, nervous instability, insomnia, overwork and anxiety. One eminent witness thought that 'neuropathic heredity' could be traced in many cases, and 'might reasonably be assumed to have been present in the remainder'.

The Committee recognised that some sources of illicit supply existed, but felt that addicts in general lacked 'the necessary determination and ingenuity' to make use of them. There was no mention of the possibility of organised crime, and the major source of supply was thought to be the medical profession. The majority of addicts had been introduced to the drugs in the course of medical treatment, and some took them as a form of self-medication for the relief of pain or emotional distress. In a few rare instances, drug use began as a result of the influence of others, or because of curiosity or indulgence. Even in these addicts—the Committee called them the 'underworld class'—drug addiction was to be regarded as a disease rather than a vice: the drugs were not taken for pleasure, but to relieve a morbid and overpowering craving. In this, as in all its general deliberations on etiology, the Committee was endorsing the prevailing medical opinion of the time: 'the taking of a narcotic drug of addiction for a few doses may be termed a vice, but if the administration is continued for a month or so a true disease condition becomes established with a definite pathology and symptoms' (Rolleston Committee, 1926).

Bean (1974) presents the following elegant summary of the Committee's rulings on the administration of morphine and heroin to known addicts:

> The Committee ... concluded that morphine and heroin should be given to addicts in the following circumstances. In the first place they could be given to relieve pain, or for the purposes of gradual withdrawal, as part of a definite plan of treatment. It was not considered that any questions would arise as to the legitimacy of prescribing in these circumstances, but they reminded practitioners that the primary object of treatment was the cure of addiction if practicable 'by steady judicious reductions of the dose'. The patient should be seen frequently and always be under sufficient medical control ...
> The other circumstances in which morphine and heroin could

be supplied are more contentious. One was where, after every effort had been made to cure the addict the drug could still not be completely withdrawn because of serious difficulties which might arise and which could not be treated satisfactorily under the ordinary conditions of medical practice ... There were other circumstances in which the patient might be capable of leading a useful and relatively normal life with a regular minimum dose, but would become incapable of doing so if the drug was withdrawn ...

Whenever the last 2 conditions existed and the medical practitioner decided to supply morphine and heroin, special precautions were thought to be needed. First, supplies should be kept within the limits of what was strictly needed. Second, the patient was to be seen not less than once a week and supplies should be no more than was sufficient to last until the next visit. Third, if a new patient asked for morphine or heroin the medical practitioner should only give that which was immediately necessary, and if further supplies were required, 'the request should not be acceded to until after the practitioner has obtained from the previous medical attendant an account of the nature of the case ...'

The Committee then added a general note on the question of the precautions to be taken when morphine and heroin were used in ordinary medical practice for persons not addicted. Their view was that other drugs should be substituted wherever possible, and if it were not possible then heroin or morphine should only be given in small doses. The patient was not to know the name of the drug, and in no circumstances should he be allowed to inject it himself. (pp. 62–4)

The Committee's report was acccepted by parliament and a set of new regulations was confirmed in 1926. These formed the basis of what came to be known as the 'British System'. For a time, any English doctor was able to prescribe morphine or heroin to addicts 'for the purposes of ministering to their medical needs', as the Home Office explained in 1953. This meant *treatment* of addiction, since addiction was a disease—an important point, since the Home Office stated unambiguously that 'prescription solely for the gratification of addiction is not regraded as a medical need'. How the distinction was to be made in practice was never specified.

There was little criticism of the *Rolleston Report*. The *British Medical Journal* was enthusiastic, not only about what was included, but about what had been left out:

> It is of interest to note that no steps are being taken to enforce notification of drug addiction, or to make compulsory the seeking of a second medical opinion in the treatment of cases of drug

addiction and that no authoritative rules have been issued for guidance in the use of scheduled drugs. The British Medical Association raised strong objections to all these proposals. Its chief contention that drug addiction is a manifestation of a disease frequently associated with nervous instability and frequently requiring treatment and not merely a vice demanding punishment appears now to be definitely recognised. (quoted in Bean, 1974, p. 68)

A number of observers commented on the relatively much greater incidence of problems in the United States, with its restrictions on prescribing to addicts, and they inferred that England's happy situation was the result of its medical response to addiction. The *British Medical Journal* itself smugly suggested that 'Britain might serve as a model for other governments which are parties to several conventions' (Bean, 1974, p. 70). In fact, as Edwards points out, 'the relaxed and gentlemanly British way of responding to drugs was witness to the small scale of the problem rather than the cause of that scale' (Berridge and Edwards, 1981, pp. 254–5). This had not escaped contemporary observers either. Bean (1974) cites the case of one physician who wanted to know where all these addicts were.

Plain men like myself want to know where the drug addicts are that call for such measures. I have never seen a case in general practice, my partner has never seen one, more than that a very eminent London neurologist . . . told me he had been asking practitioners their experience of such cases for 2 years and none of them had ever seen one! (p. 70)

Nevertheless, both the idea that the treatment of addiction was properly the province of medical professionals and the feeling that such a response would keep drug problems within manageable limits was to persist unchanged for some four decades.

Compared with the United States, England probably did have only a minor problem with opiate addiction. The reason was less the British system than the enormously different social conditions in the cities of the two nations. Even so, there is reason to believe that England's opiate problem was substantially greater than the Rolleston Committee's optimism had suggested. The size of a problem depends on how it is measured and, as Bean (1974) trenchantly remarked, 'the deviant is one to whom the label has been successfully applied' (p. 97).

Prior to 1937, England had no obligation to provide any statistics on drug addiction. Thereafter, annual returns were made to the League of Nations and eventually to the United Nations. The Home Office did keep some records and the first official estimate of addicts was reported in a discussion of drug addiction in 1931. At that time, the Home Office had the names of 250 addicts. This number rose to 300 in 1934 and 700 in 1935. Police records of prosecutions of drug offences under the *Dangerous Drugs Act* of 1920 were also available from 1921, but there was little cooperation between the police and the Home Office until the 1950s.

Basically, addicts came to the notice of the Home Office because they voluntarily reported themselves. Between 1945 and 1967, some probably believed that if the Home Office knew they were 'registered' (even though no such registration procedure even existed), they could not be prosecuted for having drugs in their possession. On the whole, though, their reasons for reporting themselves remain obscure; there seem to have been few apparent benefits for doing so. On these grounds alone, it is clear that no firm relationship can be drawn between Home Office estimates and reality. The figures were clearly underestimates. By how much will probably never be known, but some indication may be obtained from figures cited by Berridge and Edwards (1981). They estimate that between 1830 and 1869 average home consumption of opium was around three pounds per person. This equates to roughly 127 therapeutic doses of opium per year for every man, woman and child. The distribution of use was certainly uneven over the country, but this still represents a very high level of use. Opium as such gradually became less popular, both in medicine and as self-medication, but a growing spectrum of other drugs took its place. Just as the use of opium for symptomatic treatment of illness had earlier merged without clear demarcation into use for pleasure or for relief of anomie, similar mergings must have occurred for the drugs that replaced it. The incidence of drug problems, including addiction, undoubtedly remained much greater than the Home Office figures suggest.

The increase in heroin addiction in the late 1950s has sometimes been attributed to the indiscriminate prescribing the British System made possible. This is an oversimplification. There were certainly some abuses, and at that time the Home Office had no effective means other than remonstration for dealing with a doctor whose prescriptions to addicts gave rise to concern. Thus, Spear (1982) cites the 1955 test case of a London doctor who had issued over 70 prescriptions for heroin for an addict he knew was the patient of another doctor although he had never contacted that doctor to inform him of the fact. Moreover, the first doctor had only seen the addict himself on a dozen or so occasions, being content to hand the prescription to the addict's girlfriend, who was herself an addict. In dismissing charges against the doctor, the magistrate commented:

'It may well be that the patient committed an offence here. It is not for me to decide one way or the other. But to my mind, it would make nonsense of these regulations, which as I see it are designed to give duly qualified medical practitioners absolute discretion as to the way they should treat their patients, and the quantity of drugs that they should prescribe, if I were to hold that these facts amounted to an infringement of the regulations by the defendant. There is nothing in these regulations to which my attention has been directed, which limits the quantity of drugs that may be lawfully prescribed by a doctor.

'It may be that this conduct on the part of the defendant was gravely improper; it is not for me to decide any such issue. It may be that this is a matter that might properly be referred to the disciplinary body of the medical profession' . . .

Referring the facts to the General Medical Council was equally unrewarding and produced the reply that . . . the Council regretted they could not see their way to take any steps against the doctor . . . (p. 55)

Nevertheless, such abuses seem to have been few, and on the whole the British System worked well enough for some 30 years.

When heroin use began to increase in the early 1950s, there is no question that medical prescriptions fuelled its spread. However, the prescriptions did not create the demand. This came from a newly emerged, fairly cohesive group of addicts who began to seek out and exploit those doctors who could be induced to prescribe heroin in liberal amounts. Where this seminal group came from has been a matter of considerable speculation. The dramatic claim that the problem was caused by a few (variously 26 to 76) American-style addicts who fled to Britain from Canada in the wake of a harsh new drug law smacks of scapegoats. There is no evidence to suggest that their contribution was greater than that of local British addicts.

Some economic reasons for the 1950s upswing are suggested in Chapter 4. However, it does appear that a very important factor was the development of a youth culture which was, for the first time, large and affluent enough to develop certain folkways of its own. These included not only distinctive dress and music, but the recreational taking of marijuana, 'pills', and, to a limited extent, opiates. In any event, it is now clear that a relatively small number of young people who centred their lives on drugs quickly destroyed the British System as it then existed. The new-style addicts could often induce physicians to prescribe considerably more than was needed to sustain their habits, and they were able to find ready purchasers for the surplus among their friends. Still, at the end of the 1950s, the official statistics gave little apparent cause for concern. In absolute terms, the actual number of known addicts was still smaller than it had been in the 1930s, though 1958 had marked a significant upturn: 442 were reported then, as opposed to 359 in the previous year.

Nevertheless, public anxiety about the opiates was maintained by several factors. One was persistent international interest in the matter. In 1920, the League of Nations created an Opium Advisory Committee and in 1925 the Geneva Convention began to work on the regulation of international trade in drugs. The Limitation Convention of 1931 ruled that manufacture of narcotics be limited to the needs of medicine and research, and economic sanctions were prescribed for defaulting countries. Both Conventions resulted in new *Dangerous Drugs Acts* in Britain. After the war, the United Nations took over from the League of Nations, and its Committee on Narcotic Drugs continued the work of the old Opium Advisory Committee. One of its first acts was to extend international control to synthetic narcotics with the 1948 Protocol, which again resulted in changes in British domestic drug policy. All in all, international agreements were responsible for all British drug legislation up to the 1964 *Dangerous Drugs Act*, which was passed to implement the Single Convention. The Single Convention and the subsequent Convention of Psychotropic Substances (1971) are the main international treaties today, and they will be discussed further in Chapter 5.

British attitudes, then, were much influenced by international paranoia about drugs. However, what seems to have caused greatest public concern was not the international scene or the apparent size of the problem at home. Rather, it was the perceived change in the nature of the domestic addict.

As we have seen, early Home Office statistics were rather ephemeral. Nevertheless, a few inferences can be made. From 1934 to 1945, the male:female ratio among known addicts was about even, and some 20 per cent came from 'professional classes'. Most seem to have been addicted to a single drug. In 1936, for example, morphine accounted for 72 per cent of the cases, with 17 per cent and 8.5 per cent addicted to heroin and cocaine respectively. Prosecution statistics from the period add the information that the addicts seemed mostly middle-aged. Females accounted for nearly 50 per cent of the morphine and heroin offences, and half of them were shown as having no occupation, which probably means they were housewives. Among males, the largest occupational group was 'seamen', presumably opium-smoking Chinese, and most of the offenders were fined.

The people described by these statistics were no threat to established value systems. The Chinese seamen could be excused on 'cultural' grounds, particularly as they seem to have made little attempt to proselytise among the indigenous population. The addicted members of the medical profession naturally wanted to keep their habits secret and to be allowed to continue their work. The housewives were obviously good citizens in all other respects, but had unfortunately become addicted. They were more to be pitied than blamed. In other words, since the known addicts were not a problem, neither was addiction itself.

By the late 1950s, however, a new type of addict began to emerge. They were much younger and predominantly male. Increasingly, their drug of choice was heroin. They did not come from the professional classes. Far from being secretive about their addiction, they were highly visible. They congregated in particular areas, they seemed disinclined to continue or even begin working, and many seemed part of various pseudo-philosophical movements.

It is significant that the Home Office first began to differentiate between 'therapeutic' and 'non-therapeutic' addicts in 1958. In that year, 80 per cent of known addicts (349 persons) were classed as 'therapeutic', that is, people who could be seen as having become addicted through medical contact with drugs rather than through contact with other drug users, and to whom the traditional interpretations could still be applied. The size of this group subsequently remained very constant over the years. The increase in known addicts from then on was accounted for entirely by the new non-therapeutic group, which increased from 68 in 1958 to 2533 by 1969. There can be no doubt that this group was real and that it did in fact grow. However, it is interesting to speculate to what extent its early importance was exaggerated by its high visibility and vulnerability to apprehension.

It was against this background of national and international concern that the Home Office convened the Interdepartmental Committee on Drug Addiction under Lord Brain to review the Rolleston Committee's advice on addiction. As was the case with the Rolleston Committee, most of the Brain Committee's members were medical professionals. When the Committee reported in 1961, they concluded that the incidence of addiction was very small, and that the traffic in illicit supplies was almost negligible. Moreover, on examining more than 100 case histories, they found no reason to reject the concept of the 'stabilised addict' of the *Rolleston Report*. This, it will be recalled, was a person who was capable of leading a useful and fairly normal life as long as the drug of addiction was available, and who ceased to lead such a life when the drug was withdrawn. The committee also recommended that 'the Home Secretary should not establish medical tribunals to investigate the grounds for recommending him to withdraw a doctor's authority to possess and supply dangerous drugs'.

The end result of all this was that there was to be no major change in policy. Addicts continued to be medical property, and there was no formal machinery for dealing with the overprescribing doctor. It was not that the medical profession particularly wanted to treat addicts. They were then, and to some extent they still are, unpopular patients and few would treat them, let alone specialise in their problems. The issue was, rather, the threat of bureaucratic interference with professional practice, particularly with the right of doctors to prescribe as they saw fit.

In spite of the comforting picture presented by the Brain Committee, the number of new non-therapeutic addicts coming to official notice continued to rise and a flourishing black market developed. Some of the material sold on the streets had been stolen from pharmacies, drug warehouses, hospitals or doctors' surgeries. For the most part, though, addicts were disposing of their own legitimately obtained drugs. Clearly, either doctors were overprescribing or addicts were underconsuming—or both. Lord Brain's Interdepartmental Committee was reconvened in 1963 to solve the specific problem of overprescription.

In 1965, the Committee reported that the main source of supply to the new addicts 'has been the activity of a very few doctors who have prescribed excessively,' but that 'these doctors have acted within the law and according to their professional judgement' (Second Brain Committee, 1965). This was not necessarily a whitewash. Some of the problem was still due to the activities of 'script' doctors. As Lord Brain remarked to the Home Office representatives after hearing evidence of one doctor's practices, 'Your problem, gentlemen, can be summed up in 2 words—"Dr X".' However, by 1960, most of the drugs seem to have come from a few newcomers whose motives were unimpeachable. These were dedicated practitioners who felt that the young addicts presented a challenge which the rest of the profession was refusing to take up, and who were prepared to put themselves to endless trouble on behalf of the addicts. Inevitably this attitude made them easy prey for manipulative addicts.

To stem the problem, the Committee made three recommendations. First, prescribing of heroin and cocaine was to be restricted to the staff of special centres that were to be set up to treat addicts. Limitations on the supply of other narcotic drugs were thought to be both unjustified and impractical.

Second, all medical practitioners were to notify all cases of addiction they encountered to a central authority. Such notification had no legal consequences for the addict, and was not to be equated with 'registration', which 'might seem to imply that the addict is officially recognised as having a right to an approved quantity of dangerous drugs' (Second Brain Committee, 1965).

Third, there should be power of compulsory detention of addicts in the new centres 'because of the obstinacy of some addicts and the likelihood that some will not attend the treatment centres or that others may break off treatment after they have embarked on it'.

In making these recommendations, the Committee was struggling with two dilemmas. One was the simultaneous need to permit doctors to prescribe according to their professional judgement, and to curb the inevitable misuse of such freedom. All doctors were no longer seen as equally 'competent'. The Committee expressed the second dilemma as follows:

> If there is insufficient control it may lead to the spread of addiction—as is happening at present. If, on the other hand, the restrictions are so severe as to prevent or seriously discourage the addict from obtaining supplies from legitimate sources it may lead to the development of an organised traffic. The absence hitherto of such an organised illicit traffic has been attributed largely to the fact that an addict has been able to obtain supplies of drugs legally ... (Second Brain Committee, 1965)

The obvious fear was that those addicts who refused to be withdrawn and who were refused ample legitimate supplies of their drug would turn to illegitimate sources. The restriction on general ability to prescribe, it was hoped, would reduce the amount of legitimate heroin that was diverted for illicit use. At the same time, 'competitive prescribing' at the clinics should both accommodate those addicts who had been treated by general practitioners and encourage others to come forward from the anonymity of the street.

The first two recommendations were accepted and embodied in the *Dangerous Drugs Act* of 1967. The third was rejected on the not unreasonable grounds that if it became law, the great majority of addicts would shun the proposed treatment centres entirely.

It took two years to put the 1967 Act into full operation, and some have blamed the subsequent rise of the illicit drug market on this delay. It probably did contribute. The framing of the 1967 Act produced a good deal of uncertainty and speculation within the addict community. Clearly there was to be a restriction on the prescribing of heroin, but there was little information on how this would be implemented. The addicts naturally feared the worst, and they immediately began to seek alternate sources of supply.

However, other factors were also relevant. There was, during this period, a significant rise in the number of known addicts: from 521 in 1965 to 1299 in 1967. Moreover, these new addicts, together with those who chose not to become officially known, began to form a potential market of sufficient size to attract international traffickers. Where street heroin had previously been diverted pharmaceutical material, 'Chinese heroin' now began to appear in seizures. This came from Hong Kong and was probably intended primarily for smoking by London's Chinese community. However, by 1968 there was evidence that it was beginning to be used intravenously by a small number of addicts. Addicts were initially rather suspicious of this new brown powder, but its competitive price—about half that of diverted pharmaceutical heroin—undoubtedly made it attractive. The number of persons found in possession of it began to rise and it was to remain an established feature of the British opiate black market until the mid–1970s.

Illicit traffic and the spread of addiction received additional impetus from two further developments. One had to do with the concentration of the new regulations on heroin and cocaine. No controls were set on the prescribing of other drugs and a number of doctors seem to have been willing to substitute others. The amount of methedrine on the streets, for instance, increased dramatically. In May 1968, only a month after the new centres had come into full operation, Drugs Branch inspectors recovered private prescriptions for a total of 35 248 ampoules from a number of London pharmacies. These had been issued by eight doctors, one of whom was alone responsible for a total of 24 905 ampoules which he had prescribed for 110 apparently different individuals. The average rate of supply to one of his 'patients' was 46 ampoules per day. As there was still no machinery to deal with the overprescriber *per se*, this abuse had to be managed by restricting sales of methamphetamine ampoules to hospitals. A potential 'speed' epidemic was averted, but in an indirect way the episode probably increased the attraction of heroin. It brought together heroin addicts and the wider community of adolescents who were involved with amphetamines and provided the bridge between the needle culture and the kids in the clubs. According to Leech (1973), methedrine rather than cannabis played the escalator role and made the process of 'fixing' an integral part of the West End drug culture.

There was nothing in the new regulations, then, to prevent addicts from diversifying into other legally prescribed drugs. As it turned out, the operation of the clinics, when they finally did become established, actually encouraged them to do so. In the early days, clinics tended to overprescribe. It must be remembered that then, as now, addicts were unpopular patients. With very few exceptions, the only doctors with more than an academic knowledge of addicts were the very general practitioners whose involvement the new clinics were designed to eliminate. When the clinics opened, therefore, the addicts' experience in dealing with doctors usually far outweighed that of the staff in dealing with addicts. This, combined with the fact that there was no simple method of assessing how much drug an addict actually required, meant that prescriptions were initially generous. For a time, therefore, some heroin could again be diverted.

However, the clinic staff learned quickly and they soon began to reduce the size of individual doses drastically. More important, though, the clinics began to substitute methadone for heroin. Injectable methadone was, and still is, unpopular with experienced addicts, and they initially exchanged their ampoules for other drugs or sold them; the proceeds from these were then used to buy illicit heroin. The customers for these unwanted ampoules were often young persons at the fringes of the addict scene, and by 1970 there was a significant number of primary methadone addicts approaching the clinics.

The situation was not improved by the trend to replace injectable methadone with the oral form. This occurred partly because oral methadone is safer, and partly in response to pressure for greater social control over what was felt to be a new and more refractory kind of addict. Today, the few clinics that still maintain any number of addicts on heroin or morphine do so under a kind of grandfather clause. Those patients who were started on these drugs when they were originally treated for addiction, and who have made what their physicians regard as a good adjustment, may continue to receive them. New addicts, those who have returned to the clinic after temporarily dropping out of treatment, and those who have not adjusted in the sense that they have remained unemployed or been in trouble with the law, are given oral methadone, often despite strenuous objections.

The effects of this on the illicit trade really could have been predicted. Faced with small supplies of a non-preferred drug in a non-preferred form, addicts increasingly turned to illicit sources. Some attempted to supplement their prescribed heroin or methadone with other drugs capable of potentiating their effects, particularly the barbiturates. These were obtained from doctors on a casual or regular basis, through forged prescriptions, or by theft from retail pharmacies. Barbiturates themselves can cause physical dependence and this, together with the physical problems associated with injecting material intended for oral use, increased the deterioration of urban addicts.

There was also an increased incentive to seek out legally available heroin substitutes, and this refocused attention on the general practitioner as a source of supply for the black market. The case of Diconal (Spear, 1982) may be taken as an example. Its active ingredient, dipipanone, is a synthetic substance pharmacologically similar to the opiates, and it is used medically to treat pain. In 1970, a number of cases of Diconal addiction were reported in the north of England. It transpired that these were in fact patients who had been given the drug as a means of weaning them off opiates; the addicts, however, preferred to crush and inject the tablets for a short, heroin-like 'high'.

In mid−1971, an independent outbreak of Diconal misuse in the south was traced to the prescriptions of one general practitioner who appeared willing to prescribe Diconal regularly for any young person, whether on his NHS list or not, who complained of backache or dysmenorrhea. In December 1971 a further outbreak occurred in another south coast town and was similarly fuelled by the prescriptions of an elderly general practitioner. Some of his patients came from as far away as London, and some were also concurrently receiving methadone from the local treatment centre, but as far as he was concerned there was a valid medical reason, usually backache, for each prescription. Within a comparatively short space of time Diconal abuse had spread to most areas of the country where there were injecting addicts and today this preparation continues to be a major factor in the British opiate abuse scene.

There is an important difference between the Diconal situation and the period before the second Brain Committee. Diconal was prescribed by a much larger number of doctors in all parts of the country and these, with few exceptions, did not prescribe large quantities for individuals. For the most part, they simply failed to associate Diconal with addiction, and their suspicions usually only began to be roused when they realised they had suddenly acquired a sizeable group of young 'temporary residents' suffering from backache or similar conditions. Neither did these doctors realise that the tablets they prescribed had a considerable black market value and that the material would probably be injected. It must also be said that addicts showed an uncanny ability to single out the more vulnerable members of the profession. Since there was still no formal machinery for dealing with inappropriate prescription even where motives were suspect, remonstration was the only recourse. Unfortunately as soon as one prescriber was successfully persuaded to stop, addicts would discover another sympathetic and willing practitioner and the process would have to be repeated.

In sum, the effect of the move to treat addicts in clinics was to encourage black market operations on the one hand and to improve addicts' skills in conning general practitioners on the other. It also contributed significantly to the diversification of the drug scene. What had been almost exclusively a heroin and cocaine situation was changing into one in which addicts regularly used a variety of drugs obtained indiscriminately on the white, black and 'grey' markets, the last concerned with the resale of pharmaceutical preparations.

It is nevertheless inappropriate to attribute this entirely to the failure of the 'British System'. Strictly speaking, the British System never received a fair trial as far as the clinics were concerned. From the outset there has been a steady move by treatment centres away from the prescribing of heroin and more recently of all injectable drugs . At best, 'competitive prescribing' can only hope to attract addicts away from the black market at a faster rate than they are being recruited—and it can only do so if addicts are being offered the drugs they want in quantities they feel they need.

In the early and mid−1970s, incidence and prevalence of drug addiction continued to grow, supplied largely by illicitly imported heroin. Police activity and a series of bad harvests in the production areas to some extent limited availability, and prices increased steadily until 1978. From 1979, however, both incidence and prevalence increased in an unprecedented way.

Many argue that part of the reason is unemployment and the current recession. The economic growth, rising living standards and relatively full employment of the 1960s and the early 1970s have been replaced by economic stagnation. Unemployment is generally high, but especially so among the young, disadvantaged and unskilled. Along with this, many cities have experienced a steady deterioration in housing, transport and other services. Thus Ashton (1982) refers to an extensive newspaper article headlined 'Heroin On The Dole' which described 'heroin steadily creeping into deprived housing estates, particularly in unemployment blackspots in Scotland and the North of England'. Glasgow emerged as the single area of greatest concern, and the pattern of use there seemed disturbingly like that usually associated with the ghettos of American cities. The article reported almost total unemployment, little to do and increasing availability of heroin, with dealers trading on the streets of the housing estates. An Edinburgh social worker was quoted as saying: 'There are kids from 16 to their mid−20s with substantial habits . . . It takes them away from unemployment in areas of little resources . . . a lot of them say they don't want to come off it because they'll be going back to the same circumstances which led them to taking it in the first place.'

However, the situation is not quite as simple as that. The recession cannot explain the expansion of use through a wide range of social groupings, including the children of the middle and upper classes. Nor can it explain the fact that heroin addiction appears to be largely restricted to the white British or Irish population, with minimal use in black or other ethnic communities.

It is obvious that the world's worst recession since the 1930s and the presence in England alone of between three and four million unemployed must exert some effects on the patterns of drug use. But there is in fact little evidence for a causal link between unemployment and the rise in addiction, and it would be rash to conclude that the relationship must be negative. The apparent increase in addiction, for example, might be spurious: there might be a link between unemployment and addiction *statistics*, rather than addiction itself. Ashton (1982) presents the 'cautionary tale' of the massive work lay-offs in Detroit, which uncoverd the existence of an estimated 3−4 000 'blue collar' heroin users. Previously they had managed to combine work and heroin without coming to the notice of the authorities but, after losing their jobs, they could no longer support their habits. Many developed withdrawal symptoms and sought help from drug treatment centres or other facilities. In Britain this would have meant a sudden addition of 3−4 000 people to the addiction statistics, although the addicts had been there for some time.

Recession also means less spending money, and there is reason to believe that expenditure on drugs is reduced as often as it is increased. Ashton suggests that this has been one of the reasons behind the recent reduction in British drunkenness offences. The presumed psychological effect of recession is therefore complicated by its simultaneous effect on spending power, and spending power in turn has a complex relationship to drug availability.

The availability of heroin certainly did increase in the late 1970s. The reasons for this will be considered more fully in Chapter 4. Briefly, from about the mid−1970s, because of a series of regional supressions of production and trade and resulting expansions elsewhere, more and more producers and traffickers were actively seeking to maintain and, if possible, expand their markets. Heroin became increasingly available, its purity was reasonable and cost was relatively low. Hartnoll and his colleagues (1984) estimate that relative to inflation, the price of heroin has halved since 1978.

However, it cannot be assumed that ready supply in itself created demand. There were also a number of domestic developments which ensured that the increased supply would find a ready market, even in a depressed economy. One of them, ironically, is the continued existence of the 'British System' (Ashton 1982). Even if heroin has become cheaper, an addict might still use half a gram each day. Supporting a habit of this size on the illicit market requires a disposable income of at least £200 a week. Many of the estimated 20−30 000 opiate dependents in the United Kingdom manage because all or part of their opiate supply consists of legally manufactured substitute opiates like methadone and dipipanone. Something like one-fifth of all heavy users of opiates are prescribed these drugs as part of their treatment, and many of these sell part of their prescription to others.

Another factor has been the relative unavailability of earlier alternatives, especially cannabis. The cost of cannabis has risen markedly over recent years and at times supplies have been limited. The price of heroin is currently low and its purity relatively high, and this makes it relatively more attractive.

Probably the most important factor, however, has been the breakdown of a number of personal and social barriers. Drug-taking circles are no longer as insular as they were. The youth cultures of the late 1960s and early 1970s had disintegrated. In their day, they had exercised a good deal of informal control over which drugs were acceptable and which were not, and heroin was perceived as a relatively unglamorous drug. No really coherent youth cultures have risen to replace them. Moreover, the new generation of users is very much more accustomed to the idea of drug use. Many use alcohol and tobacco routinely, as well as a variety of quasi-legitimate substances such as prescription drugs, over-the-counter medicines and solvents. Multidrug use has become the norm not only for the drug scene, but for the general community as well.

In the drug scene itself, most dealers are now prepared to supply a variety of drugs, though a few purists continue to deal only in cannabis as a matter of principle. Familiarity breeds, if not contempt, then at least an increased willingness to experiment, and the experiences may generalise. Sniffing cocaine, for example, has become a very glamorous activity. As we have seen, in the late 1960s there was a cross-fertilisation between intravenous heroin users and oral amphetamine users. In the 1980s, cocaine sniffing is encouraging the sniffing or smoking of heroin—sniffing one powder seems much like sniffing another. Sniffing or smoking heroin is less cost-effective than injection, but then, the cost of heroin has fallen. Perhaps more important, sniffing or smoking largely avoids the 'junkie' stigma. It leaves no visible marks—in fact, it sidesteps self-injection altogether—and it is widely believed that using the drug this way cannot lead to addiction.

Even allowing for journalistic and academic hyperbole, it seems clear that more British residents are using heroin regularly. In 1984, Harnoll and his colleagues put the figure at around 40 000. How many of these could be classed as addicts is almost impossible to determine. Far fewer also seem to be in treatment than formerly—the 1984 estimate was about one-fifth of the total user population. This could mean that most are only experimental or occasional users. But an equally valid explanation would be that many find the formal treatment offered unacceptable and/or that they choose to deal with non-specialist practitioners who may be a more generous source of drugs.

As Hartnoll et al. (1984) see it, Britain's prospects for heroin use in the 1980s include an increasing predisposition of large parts of the population, especially those caught in the unemployment limbo between school and work, toward heroin. They also foreshadow the development of a heroin supply system capable of increasing the quantity delivered, reducing price without reducing the quality, and adapting to political and military disruptions without significantly interrupting deliveries. 'Suffice it to say', they conclude, 'that expressions of confidence are very hard to find and unconvincing; to quote the recent circumspect statement from a senior Home Office drugs officials, we are, at the least, "in for a fairly interesting period"'. (p. 5)

Opiates in America

Opiate addiction became visible in the United States with the end of the Civil War as the 'army disease', but its incidence was undoubtedly already considerable. The majority of those addicted had formed the habit for health reasons, either through medical treatment or in the course of self-medication with patent medicines. Doctors clearly used opium and eventually morphine widely and for diverse ailments. In 1899, for example, one doctor was able to put forward reasons for transforming chronic alcoholics into opiate addicts that are persuasive even by today's standards:

> The only grounds on which opium in lieu of alcohol can be claimed as reformatory are that it is less inimical to healthy life than alcohol, that it calms in place of exciting the baser passions, and hence is less productive of acts of violence and crime; in short, that as a whole the use of morphine in place of alcohol is but a choice of evils, and by far the lesser. To be sure, the populace and even many physicians think very differently, but this is because they have not thought as they should upon the matter.
> On the score of economy the morphine habit is by far the better. The regular whiskey drinker can be made content in his craving for stimulation, at least for quite a long time, on two or three grains of morphine a day, divided into appropriate portions, and given at regular intervals. If purchased by the drachm at fifty cents this will last him twenty days. Now it is safe to say that a like amount of spirits for the steady drinker cannot be purchased for two and one-half cents a day, and that the majority of them spend five and ten times that sum a day as a regular thing.
> On the score, then, of a saving to the individual and his family in immediate outlay, and of incurred disability, of the great diminution of peace disturbers and of crime, whereby an immense outlay will be saved the State; on the score of decency of behavior instead of perverse deviltry, of bland courtesy instead of vicious combativeness; on the score of a lessened liability to fearful diseases and the lessened propagation of pathologically inclined blood, I would urge the substitution of morphine instead of alcohol for all to whom such a craving is an incurable propensity. In this way I have been able to bring peacefulness

and quiet to many disturbed and distracted homes, to keep the head of the family out of the gutter and out of the lock-up, to keep him from scandalous misbehavior and neglect of his affairs, to keep him from the verges and the actualities of delirium tremens and horrors, and, above all, to save him from committing, as I veritably believe, some terrible crime that would cast a lasting and deep shadow upon an innocent and worthy family circle for generation after generation. Is it not the duty of a physician when he cannot cure an ill, when there is no reasonable ground for hope that it will ever be done, to do the next best thing—advise a course of treatment that will diminish to an immense extent great evils otherwise irremediable? . . .

The mayors and police courts would almost languish for lack of business; the criminal dockets, with their attendant legal functionaries, would have much less to do than they now have—to the profit and well-being of the community. I might, had I time and space, enlarge by statistics to prove the law-abiding qualities of opium-eating peoples, but of this anyone can perceive somewhat for himself, if he carefully watches and reflects on the quiet, introspective gaze of the morphine habitué and compares it with the riotous devil-may-care leer of the drunkard . . . (Black, 1889)

Opiates in varying forms, including morphine and, after 1898 heroin, could be bought freely from pharmacists and local stores and even by mail order. In the 1880s, Sears-Roebuck offered two ounces of laudanum for eighteen cents, or one and a half pints for two dollars. In 1906, their mail-order paregoric ('always useful for children and adults') was still only fourteen cents—and pure alcohol cost 75 cents a quart.

Patent medicines, originally imported from England, had been available at least since the late 1700s. The level of health care was generally poor, the public relatively unsophisticated, and there were few government regulations on the industry. The influx of large numbers of maimed and diseased veterans added further incentive, and within a decade after the Civil War morphine was included in a vast number of preparations sold as household remedies. Most were for pain, digestive ailments, coughs and asthma, but there were also many cholera specifics, treatments for men's diseases 'caused by excesses', 'general weakness' (a female problem), fatigue and nerve disorders. Few of these conditions were either understood or treatable by the medical profession of the day, and the patent medicines merely echoed what a doctor might have done: they made the sufferer feel better, either through faith or because of a central nervous system action on pain or anxiety. Both the opiates and alcohol have major effects of the latter sort, and they were used liberally. If addiction became a problem, users could always purchase an addiction cure. Since labelling of contents was not required, the majority of the 'cures' contained much the same ingredients as the original tonic that had caused the addiction.

Predictably, American consumption of opiates during the last half of the nineteenth century was enormous. According to Lindesmith (1968), medical practitioners and patent medicines between them required the importation of 110 305 pounds of opium and 588 ounces of opium alkaloids like morphine between 1860 and 1869. In the last decade of the 1800s, this had risen to 513 070 pounds of opium and 20 193 ounces of opium alkaloids. Opiate addiction was relatively widespread. The most reliable estimates suggest that two to four per cent of the population had opiate habits. In proportion to the population, this means that addiction was at least five times more prevalent than it is in America today.

Many doctors were aware of the possibility of opiate addiction and some were alarmed, but on the whole there was little real concern. Doctors were opposed to the excesses of the patent medicine trade primarily because it presented a threat to their own and, to some extent, because of Temperance Movement sympathies. Certainly the alcohol content of most of the nostrums was sufficient to outrage prohibitionists. The newspapers were concerned about loss of revenue should they alienate their patent medicine and other drug advertisers, and so remained generally silent on the issue. The general public, of course, was deriving undeniable benefits: their aches and anxieties were genuinely if temporarily lessened.

However, the most important reason for the general lack of concern about addiction was the phenomenon itself. Opiate addicts, on the whole, really were no problem. With the exception of opium smoking, addiction was not linked with crime to any appreciable extent. There are a few references to the use of laudanum by prostitutes, but there were no suggestions that women became prostitutes because of the drug, and at the time women addicts outnumbered men by about three to two. There was little emphasis on evil associations, and dope peddlers were hardly mentioned. Most important, addiction to drugs was a 'vice of middle life, the larger number by far being 30 to 40 years of age'. Upper and middle classes predominated among opiate addicts, with the medical and related professions well represented (Terry and Pellens, 1928). The habit was not approved, but neither was it regarded as criminal or monstrous. Some of the most respectable citizens of the community, pillars of middle-class morality, were addicted. In cases where this was known, the victim was seen as having a physiological problem, much as we see diabetics today. Acquaintances might feel somewhat sorry for them, but they could still be admitted to positions of respect and authority.

What changed this state of affairs was to some extent moral indignation. On the one hand, there was an international movement against the opium trade in which churchmen took a leading role. On the other, there was the growing conviction among religious leaders concerned with the Temperance Movement that opium was an evil akin to alcohol—another unearned pleasure leading to degradation. By far the most significant changes, however, arose from one of the nation's recurrent racial problems.

Chinese labourers were brought to the United States in the 1850s to build the western railroads and to work the mines. They stayed on to compete with white Americans for jobs. From the beginning, the anti-Chinese movement was led by the labour unions. In the course of this smear campaign many unpleasant practices were ascribed to the Chinese and their characteristic habit—smoking opium—became a leading symbol of their dangerousness. 'After all', Szasz (1975) comments, 'Americans could not admit that they hated and feared the Chinese because the Chinese worked harder and were willing to work for lower wages than they did' (p. 76).

There is in fact no evidence that opium use was very extensive among the Chinese immigrants, or that it greatly affected the health or social functioning of those Chinese and the few white users who did indulge. Nevertheless, propagandists quickly created the image of the Chinese opium fiend, complete with innocent boys and virgin girls lured into dank backs of laundry rooms for unspeakable purposes. In 1875, San Francisco enacted an ordinance forbidding the keeping of opium dens, and similar prohibitions on opium smoking were gradually adopted and extended by most western states. The results were predictable.

> The very fact that opium smoking was a practice forbidden by law seemed to lead many who would not otherwise have indulged to seek out the low dens and patronize them, while the regular smokers found additional pleasure in continuing that about which there was a spice of danger. It seemed to add zest to their enjoyment. Men and women, young girls, virtuous or just commencing a downward career, hardened prostitutes, representatives of the 'hoodlum' element, young clerks and errand boys who could ill afford the waste of time and money, and young men who had no work to do were to be found smoking together in the back rooms of laundries in the low, pestilential dens of Chinatown, reeking with filth and over-run with vermin, in cellars of drinking saloons, and in houses of prostitution.
> (quoted in Lindesmith, 1968, p. 214)

Congress responded by raising the tariff on smoking opium in 1883, prohibiting its import by Chinese (though not by Americans) in 1887, and prohibiting import completely in 1909. Opium for oral use, and all its derivatives, remained legal.

While much of the sentiment against opium smoking was hyperbole and pure fabrication, some white people undoubtedly did learn the habit, first from the Chinese, then from each other. Unlike opium eating, smoking did not involve contact with the medical profession. Opium for smoking was prepared in a distinct way, and doctors did not prescribe it. The white opium smokers of this period were generally described as 'sporting characters', hoodlums, and 'women of the town'. Nevertheless, they seem to have represented the upper crust of the underworld and they regarded themselves as much superior to the hypodermic user or 'opium eater' of respectable society. These they called 'dope fiends', and Lindesmith (1968) reports an incident that sums up their attitude. Early in the twentieth century, a habitué of a New York smoking joint apparently discovered a hypodermic user injecting himself in the toilet. He immediately reported to the proprietor that there was a 'God-damned dope fiend in the can', and the offender was promptly ejected (p. 215).

Beside the underworld, white opium smokers seem to have included a liberal representation from the socialite class, theatre, financiers and the professional classes. In the main, opium smoking was considered a gentleman's vice. Still, it was the connection of opium with the underworld, together with the picture of those 'tiny lost souls yielding up their virgin bodies to their maniacal yellow captors' (Szasz, 1975, p. 79) that caught the public's attention, and began to change attitudes toward addiction. The need to reconcile the image of the vicious dope fiend with the reality with which many were personally acquainted gave rise to the idea that there were two sorts of addicts: good citizens who were innocent victims, and villains for whom opium use was yet another vice.

Against such a domestic background, missionary agitation about the opium trade in China began to find receptive listeners. China had been a prime target for American missionaries and these, like their British colleagues, were vehement about the evils of opium. Also, with the annexation of the Philippines in 1898, the United States for the first time felt responsible for an Asian colony. Manila had a large number of opium dens and was, in fact, one of the places where opium smoking had begun. And finally, for many Americans, the earlier anti-Chinese sentiments had generalised to become simply anti-opium feelings.

So when Charles Brent, episcopal bishop of the Philippines, sent a letter to President Roosevelt in July 1906 deploring the opium trade and suggesting 'international action' in view of the 'manifestly high' principles of the United States in relation to the traffic in opium, the President was willing to act. Long negotiations led to the first international conference on opium in Shanghai in 1909, and the Shanghai

Conference eventually led to the Hague Conference of 1912.

The articles of the Hague agreement were vague and did not bind the signatories to anything very definite, but the intent was to limit importation of opium into China, to limit trade in opium in other countries to medical purposes and to initiate international exchange of information on opium-related matters. As a result of the Hague Conference, the United States found itself in the embarassing position of being the only major power among the nations represented without any law covering the distribution of medicinal opiates within its borders. The *Harrison Narcotic Act* of 1914 was passed in this climate of both domestic and international concern.

The *Harrison Act* had three central provisions. The first was to provide information about legal opiate traffic. It stipulated that producers and distributors of narcotics must register with the federal government, and keep appropriate records. The second provision required that all parties handling the drugs through either sale or purchase were to pay a tax. This reinforced the intent of the first provision, and provided substantial revenue. Finally, the Act ruled that unregistered persons could purchase the drugs only upon the prescription of a physician, and that such a prescription must be for a legitimate medical purpose. The intent of this provision was to place the addict entirely in the hands of the medical profession, but the eventual consequences were exactly the opposite. The problem was the definition of 'legitimate medical purposes'.

As Duster (1970) has pointed out, passing a law cannot change the strong feelings that people have about right and wrong. Laws are secondary to the more basic reference point of the moral order. When the *Harrison Act* was enacted, the moral position on opiate addiction was already ambivalent. In 1918, the following classification of addicts appeared in the *American Journal of Clinical Medicine*:

> In Class one, we can include all of the physical, mental and moral defectives, the tramps, hoboes, idlers, loafers, irresponsibles, criminals, and denizens of the underworld ... in these cases, morphine addiction is a vice, as well as a disorder resulting from narcotic poisoning. These are the 'drug fiends'. In Class two, we have many types of good citizens who have become addicted to the use of the drug innocently, and who are in every sense of the word 'victims'. Morphine is no respecter of persons, and the victims are doctors, lawyers, ministers, artists, actors, judges, congressmen, senators, priests, authors, women, girls, all of whom realize their conditions and want to be cured. In these cases, morphine-addiction is not a vice, but an incubus, and, when they are cured they stay cured. (quoted in Duster, 1970, p. 11)

The immediate consequences of the new legislation swung public opinion decidedly against addiction. When physicians became the only legal source of opiates, hundreds of addicts suddenly appeared outside their offices. It seems reasonable to assume that the majority came from the law-abiding 'class two'. The relatively small number of doctors in the country were hard pressed to handle over half a million new patients in any manner, let alone individually. The doctor's office became little more than a dispensing station for addicts, and only a tiny fraction received personal care.

There was some recognition that the situation was impossible. Beginning in 1918, a number of Narcotics Clinics were opened in many of the major cities, and some undoubtedly helped addicts to continue their normal lives without being drawn to drug peddlers. However, there were also some abuses, many of them the fault of the available facilities rather than of the system. New York, with its large addict population, was a case in point:

> Hundreds and hundreds of addicts would line up outside the clinic in the early morning for their supply, the queue stretching for several city blocks on some days. The staff physicians simply prescribed as quickly as they could, not being able to afford to take the necessary time to check records thoroughly for complete identification, registration, and the like. So, some addicts would get their supply for the day, then go back and get in line a few more times so that they would not have to come back so often. The New York newspapers of the time, in the heyday of yellow journalism, sent out reporters. They documented some of the abuses of the New York clinic, but gave such sensational accounts that clinics in general were portrayed as sinful places where the addict could go to satisfy his 'morbid' desires and pursue the thrills and pleasures of narcotics. The stories were picked up by papers in various parts of the country, and the public responded with *moral* outrage. (Duster, 1970, p. 18)

The government began to close the clinics in 1920, and virtually all were disestablished by 1921.

In the meantime, government agents decided to prosecute some of the private physicians who were prescribing to addicts *en masse*. In 1919, the Supreme Court, ruling on the Webb case, decided that a prescription of drugs for an addict 'not in the course of professional treatment in the attempted cure of the habit, but being issued for the purpose of providing the user with morphine sufficient to keep him comfortable by maintaining his customary use' was not a prescription in the meaning of the law. In other words, doctors who prescribed for addicts on anything but the most individual basis suddenly faced the demonstrated possibility of real fines and prison sentences. In 1922, the Behrmann case went on to declare that prescribing for an addict was not legal even if it was part of a cure program.

Between them, these two Supreme Court decisions made it impossible for an addict to continue using legally at any level, and the illicit market became the only alternative. Faced with this, many addicts did stop. These, however, were probably the least addicted. Goode (1984) argues that 'the legislation probably "helped" only those who were most capable of being helped, and who constituted the least troublesome problem anyway' (p. 221).

He also suggests that a substantial proportion of former opiate users may simply have turned to other drugs. The first barbiturates had been introduced in 1903—just in time to substitute for the now unavailable opiates. Those addicts who in 1900 were in the majority, that is, middle-aged, middle class white women with various quasi-medical problems, undoubtedly found the new sedatives an attractive and legal functional equivalent of their earlier drugs.

Finally, there were the addicts who refused to stop, and since they did not or could not obtain drugs legally, the public could with truth begin to talk about all addicts as consorting with criminals. Who stopped and who continued (or was seen to do so) is rather predictable: the 1920s addict was a young male from the highly visible lower classes, or the non-respectable parts of society. Imputing actual criminality to him was an easy step. These shifts in public opinion are graphically illustrated by a report on cases treated in 1920 at the Riverside Hospital in New York City. The author concluded that drug addicts fell into two general classes:

> The first class is composed of people who have become addicted to the use of drugs through illness, associated probably with an underlying neurotic temperament. The second class, which is overwhelmingly in the majority ... is at the present time giving municipal authorities the greatest concern. These persons are largely from the underworld, or channels leading directly to it. They have become addicted to the use of narcotic drugs largely through association with habitués and they find in the drug a panacea for the physical and mental ills that are the result of the lives they are leading. Late hours, dance halls, and unwholesome cabarets do much to bring about this condition of body and mind ... (quoted in Duster, 1970, p. 11)

Note that even the first class now attracts a certain amount of moral judgement. As for the second class, it is clear that this type of addict was no longer a victim of drugs, an unfortunate deserving of society's sympathy and help. These were weak and self-indulgent degenerates who contaminated all about them and who deserved nothing short of condemnation. The law enforcement approach was accepted as the only workable solution to the problem of addiction.

What few people seem to have realised at the time was that this new criminal class owed its existence to the very law that was supposed to eradicate it. As Goode (1984) points out, it was the criminalisation of addiction that created addicts as a special and distinctive group, that is, an emerging subculture. Prior to this, addicts had no special reason to show cohesion or loyalty as a group. They possessed no lore concerned with the acquisition and administration of drugs, no ideology elaborating the qualities of various drug highs, no justification for using drugs and no status ranking unique to the world of addiction. There was no need to reject the non-addict world. Under the new rules, all these things became advantageous, and indeed essential. They were also the things that gave the subculture its recruiting power.

It was early noted by a number of overseas observers that the implementation of the provisions of the *Harrison Act* was less than constructive. In 1922, for example, an English physician commented:

> In the United States of America a drug addict is regarded as a malefactor even though the habit has been acquired through the medicinal use of the drug ... In consequence of this stringent law a vast clandestine commerce in narcotics has grown up in that country. The small bulk of these drugs renders the evasion of the law comparatively easy, and the country is overrun by an army of peddlers who extort exhorbitant prices from their helpless victims. It appears that not only has the Harrison Law failed to diminish the number of drug takers—some contend, indeed, that it has increased their numbers—but, far from bettering the lot of the opiate addict, it has actually worsened it; for without curtailing the supply of the drug it has sent the price up tenfold, and this has had the effect of impoverishing the poorer class of addicts and reducing them to a condition of such abject misery as to render them incapable of gaining an honest livelihood. (quoted in Lindesmith, 1968, p. 233)

The *Harrison Act* could have been interpreted differently, and the social results would doubtless have been different. One result that *cannot* be assumed, though, is that the United States would have had no problems with opiate addiction without it. The British experience demonstrates that allowing physicians to prescribe freely for addicts brings its own difficulties and, in any case, too many other factors are relevant. In the event, where Britain espoused a disease model, the United States took an essentially moral stance on opiate addiction, and that stance remains basically unchanged.

There were some attempts to reinterpret the *Harrison Act*, but they met with little success. In 1925, for example, the Supreme Court reversed itself and declared, in the Lindner case, that addiction was an illness and that physicians might prescribe narcotics for addicts after all, provided that this was part of a program to eliminate the addiction. But the damage had been done. The doctors had been harassed too much, and the view of addicts as immoral, weak, psychologically inadequate criminals who prey on an unsuspecting public to supply their morbid appetites had passed into national folklore. To this day, the basic concept of 'offence' remains as part of the United States view of addiction. As the Secretary of the United Nations remarked in 1978, 'only the ways in which the offence may be dealt with have changed'(U.N. Secretariat, p. 43).

Illegal traffic had been gaining ground even while the Narcotic Clinics were still open, and the *James-Miller Act* of 1922 doubled the maximum penalties for dealing, with mere possession becoming grounds for conviction. It was a 1924 amendment of this Act, incidentally, that first formally mentioned possession or manufacture of *heroin* for other than medical purposes as illegal. Its use in medicine was eventually prohibited as well by the 1956 *Narcotic Drug Control Act*, and remains so to this date. Possession of heroin in the United States is currently legal only for some research purposes.

Enforcement of the anti-opiate laws was clearly very vigorous. Despite the fact that alcohol prohibition (1920–33) focused the activities of organised crime on the distribution of liquor rather than narcotics, individuals sentenced for narcotic drug offences made up one-third of the total prison population in 1928: twice as many as those imprisoned for liquor law violations. This created a major problem in federal prisons and in 1929 Congress responded by establishing two 'farms'—one at Fort Worth and one at Lexington—for the incarceration and treatment of addicts convicted of breaking a federal law. For the purposes of this exercise, an addict was defined as 'any person who habitually uses any habit forming narcotic drug ... so as to endanger the public morals, health, safety, or welfare, or who has been so far addicted to the use of such a habit forming drug as to have lost the power of self-control with reference to his addiction'. Among the habit forming drugs listed were opium and its derivatives, marijuana and peyote. Soon after, in 1930, Congress took several actions that culminated in the formation of a separate Bureau of Narcotics within the Treasury Department. Its first commissioner was the redoubtable Harry Anslinger, who came to exert a powerful influence on subsequent non-medical drug legislation.

All this activity, coupled with the Depression of the 1930s, had a delaying effect on the growth of the addict subculture. According to Preble and Casey (1969), prior to World War II the use of heroin was limited, for the most part, to the entertainment and underworld trades. Those who controlled the heroin market sold mostly to these people, and there was little knowledge or publicity about it. Part of the lack of publicity was due to the fact that the public now had a new drug menace to worry about, courtesy of Harry Anslinger—marijuana, the 'assassin of youth'. Still, the heroin subculture was probably not large, and the disruption of drug supplies caused by World War II further slowed the recruitment of new addicts.

When the war ended, the increase in use seems to have been due initially to the recruiting powers of a small subculture of intensely committed addicts. It is not impossible that their motives may even have been defensible. Their recruits came predominantly from the greatly expanded populations of Negros and Puerto Ricans who had come to the cities, especially New York, in response to the wartime manpower shortages. Like all new immigrants, they worked at the lowest economic levels, settled in slum neighbourhoods, and endured unemployment, poverty and discrimination. From 1947 to 1951 the use of heroin spread steadily among these and other lower class, slum dwelling people, mainly the Irish and Italians. The increase was gradual and did not attract much attention. Most of the users were in their twenties and thirties. They were more or less circumspect in their drug consumption, and the drug-using groups showed social cohesion, identification and ritual.

> Since heroin was so inexpensive during this time, no addict had to worry about getting his fix; someone was always willing to loan him a dollar or share a part of his drug. The social relationships among these addicts were similar to those found in a neighbourhood bar, where there is a friendly mutual concern for the welfare of the regular patrons. The most important economic factor in these early postwar days of heroin use was that heroin users were able to work even at a low-paying job and still support a habit, and many of them did. Relatively little crime was committed in the interest of getting money to buy heroin. A habit could be maintained for a few dollars a day, at little social or economic cost to the community. (Preble and Casey, 1969, pp. 4–5)

This scene began to change around 1951 with the emergence of younger users. According to Preble and Casey (1969), this experimentation with heroin by youths usually began at their initiative and not through proselytism. They were street gang members who were tired of gang fighting and looking for a new high.

> Also, contrary to professional reports about this development, it was not the weak, withdrawn, unadaptive street boy who first started using heroin, but rather the tough, sophisticated and respected boy, typically a street gang leader. Later, others followed his example, either through indoctrination or emulation.

By 1955 heroin use among teenagers on the street had become widespread, resulting, among other things, in the dissolution of fighting gangs. Now the hip boy on the street was not the swaggering, leatherjacketed gang member, but the boy nodding on the corner enjoying his heroin high. He was the new hero model.

As heroin use spread among the young from 1951, the price of heroin began to rise in response to the greater demand, and the greater risks involved in selling to youths. Those who started using heroin as teenagers seldom had work experience or skills, and resorted to crime in order to support their heroin use. They were less circumspect in their drug using and criminal activity, and soon became a problem to the community, especially to those who were engaged in non-narcotic illegal activities, such as bookmaking, loan-sharking and policy ... The activities and behavior of young drug users brought attention and notoriety to the neighbourhood which jeopardized racketeer operations. It was not uncommon for a local racketeer to inform the parents of a young heroin user about his activities, hoping that they would take action. (p. 6)

The youngsters involved, unfortunately, were very inexpert criminals, and their activities spurred the authorities to take a hard-line attitude directed primarily at crime control. The 1951 Boggs amendment to the *Harrison Act* established minimum mandatory sentences, and it prohibited suspended sentences and probation for second offences. In 1955, a subcommittee of the Senate Judiciary Committee (Senate Report No. 1440, 1956) suggested that addiction was responsible for 50 per cent of all urban crime, and was one of the ways in which Communist China planned to demoralise the United States. Against such a background, the 1956 *Narcotic Drug Control Act* becomes more understandable. Among a general tightening of all penalties, this law included the death penalty for anyone selling heroin to a person under 18. Commissioner Anslinger's comment on that provision was 'I'd like to throw the switch myself on drug peddlers who sell their poisons to minors.' (U.S. News and World Report, 1956)

Meanwhile, back on the streets, flower children, hippies and psychedelic drugs began to suffuse the media, and rising concern eventually gave birth to the 1965 *Drug Abuse Control Amendment*. This brought barbiturates, amphetamine and psychedelics under federal control. At the same time, white mainstream Americans were not especially concerned about heroin. Heroin addicts were believed to be mostly Black or Latin, and restricted to a few urban ghettos in any case. Within these ghettos, however, heroin addicts were having problems of their own. Late in 1961, a critical shortage of heroin developed. Although it lasted only a few weeks, this 'panic', whatever its cause, profoundly altered the heroin scene. Demand for the meagre supplies was so great that those who had heroin were able to double and triple their prices and further adulterate the quality, thus realising sometimes as much as ten times their usual profit. By the time the panic ceased, dealers had learned that even inferior heroin at inflated prices could find a market, and prices continued to climb. By 1969, an average habit that had cost $2 a day twenty years earlier was costing $20.

As Chapter 4 will show, the relationship between drug use and crime is extremely complex and a price rise can have quite unpredictable results. In the ghetto situation, however, drug users are typically uneducated and unskilled and alternatives like escape into treatment may be unavailable. When faced with the need to raise money for their drugs, they tend to engage in fairly basic forms of criminal activity. And they tend to operate outside their own community, not out of loyalty but simply because wealthier neighbourhoods offer better pickings. From the 1960s on, then, ghetto addicts were increasingly identified with urban crime. Indeed, they became scapegoats in this regard. In 1972, for example, Governor Rockefeller justified his argument for harsher criminal penalties for drug users by citing statistics collected by the New York State Narcotic Addiction Control Commission to the effect that drug addiction was costing New York State an annual $6.5 billion in thefts. Commenting on this, the Fellows of the Drug Abuse Council noted that in that year, stolen property actually reported to the police in New York City—where over 80 per cent of the state's addicts then lived—totalled a mere $238 million. 'It is unlikely, we believe', wrote the Fellows acidly, 'that addicts steal over twenty-five times the amount of all property reported stolen'.

Nevertheless, the ghetto addicts' predation upon surrounding communities was real and substantial. Moreover, the pressures placed on addicts by recurring heroin panics altered the ghettos themselves. In 1969, Preble and Casey noted that

> The competition and struggle necessary to support a habit has turned each one into an independent operator who looks out only for himself. Usually, addicts today will associate in pairs (partners), but only for practical purposes ... There is no longer a subculture of addicts based on social cohesion and emotional identification, but rather a loose association of individuals and parallel couples. Heroin users commonly say, 'I have no friends, only associates'.
>
> The economic pressures on heroin users today are so great that they prey on each other as well as on their families and on society at large. An addict with money or drugs in his possession runs a good risk of being *taken off* (robbed) by other addicts. (p. 8)

The rising crime rate attributed to addicts and the increasing social disorganisation of the ghettos was undoubtedly partly responsible for the turn drug legislation took in the early 1970s. In 1969 deliberation began on legislation that was to replace and update all previous laws concerned with narcotics and dangerous drugs. As first proposed, the changes were remarkably liberal, with emphasis on education, rehabilitation and research. What was finally submitted to Congress and signed into law as the *Controlled Substances Act* of 1970 minimised both education and treatment and focused heavily on law enforcement. The ghetto situation notwithstanding, the main reason for this reversal was Vietnam.

Drug use by American troops in Southeast Asia seems to have been substantial from the beginning of the conflict. It could hardly have been otherwise. The men went straight from a drug-oriented hippie scene at home to an unpopular 'non-war' in an area where drugs of all kinds were cheap, pure and freely available everywhere. The Department of Defense had established a Task Force on Drug Abuse in 1967, and its main concern was initially marijuana. By 1969, however, it was heroin, and both Congress and the American public were galvanised into activity. Addiction could no longer be dismissed as something indulged in by coloured ghetto minorities. The white middle class, it seemed, was vulnerable too. In July 1969, President Nixon stated that 'within the last decade, the abuse of drugs has grown from essentially a local police problem into a serious national threat to the personal health and safety of millions of Americans'; in June 1971, he declared a 'national emergency' and asserted that drug abuse was 'America's Public Enemy No. 1'.

That a large number of American servicemen experimented with heroin in Southeast Asia is unquestioned. They were of a susceptible age, removed from usual social constraints, bored, anxious and disaffected. Since the heroin was about 95 per cent pure, it could be smoked or sniffed, thereby circumventing the inhibitions of many about self-injection. Since there is a persistent myth that addiction can only occur with intravenous use, the possibility of smoking and sniffing probably increased willingness to experiment.

How many of these actually became addicted, though, is something else again. Without a doubt both the estimates of addiction rates and the reactions they produced at home were exaggerated. Early reports (Committee on Armed Services, 1971) suggested that 10 to 15 per cent of all troops in Vietnam were heroin addicts. However, a urine screening program that was hurriedly inaugurated found traces of opiates in only 5.1 per cent of the 100 000 servicemen tested. Back home, massive rehabilitation programs were prepared by the Veterans Administration to deal with returning addicts. They did treat some 26 000 veterans for drug addiction (97 000, incidentally, were treated in separate programs for alcohol dependence), but many of the new treatment facilities were closed again by 1974 because they were not being used. And a series of excellent follow-up studies (Robins et al., 1975) showed that most of the Vietnam heroin users spontaneously gave up their habits once they returned home. Eight months to a year after returning, the rate of use in this population was back to one to two per cent, that is, about the rate found at induction into service.

The Vietnam heroin use mountain may have been a molehill, but its effect on public and political perception of illegal drug use was enormous. The Controlled Substances Act of 1970 contained a plethora of new and increased controls. All aspects of the manufacture, movement and use of controlled substances came under rigid and continuing scrutiny. While this did decrease the amount of diversion of legitimately produced drugs into the illegal market, it decreased illegal use not at all—it merely shifted users more firmly toward illicit sources. The law also dramatically increased penalties for distributing drugs to minors, for persons engaged in 'continuing criminal enterprise' and for 'dangerous special drug offenders'. The last two categories were aimed at the illegal entrepreneurs.

Unfortunately, one of the things that determines the effectiveness of a law is the probability first of being arrested and, subsequently, of being found guilty. In practice, most dealers are released on bail for a period between their arrest and trial. It should come as no surprise that a number are never heard from again. Where some further information is available, it appears that a good many are far from idle during their wait. In 1974, for example, of those arrested for dealing 47 per cent were implicated in selling narcotics while on bail, and 12 per cent were actually rearrested for narcotics sales (United Press International, 1974). Sentencing is equally problematic. In 1978, Ray estimated that 'one out of every three individuals convicted in federal courts of a heroin or cocaine charge is placed on probation. Of those sentenced to prison, one out of three receives a sentence of three years or less and is eligible for parole after one year of prison ... At this time the odds seem overwhelmingly against [even] being arrested' (p. 45). The real effect of all this on the street scene is a simple increase in price, as the extra overhead is passed on to the customers.

Where the law did reduce controls somewhat was in the case of first offenders charged with possession and/or use. For these, there was to be no mandatory federal sentence and under certain circumstances records of the conviction might be expunged. Some cynics have suggested that this was less a result of enlightenment than of the drug scene moving into white suburbia. 'Since the sons and daughters of prominent persons—including senators—started getting busted for crimes previously associated with lower-class blacks, compassion for

[drug] criminals was sure to arise' (New Republic, 1969). Whatever the reasons, the law now saw the 'pusher' as the main villain of the piece and the problem as being elsewhere—in the Turkish poppy fields, or French heroin factories, or whatever was topical and convenient. Righteous indignation could thus still be vented, while a certain amount of sympathy could be shown for the addict.

From the 1970s on, the picture in the United States is remarkably similar, in broad outline, to the one we have already explored for Britain. Only the numbers are significantly different. For several years in the early 1970s heroin activity seemed to decline. The new federal laws sparked a rash of parallel or even tougher state laws, and for a time many users and dealers adopted a conservative wait-and-see attitude. Dealers, for instance, both increased their prices and sold only to known users. In this sense, the laws 'discouraged amateurs' (Raab, 1977), but there was no real difficulty in buying drugs, no great increases in arrests or convictions, and certainly no rush by addicts into treatment programs.

It was during this period that poppy growing was temporarily banned in Turkey, and the morphine-to-heroin laboratories of southern France were eliminated. The situation is examined more fully in Chapter 4. Predictably, other poppy growers and processors rose to the challenge. The combination of a world shortage of legal opium and the rising demand for it and its products on the black market was irresistible. By 1975, Mexican brown heroin was well established in the United States, and the size of the trade may be estimated from the fact that between 1966 and 1976 the Mexican government, with American help, destroyed 14 000 acres of poppies. Presumably they missed some—and the way the Mexicans grow it, each acre yields about 8 kg of opium, and there are two crops a year (Ray, 1978). In 1977, a Congress committee reported that the flow of narcotics into the United States from Mexico was 'almost entirely out of control' (*Science*, 1977).

As in England, 1979 saw a dramatic upsurge of heroin use—in much the same pattern and probably for much the same reasons. In that year, the New York State Division of Substance Abuse Services, which monitors a variety of drug use indicators, received reports from its street studies unit that more white heroin was appearing on the streets than Mexican brown and that dealers were talking glowingly about its quality. Early in 1980, 150 heroin users and/or dealers were interviewed at 30 locations in New York City. Quality was reported to be excellent:

> Many informants compared it to the heroin of the past: 'The stuff out there is like the O.D. bags of the sixties'. 'The shit is so good

it makes you think you are back in the days'. Furthermore the purity was so high that a series of dealers were able to dilute the heroin many times and still preserve the 'kick'. Some dealers said:

'I got it man, I got the real deal. I can give you a good play on some pure (i.e., unadulterated heroin). This is on a fifteen (i.e., can be diluted 15 to one and still have strength). So now I give it a 20 or a 22 and sell it for pure; they can put a five or a three on it and still get over'.

The dealers and users recognized the fact that it was heroin coming from a new source—Southwest Asia. For instance, this dialogue was reported:

'Wow I haven't seen or heard of that kind of shit for years'.
'Well my people got it man. Straight off the boat'.
'I wonder where it comes from?'
'Man I think its from Iran! Yep Iran man!' . . .

Heroin dealing was taking place throughout the city and street bags were averaging about $10 per bag. What was most disconcerting was [the] finding that six or seven dealers were selling heroin for $4 per bag, a price that was unheard of since the 1960s. (Frank and Lipton, 1984, pp. 96–7)

Like their British colleagues, workers at the Substance Abuse Services commented on the fact that heroin was increasingly being smoked and sniffed. Their final conclusion, too, is remarkably similar:

From emergency room data, treatment admissions, death data, it appears that the addicts currently most visible are those over the age of 30. Many of these are probably former addicts who have been lured back by the white heroin; some probably had been using all along but the heroin now available may have brought their use to dysfunctional levels. Whatever the pattern, many of these users have already had an immediate and overwhelming impact on the treatment system.

We expect, however, a second wave of users to impact the treatment system. These are the new abusers. The usual history of heroin addiction shows that it takes a year or two (what is euphemistically called the 'honeymoon' period) before the addict surfaces in treatment. We may have begun to see these users surfacing in the criminal justice system among adolescent inmates in New York City admitted to the detoxification program on Riker's Island and in the health system in the recent increase in cases of serum hepatitis B.

There may even be a third wave of abusers who will be seeking treatment, those who start by snorting and smoking heroin and whose addiction histories may take a longer time to develop.

In any case the overall epidemiological implications of the current heroin crisis are grave. (Frank and Lipton, 1984, p. 99)

3
Heroin the drug

Mr Michael Patterson's youngest daughter, Irene, is a heroin addict ... Mr Patterson, a 63-year-old invalid pensioner, tells of the decline of his 19-year-old daughter ...

'She was a pretty girl, but she got worse and worse.

'If she hadn't have got into drugs, she would have turned out OK. She's got nouse. She would have gone to work. But who'd have her now?

'No one will give her a job when she's taking drugs and when she is not on drugs she gets the shakes.

'It's hurt her health. They don't eat, see, when they're on drugs.

'Last Monday week Irene came home for a day. She came to the door and fell in the doorway, out of it on heroin. She was just walking around looking like a rotten corpse.

'When she left she took away the iron, the brand new iron I bought for her mother. They just can't stop thieving.

'I can't find her now to put her into a clinic. If I did put her in she wouldn't stay there. She can't get a needle in there.

'Now, there's not much I can do.'

Sydney Morning Herald, 18 June 1984

... I understand that heroin not only reduces the physical pain, it also produces a feeling of well-being ... Just a few days before his death, when he was no longer able to speak, nurses were still telling my husband that they would give him pain-killers only when he asked for them.

In retrospect, I wish I had had the courage to break the law and endeavour to obtain drugs for a dying man which would have allowed him to die with some dignity (A.M., Cambridge Park)

Sydney Morning Herald, 24 January 1985

Heroin is variously referred to as a narcotic, an opiate or an opioid drug, and this confusion requires some clarification.

The term *narcotic* is derived from the Greek word for stupor and it was once applied to any substance that induced sleep. Heroin can do this, but so can a wide range of unrelated substances including alcohol. In time, 'narcotic' came to mean a strong morphine-like analgesic, and since these were generally opium derivatives, 'narcotic' and 'opiate' were for a time more or less interchangeable. From a pharmacological standpoint, however, both terms rapidly became inadequate. Moreover, 'narcotic' was increasingly used in legal contexts to describe drugs that societies were currently upset about, and that were thought to be 'habit-forming'. Initially, these were again opium derivatives, but cocaine, pharmacologically a stimulant, was included from the earliest stages of most drug legislation. Today, the list of illegal 'narcotics' includes a pharmacological potpourri ranging from heroin to LSD and, under the circumstances, if the term is to be retained at all it should be restricted to legal contexts. It has relevance only in what Sapira and Cherubin (1975) have called 'federal pharmacology'.

Opiates were once drugs derived from opium. Some 25 per cent by weight of dried opium is made up of a variety of alkaloids. Only a few of these 'natural' opiates are clinically useful; the most important are morphine and codeine. These form 10 per cent and 0.5 per cent by weight of dried opium respectively. Relatively simple pharmacological modifications of the natural opium alkaloids result in a number of 'semi-synthetic' opiates. Thus heroin is made from morphine and modification of the opium alkaloid thebaine produces the opiate antagonist naloxone.

In due course, a variety of totally synthetic drugs with morphine-like actions were created, among them methadone. Since their chemistry was quite unlike that of opium derivatives, the alternative term *opioid* was proposed for the entire group. This was made especially attractive by the discovery that all opioid drugs seemed to act by combining with a unique group of receptor sites. Drugs that meet these specifications may or may not have pharmacological profiles similar to opium derivatives; for the most part, though, the terms 'opiate' and 'opioid' are still reasonably interchangeable. 'Opiate' will be used throughout this discussion.

The positive side: uses of heroin

The pharmacology of heroin must be discussed in the larger context of the opiates as a group. As we shall see, heroin itself acts primarily through its parent drug, morphine. Several other opiates, notably methadone and some of the opiate antagonists like naloxone, are important in the diagnosis or treatment of heroin addicts. And, either by preference or through necessity, many street addicts supplement their heroin with a variety of other licit opiates like dipipanone (Diconal), dextromoramide (Palfium) and meperidine (Pethidine), as well as an increasing number of illicit opiate-like 'designer drugs'.

The opiates, and especially heroin, have acquired so much mythological baggage as *the* drugs of addiction and the source of a multitude of evils that even their pharmacology is sometimes treated as suspect. Yet they are drugs like any others and, in medicine, more important than many. Despite intensive research few other drugs have come even close to their effectiveness in the management of either pain or diarrhoea. They are also superb sedative and anxiolytic drugs, and only their so-called addiction liability and their tendency to produce vomiting prevents their use for these purposes.

All opiates act on the *gastrointestinal tract*. The peristaltic movements which normally propel food downwards are markedly diminished, while the tone of the intestine is greatly increased. This is accompanied by dehydration of the feces. All these effects combine to control diarrhoea, however caused. They are also responsible for the chronic constipation experienced by the majority of opiate addicts.

Opiates *decrease the size of the pupil* (miosis). The precise mechanism is unknown, but it appears to originate within the brain rather than in the eye itself.

The effects on *brain, mind* and *mood* are predominantly depressant. There is drowsiness, mental clouding, sedation and lethargy. While some people respond to their first oral dose of an opiate with fear, anxiety and dysphoria, the experience is pleasant for the majority. There is a feeling of warmth, well-being, peacefulness and content. This is often accompanied by a dream-like state, a turning inward and sleep.

Depressant effects also underlie a major potential problem. Opiates depress the activity of the brain's *respiratory* centres. At high doses, respiration may become inadequate and death from opiate overdose is almost always secondary to failure of respiration.

There are some excitatory effects as well. One is stimulation of the brain's *'vomiting centre'*, and nausea and vomiting are frequent side effects of the opiates. Since these can be significantly reduced if the user lies down, there is probably some action on the balancing centres too.

A few individuals are stimulated by opiates, sometimes with accompanying feelings of boundless energy, strength and capability. This occurs fairly rarely in humans, and the reaction is unrelated to the 'rush' that intravenous users describe so ecstatically. In fact, the rush is something of a mystery pharmacologically. Most opiates exist in the blood in a fat-insoluble form and as such penetrate the brain with difficulty and quite slowly. Only about 20 per cent of the total amount of morphine given intravenously reaches the brain, and that only after many minutes. Heroin is much more fat-soluble than morphine and so reaches the brain more quickly, but still too slowly to account for the instant sensation of the rush. Some argue that the effect is due to action on the cardiovascular system, or to some as yet unknown peripheral nervous mechanism (Julien, 1981).

The major medical action of the opiates, however, is *analgesia*, and this can usually be achieved at doses smaller than those that would produce significant sedation or respiratory depression. The analgesia produced by opiates is unique in that sensory abilities remain unaltered. The pain is still present and felt, but it no longer bothers the patient. In other words, opiates decrease the suffering associated with pain rather than pain itself. Continuous, dull pain is relieved more effectively than sharp, intermittent pain but it is generally possible to ease even very severe pain with sufficiently large doses. Mental suffering—that is, psychological pain—is relieved at least as well as physical pain.

The potential role of heroin as an analgesic has been much debated recently, especially with regard to the management of terminally ill cancer patients. Heroin has always been available to medicine in Britain, but both the United States and Canada have so far resisted its reintroduction.

In both countries, opponents of the move claim it would open the way to further legalisation, and that it would give the 'wrong message' about drugs to the public. Both countries are also concerned about possible use by physicians and nurses. A meeting of the Royal College of Physicians and Surgeons in Montreal was told that while there were no statistics on heroin addiction among Canadian doctors before the drug was banned in 1954, 'it would not be too far fetched to conclude that if it becomes available again ... emotionally impaired physicians who tend to abuse drugs would move away from tranquillizers and other analgesics and onto heroin' (Arboleda-Florez, 1984). And both countries are panicky about the possibility of diversion of legitimate heroin into the illegal trade.

Is heroin a superior analgesic? It is certainly a very good one. Still, heroin is simply morphine with two small chemical groups attached. Once the heroin is in the body, these chemical groups are quickly stripped away, morphine is recreated and it is the morphine that produces the majority of heroin's pharmacological effects. Heroin penetrates the brain more readily than morphine, and if it is given intravenously, some of the conversion to morphine will actually occur there. This means that heroin can produce a greater and speedier morphine effect than would occur if morphine itself was given. However, the route of administration is crucial. When heroin is given in any way other than intravenously, even experienced heroin addicts cannot tell whether they are receiving it or morphine.

The fact remains, though, that under special conditions the actions of heroin and morphine are distinguishable. It is also true that while morphine can control the pain of advanced malignant disease in over 90 per cent of the sufferers, it is inadequate in the rest. Is there a role for heroin in the treatment of these remaining patients?

There are two aspects to this issue. First, no amount of research will ever produce a clear statement that any drug, including heroin, is unequivocally superior to all others as an analgesic. The reason is individual variability—both between the drugs, with respect to the several effects they as a class have in common, and between the patients, with respect to each one's unique physiology and psychology. Thus, one drug may relieve pain quickly, but causes severe nausea. Another may have no bad side effects, but acts too briefly. And while there is ample evidence that some patients respond better to heroin than to other opiates, there is no way to predict who these will be. As Trebach (1984) points out, 'The only way any doctor can tell if a patient may be helped by heroin is to provide it to that person and observe the results' (p. 6).

Trebach is a strong supporter of legalising heroin for medical use. He argues that if even a few patients are greatly helped by heroin, it should be available. The problem of diversion, he feels, would be real but insignificant. He reasons as follows. In Britain, where heroin may be legally prescribed, physicians use approximately 3 kg of heroin for every 7 kg of morphine for pain management. Assuming that American doctors were to prescribe similarly, in 1982 they would have used a hypothetical 228 kg of heroin, since their actual morphine use for that year was 533 kg. In 1982, the estimated consumption of illicit heroin in the United States was 8 metric tons. In other words, were all the hypothetical 228 kg of legal heroin to be somehow diverted into the black market, it would amount to only 2.9 per cent of what was already being consumed illegally.

Trebach's logic is far from watertight. Too many factors other than its expected usefulness determine whether a given drug will be chosen in therapy. The opiates tend to be placed in a sort of unofficial hierarchy. In countries that forbid the use of heroin, injectable morphine is usually regarded as the biggest gun, to be saved for the direst need. Were it to become legal, how many patients currently on morphine would move into the heroin group, and how many now treated with 'softer' opiates would graduate to morphine? Would heroin become simply the biggest gun, instead of a drug to be given selectively to those patients who benefit from it most—assuming that we could somehow determine who these are?

Nevertheless, the substance of Trebach's argument is extremely important. It focuses attention on a crucial moral question: do we hate the thought of addicts using diverted heroin so much that we are willing to accept the risk of allowing some terminally ill people to suffer unnecessary pain? If heroin were made available for medical purposes in the United States, an amount would certainly be diverted and an unknown number of both addicts and experimental users would benefit. At the same time, one quarter of Americans now living—some 50–60 million people—are expected to succumb to cancer. Approximately half of these will need some form of analgesic medication and although there is currently no way to predict who or how many would fall into this group, a proportion would respond better to heroin than to alternative drugs. Where is the balance to be struck? Trebach's answer is uncompromising:

> Using our present set of operational values, we seem to be saying: the cancer patients must suffer so that we can keep this drug away from dope fiends. In practical terms, this position represents a cruel irony because our massive interdiction and enforcement programs are failing, utterly, to keep heroin out of the veins of street addicts. In ethical terms, this position is a perversion of every moral principle that rests close to the gentler hearts of our people. (p. 6)

How would you vote?

The second issue in the medical heroin controversy actually has very little to do with heroin itself, although it does depend critically on social perceptions of the opiates as a group. Current pain control is inadequate, but this is more than a matter of the availability or otherwise of particular drugs. Some people lack access to adequate pain control services because of linguistic, financial, ethnic, religious and other barriers. There is also inadequate application of existing knowledge. Pain control is nobody's specialty, therefore nobody's responsibility.

More important, there are entrenched attitudes that the addictive potential of pain-killing drugs is enormous and that addiction must be avoided at all costs. Patients themselves sometimes refuse to accept prescribed medication for fear of becoming addicted, and the healing professions as a group have been positively terrorised. Even 'soft' opiates like codeine are often given in doses too small to be effective. With the 'hard' opiates, the situation is sometimes little short of the macabre. Jaffe (1984) offers the following vignette:

> Five years ago my father-in-law, age 73, was dying of disseminated carcinomatosis. He had lost the use of his lower limbs, and he was hemorrhaging from the GI tract. He was

attended by a general practitioner whom he had known for many years. My father-in-law rarely used the word pain. Having suffered from multiple illnesses over the years, he had learned that those around him were less disturbed when he spoke of discomfort rather than pain. During his last few days of his life, with the i.v.'s running and tubes protruding, he complained to me of 'great discomfort'. His spirits were lower than they had ever been. At one point the reluctant attending physician was persuaded to give him an injection of 75 mg of meperidine.

His face brightened—the drug obviously relieved both his pain and his depression. The next day he bled again and was moved to the intensive care unit; the end was nearer. He was even more 'uncomfortable'. The multiple special consultants never stopped drawing blood and/or inserting their tubes and viewers. His attending physician, however, refused to order any more meperidine—'Your father-in-law is not having that much pain,' he said to me, 'and besides, meperidine is addicting.' As a concession to my pointed remark that his spirits were quite low, the attending [physician] prescribed a benzodiazepine, which was without any visible effect. The next day, my father-in-law died: in pain, depressed, but unaddicted—with his pharmacological virginity, so to speak, intact. (p. 12)

What is this 'addiction', that the threat of it is enough to make a physician unwilling to prescribe pain-killers to a dying man? The process is touched on in Chapter 7, and a more comprehensive discussion may be found in Krivanek (1988). Briefly, it is an exceedingly complex phenomenon whereby some thing, person or activity becomes enormously important to someone. Very often this means that the addict actively enjoys the thing, person or activity, but not always. The overt objects of an addiction may be mere stepping stones to something else that is intensely desired, or they may simply be the least of several possible evils, or they may serve to lessen the threat of some unpleasant experience. Drugs are simply one of the infinitely varied things around which an addiction can develop. Why addiction to drugs produces such hysteria while other addictions are either ignored or actually valued is essentially a social and historical matter, and has little to do with the pharmacology of drugs. In any case, addiction is a property of the addict; drugs merely have effects.

Likes and dislikes are very personal matters and almost any effect can be attractive to someone. As a group, the opiates produce several that are attractive to many. Their ability to relieve physical pain is very important, but there is that 'psychic' pain as well. Tom Field, an ex-heroin addict, has this to say:

> Just as heroin cocoons the mind from pain, so it does from the cares and anxieties of life ... By slowing down the mind, it

> prevents that crowding in of anxieties that makes rational thought and hence solutions so difficult. When financial, work and emotional pressures arrive simultaneously, it is often hard to separate them and confront them individually. Heroin removes the pressure of problems. However, it also tends to minimise them and thus also removes the pressure for solutions . . .
>
> Heroin's ability to push problems out to arm's length until they seem simplistically soluble is a part of its general self-confidence inspiring action . . . Depending on the personality or the mood of the user, this confidence can be exaggerated into an overbearing arrogance and aggressiveness. The drug acts then as a stimulant rather than a depressant. I remember an occasion when this feeling took hold of me while I was driving. I began to drive with outrageous aggression, running red lights and screaming abuse out of the window at anyone who got in my way. I was spoiling for a fight.
>
> For the user this feeling is marvellous: he is Caesar with the world at his feet. For others it can be insufferable . . . Similarly, although heroin is a relaxant, it can make users very short-tempered and irritable. Occasionally it is because the user resents any intrusion on the inner tranquility that the drug has given him. Usually, however, it is only an aspect of the egocentricity of the drug: no one has the right to approach Caesar without Caesar's permission. (Field, 1985, pp. 50–1)

Some enjoy the 'nodding out' that occurs with a large dose—a dream-like state in which the user can still exert some conscious control over the images that pass through the mind. Still others appreciate the way heroin seems to lessen boredom. Part of this is a result of the special state of mind described above, but there is an amnesic effect as well. Memory is clouded; the user lives almost entirely in the present and the future is far away and unimportant. 'Heroin time differs from usual time, because, in retrospect, it barely exists if at all. Like the time spent sleeping, it is time out of life' (Field, 1985, p. 49).

Things seem better with smack, and the user finds more and more things that would be better with smack until life itself seems increasingly dull without it. Tom Field again:

> He finds that certain events are not merely better on the drug but cannot be faced without it: a visit to the bank manager, a job interview, a meal with his parents. Each time he surrenders to the temptation this feeling increases so that the next time it is harder to resist. Even his increasingly brief glimpses of the trap into which he is walking serve, perversely, not to strengthen his resolve but to weaken it: he wants the escapism of heroin to forget what he is doing.

The user is now psychologically addicted. Life without the drug is perceived as worse than it was before he tried heroin:

there are mental deprivation symptoms ... Once discovered, it is impossible, ever, to forget how nice heroin is.

A user aware that he is psychologically addicted will typically attempt to fight it by making rules for himself. I did it myself: I decided to have a two-day break for every two days I took it consecutively. Such rules are far easier to make than to keep. There is always some special, overwhelming reason to take it on one of the days off. Each extra time is just an 'exception'. The rule disintegrates. (Field, 1985, p. 56)

Mechanisms of action

Drugs act by interacting with one or more of the chemicals that make up the tissues of the body. Tissue changes result and in due course these may produce observable physical or behavioural change. Each drug will typically participate in many such changes in different parts of the body. No drug has a single effect. In this discussion we will be concerned mainly with heroin's 'central' effects, that is, those that depend on its interactions with the brain.

Some central drug effects involve generalised changes in brain tissue and the results of such action will also be very generalised. More often, though, a drug will combine with discrete active sites, the 'receptors'. Receptors are normal components of tissues and they are there for a purpose. Usually, they react with one or more endogenous 'ligands', and the result of such an interaction is an integral part of the tissue's normal functioning.

Information processing in the brain may be taken as an example. Within each nerve cell, information is coded as a travelling electrical change. At the synapses (the points where cells come into close physical contact), the information-carrying impulse in the sending cell releases a special transmitter substance which moves across the gap between the cells and binds chemically with receptors on the surface of the receiving cell. This binding changes the electrical character of the receiving membrane and regenerates the information-carrying electrical impulse. In this series of events, the transmitter is acting as an endogenous ligand for the receiving cell's receptors.

Many receptors are highly specific in their binding, but all will accept a range of substances. In this range, some ligands will bind more eagerly than others. Also, some ligands (agonists) activate receptors, while others (antagonists) block or inhibit them. Either way, there will be an 'effect', and this effect will last a variably long time. Some substances occupy receptors quite briefly—in the case of a bonding between a transmitter and its receptor, for only a fraction of a second—and the receptor is soon available again for re-bonding.

Other substances may occupy a receptor site for many minutes, occasionally for hours.

Many psychoactive drugs act by mimicking the action of the brain's own endogenous transmitters at synaptic receptors, or by blockading these receptors so that transmitter access to them is limited for as long as the drug remains in the body. Others alter the mechanics of transmitter production, distribution, release or termination. The important point is that when drugs act on the brain, they do so by altering processes that are already there. No drug can make the brain—or its owner—do something it cannot do in the undrugged state. Drugs add nothing new to the brain's behavioural repertoire.

Work on the identity of the receptors for opiate drugs began in the mid−1960s and expanded explosively from the 1970s on. At present, the best guess is that the opiate receptors are proteolipids, perhaps cerebrosides. As such, their number would be to some extent under genetic control and this in turn means that each individual's sensitivity to the effects of opiates might be partly determined by his or her genes. As is often the case, there is not a single type of opiate receptor but several. To date, three subspecies have been identified, the *mu*, *kappa* and *sigma* (Gilbert and Martin, 1976) and there may be others.

The discovery of multiple opiate receptors helped make sense of the puzzling effects of a class of drugs called *opiate antagonists*. These drugs bind to opiate sites, but do not activate them. Moreover, once in the system, they prevent agonistic opiates like heroin or morphine from binding with their receptors and, should the agonist drug have been in possession of the receptors beforehand, they are able to displace it. In other words, opiate antagonists either prevent or promptly reverse the effects of morphine-like drugs.

This phenomenon has many-sided implications. First, and most important, opiate antagonists permit reversal of such opiate overdose effects as respiratory depression. Second, and by the same mechanism, they may be used to unmask opiate dependence. Thus, if a person who is physically dependent on a drug like heroin is given an opiate antagonist like naloxone (Narcan), a moderate to severe withdrawal reaction will be precipitated within minutes. We will discuss this further presently. Finally, since the presence of an opiate antagonist prevents any opiate drug used subsequently from producing its usual effects, there is a potentially important role for these drugs in the treatment of opiate addicts.

Opiate antagonists may be produced by making relatively minor modifications to the chemistry of opiate agonists. The antagonist naloxone differs only slightly from morphine, and it is in fact manufactured directly from the opium alkaloid thebaine. Naloxone is a 'pure' antagonist, that is, it appears to have no action of its own other than binding passively with opiate receptors (and displacing other opiates, should the receptors be occupied). Most opiate antagonists, however, are 'partial' antagonists. They are able to displace opiate agonists, but at the same time they have agonist actions of their own. These effects are opiate-like for the most part—and this was the puzzle. Thus, drugs like pentazocine (Fortral, Talwin) and buprenorphine (Temgesic) can displace opiates, yet they are good analgesics and they can produce both sedation and euphoria. In fact, people can become as dependent on them as on heroin or morphine, and for much the same reasons. What is happening?

It appears that different receptors are involved. The opiate agonists like morphine and heroin seem to combine primarily with mu receptors. It is this interaction that is involved in the analgesia, the euphoric effects and the respiratory depression produced by opiates. Heroin and morphine also have a much smaller effect at the kappa receptors, and this seems the basis for the pupil constriction and most of the sedative effects. Pure antagonists like naloxone seem to exert antagonistic actions at all opiate receptors. They can therefore reverse all the actions of agonistic opiates. The partial antagonists, however, have antagonistic actions at the mu receptor only in the presence of opiate agonists; in their absence, they themselves produce a milder agonistic action there. At the same time, they have a strong agonistic action at the kappa and sigma receptors. It is the sigma receptors that are involved in the anxiety, 'crazy feelings', vivid dreams and occasional hallucinatory experiences that accompany addiction to the partial antagonists. These never occur with heroin or morphine, since these drugs have no action at sigma receptors.

As might be expected from the actions of the opiates, some opiate receptors are located in the gut. However, the majority are within the brain, where they form part of the membranes of nerve cell terminals—those points where information transfer occurs. Their distribution in the brain is rather specific. There are substantial numbers in areas concerned with the physical and psychological perception of pain. However, the greatest concentration occurs in the subcortical areas concerned with emotion, motivation, learning and memory. Opiates generally do not affect cognition or intellectual functioning, so it is entirely in keeping that cortical regions seem to contain very few opiate receptors.

Opiate receptors have been demonstrated in all vertebrates. This alone suggests that they have some important role in the normal functioning of organisms. The immediate implication is that there must be one or more endogenous ligands for these sites—substances that are produced by the body, like the transmitters, for particular purposes. Simultaneous research in several laboratories culminated in the identification of two opiate-like peptides that the discoverers named *met-* and *leu-enkephalin* (Hughes et al., 1975). Several other endogenous opiates were discovered in quick succession, and the term *endorphin*—a contraction of 'endogenous' and 'morphine'—was coined to describe this new group.

Both the endorphins and the enkephalins have opiate-like effects. Injected directly into the brain, they produce a profound analgesia that is reversed by naloxone, as well as a host of less well explored effects on mood, movement and hormonal function. The interested reader is referred to reviews of the subject by Guillemin (1978) and Beaumont and Hughes (1979).

While their general effects are the same, the two groups of substances probably have somewhat different functions. *Enkephalins* are found in basically the same areas of the brain as opiate receptors. Their pharmacological activity is short, a matter of minutes only, so their effects in the brain would not spread much beyond the immediate area of release. All this suggests that they act as transmitters and the best guess currently is that they regulate the function of neuronal systems. The *endorphins*, on the other hand, seem to be made only in the pituitary-hypothalamic regions of the brain. Their effects develop quite slowly, but they last three to four hours. This suggests a hormone-like action through the bloodstream. Dual control of this sort—a fast, highly accurate system suitable for fine adjustments, teamed with one that is slower and responsible for a more general tuning—is quite common in the brain. The clearest example is the adrenergic fight–flight system, where general tone is set by the hormones of the adrenal gland, while fine control comes from their analogue transmitters in the sympathetic nervous system.

The actual mechanism through which the endogenous opiates alter neuronal transmission is still unclear. However, since they can act on a wide variety of neurons which use several different transmitters, the mechanism is probably very basic. One currently popular suggestion is that they interfere with movements of calcium. Nerve terminals must take some of this in before they can release their transmitters. Morphine certainly lowers calcium availability; perhaps the endogenous opiates work similarly.

The role of endogenous opiates in modulating pain has so far received most attention. However, it seems clear that these substances are also critically important in the mechanisms of reward. Rats, for instance, will work for self-injections of enkephalin and the phenomenon is reversed by naloxone. Given the crucial role of reward, motivation and emotion in learning and information processing generally, it therefore seems likely that the endogenous opiates affect even the highest cognitive functions.

It is also clear, however, that the endogenous opiate systems are not always active: they are quiescent until activated by appropriate stimuli. Perhaps this could have been predicted. A moment's thought will show that it would be unadaptive to block pain completely—it is an important alarm system. Blockade would only be useful if the pain was likely to intefere with normal functioning.

Under natural conditions, the releasing stimuli for the endogenous opiate system are probably emotional. When individuals perceive great threat to themselves or to something they value greatly, fear and pain are forgotten. Cornered animals will attack, females will defend their young, males will battle for females in breeding season. We humans have a vast folklore of superhuman feats of pain endurance and apparent loss of all fear under conditions of stress. Ongoing, rhythmic activity—like jogging—may tap into the system, and so may strong belief. Analgesia produced by placebo, a substance that the recipient believes will kill pain but is in fact pharmacologically inert, can be reversed by naloxone (Pomeranz and Chiu, 1976). Placebo reactivity is not something limited to gullible neurotics: it is a large and common effect, as Beecher (1959) showed almost 30 years ago. In his studies, a great many non-addicted and otherwise normal people had their post-operative pain relieved adequately by placebos. Their belief in the effectiveness of the medication may well have released enough of their own endogenous opiates for a real physiological effect on their pain.

The endogenous opiate system can also be released artificially. In man, direct electrical stimulation of particular brain areas will do so. Such stimulation-induced analgesia is reversed by naloxone; it is also subject to tolerance and there is cross-tolerance between it and opiate-induced analgesia.

Electrical or mechanical stimulation of peripheral nerves, for example through acupuncture, also produces naloxone-sensitive analgesia. Interestingly, the analgesic effects of acupuncture are slow to develop but they persist long after the stimulation is discontinued—which suggests the involvement of endorphins rather than enkephalins.

Finally, the endogenous system can be activated by drugs, and exogenous opiates like morphine and heroin presumably operate by taking the place of endogenous opiates at the opiate receptors. Obviously such unnatural ligands cannot match the fine tuning the system shows when it operates under natural conditions, using its own endogenous chemicals. The effect of exogenous opiates is likely to be too gross, too inflexible. At the same time, since their administration is under external rather than situational control, opportunities for 'misuse' will be very much greater.

Inherent problems: tolerance and physical dependence

All drug effects are dose-dependent. A certain minimum amount is needed for an effect to appear and different effects have different thresholds. Thus, 10 mg of morphine (or 3 mg of heroin or 8 mg of methadone) given by subcutaneous injection will provide adequate analgesia in about 70 per cent of patients with moderate to severe pain. At that dose, sedative effects and respiratory depression should both be minimal. As dose increases, they become more pronounced, and the respiratory depression will become life-threatening with about 30 mg of morphine. If the drug is taken orally, the dose needs to be about ten times larger for an equivalent effect, since some of the drug is destroyed by the liver. Intravenous doses, on the other hand, can be considerably smaller—about one-fifth of the subcutaneous dose. Street users, of course, have no control over the purity of the drug they use, so these figures have little meaning for them.

Once the threshold dose for a particular effect is reached, the effect builds gradually to a maximum that will be determined by the amount of drug and number of receptors available. The rate at which the effect builds depends on a number of factors, including the ease with which the drug moves through the body to its site of action.

The user obviously wants the desired effect to happen as soon as possible. Because of its chemistry, heroin has a far more positive slope than either morphine or methadone—that is, its effects begin and reach a peak more rapidly—and this is one of the reasons users prefer it. The eventual preference of many for the intravenous method of use may also be related to this. As the relative doses given above suggest, substantially less drug is needed to produce an effect when it is given this way, and many users claim that financial pressure forces them into 'mainlining'.

Tom Field disagrees. He argues that while intravenous injection makes financial sense in the short term, over the longer term the opposite is true: tolerance builds more quickly this way, and with it the need for larger doses and more money. In his opinion, users really switch to mainlining because of the rush, and the fact that they need to justify their action in some other way indicates their belief that injection characterises a junkie, someone no longer in control of the drug.

Once in the body, drugs begin to be broken down by metabolic processes, often at very different rates. Morphine and heroin are cleared quite quickly, within about six hours after adminstration. Clearance of methadone takes at least three times as long. While there is an obvious relationship between the length of a drug's stay in the body and the duration of its effects, it is not a simple one. An effect ceases when the amount of drug available falls below a certain threshold. The subjective effects of morphine and heroin—analgesia, sedation and the like—last about four to five hours, that is, they parallel the rate of elimination quite closely. But the same effects produced by methadone also last four to five hours, though this drug stays in the body much longer. The reason is that a substantial portion of each dose of methadone binds firmly to various tissues, including parts of the brain, and the drug is released slowly from these sites in amounts too small to maintain the usual subjective effects. This slow release is nevertheless sufficient to prevent withdrawal signs in dependent individuals for quite a long time.

The subjective effects of heroin—presumably the ones a user is attracted to—thus last a relatively very short time. If the user discovers, as Field suggests, that more and more things go better with smack, there will be a tendency to use the drug more and more often. Not all of a drug's effects are due to the drug. Many, perhaps most in some users, come from the ritual of drugging. Still, if the substance used contains an active opiate and if use becomes frequent, tolerance will begin to develop.

Tolerance develops with most drugs. It seems to be a basic adaptive process through which the functions altered by the presence of the drug strive to return to normal. Several mechanisms are involved. To begin with, each individual has an innate sensitivity to drugs and this varies within a range that depends on the circumstances. Thus, the more 'normal' a person feels, the less he or she will generally respond to drugs. Depression, fatigue, illness or any physical or psychological disequilibrium usually means that drugs will be more effective in smaller amounts. Tolerance builds from this innate baseline.

'Dispositional' tolerance is probably the simplest form. The body becomes more efficient at removing the drug, so that less reaches the receptors. The user may also show 'pharmacodynamic' tolerance. Here systems affected by the drug show adaptive changes to its presence. They become less reactive, and more drug is needed to produce the original effects. In the case of the opiates, little dispositional tolerance develops and the changes are mostly pharmacodynamic. Not all effects show tolerance. The pupil constriction and the constipation usually persist. However, analgesia, sedation and euphoric effects all show tolerance, as does respiratory depression, though here there is a ceiling—*some* dose will always kill.

Tolerance develops most readily when the drug is given on a regular schedule, at intervals short enough to maintain some drug in the body constantly, and with the dose raised as often as necessary to achieve the desired effect. For heroin, this means that the drug would need to be used more than once a day. Under such conditions, tolerance can develop very rapidly. Martin and Fraser (1961) placed 'post-addict' prisoners on a schedule of 7.2 mg of intravenous heroin given four times a day, and the dose was then increased daily. Some tolerance was evident even with the second dose. In two or three weeks, the reported subjective effects were markedly diminished, even though the dose had increased tenfold. For some, doses 20 times higher than those used initially failed to give the desired effects. The development of tolerance would probably be less dramatic in neophytes. Previous tolerance seems to change the body rather permanently, even though use may be interrupted for a substantial period. Former addicts, like the group in Martin and Fraser's study, can return to very high doses remarkably quickly though not immediately.

If drug use is discontinued, tolerance falls dramatically with time, though it may not quite reach zero. A substantial percentage of overdoses result from users taking their usual dose after a period of abstinence. At the same time, many addicts also take advantage of this phenomenon. They periodically withdraw to reduce the amount of drug they need and so alleviate some of the financial pressures on them. This should be carefully distinguished from attempts at 'cures'. These addicts fully intend to use again and there is no question of giving up the drug permanently.

Beside tolerance to the effects of the opiate actually used, repeated administration will also produce some degree of *cross-tolerance* to other opiates. Thus, a person tolerant to heroin will automatically show tolerance to morphine or methadone. However, this tolerance does not extend to other classes of drugs and a particular problem occurs with various general depressants. These drugs tend to potentiate opiate effects and they are often used by addicts to supplement or increase effectiveness of street drugs, especially when drugs are scarce and price is high. Unfortunately, negative effects are potentiated as well as positive ones. Thus, if an individual takes a moderate dose of an opiate and then either deliberately or in ignorance drinks alcohol or takes a barbiturate or tranquilliser, additive depression of respiration will occur. This may result in coma, and deaths from the combined effects of opiates and general depressants are fairly common.

The body, then, adapts to the repeated presence of a drug by decreasing its sensitivity to it. But tolerance cannot be explained simply as an interaction between the drug and an individual's physiology. Psychological factors are also extremely important, especially those related to learning. Thus, tolerance develops much more rapidly if the person knows that he or she will have to perform some significant task while under the drug's influence. This can be interpreted in several ways, but the most favoured explanation is that the observed tolerance is in fact a learned compensation for the drug's effects.

Tolerance also develops more rapidly and lasts much longer if both drug administration and tolerance testing are carried out in the same environment. And, as we have already noted, exposure to repeated cycles of drug administration and withdrawal apparently accelerates the reacquisition of tolerance. A psychological explanation for these phenomena could be made just as easily as the suggestion that the adaptation is a physiological one. The point is that tolerance cannot be regarded as some sort of physiological constant.

While tolerance occurs with a wide variety of drugs, a much smaller number produce physical dependence. *Physical dependence* is not fully understood, but most agree that it represents some form of counter-adaptation to the presence of a drug. Where at least some forms of tolerance can be explained as a decrease in the body's reactivity to a drug, physical dependence seems to involve the development of an active mechanism to counteract its action. Thus, when a high degree of tolerance has been attained, even very large doses of heroin may fail to produce any euphoriant effect and the user merely feels 'normal'. However, if intake is stopped, a profound derangement known as the withdrawal or 'abstinence' syndrome quickly ensues.

Withdrawal begins with a slight depression and a vague depletion of energy, and in the experienced user these symptoms signal that a new dose is required. Following the administration of the drug, energy returns, both physical and mental efficiency is restored and the user is again ready to go about his or her ordinary affairs. If administration is delayed too long, or if the drug is unavailable, withdrawal will begin in earnest. The symptoms are generally opposite to the effects of the drug, and this suggests that compensatory mechanisms have been established against its action. In the case of heroin, the more the drug depresses various functions, the harder the body tries to bring them back to normal. With the heroin gone, the body continues to fight an enemy that is no longer there, and both it and the mind will be hyperactive until the compensatory mechanisms are dismantled.

What these compensatory mechanisms are remains unclear. Both the adaptive adjustments that constitute physical dependence and the disorganisation of these that occurs during withdrawal depend on the integrity of certain transmitter systems. As we have seen, exposure of nerve cells to opiates lowers their ability to use calcium, and therefore to release their transmitters. It also appears that opiates inhibit transmitter receptors directly, so that the effects of such transmitters as the cells manage to release would be reduced. Both these mechanisms show compensatory adaptation on repeated exposure to opiates, and this could account for their hyperactivity when the drugs are withdrawn.

There have also been attempts to relate the development of physical dependence to the endogenous opiate systems. The idea is that flooding the opiate receptors with exogenous opiates inhibits the production of the enkephalins and endorphins, so that in time the system becomes wholly dependent on the exogenous opiates for the maintenance of its function. When the opiate is withdrawn, both the pain relief and pleasure systems would be inactive until production of natural opiates was reestablished. It is an attractive theory, with sound biological precedents—many glands, for instance, are deactivated when their own hormones are given artificially—and it does have some empirical support (see Su et al., 1978; Ho et al., 1980). On the whole, though, the potential role of the endogenous opiates in the development of physical dependence must remain an exciting speculation for the time being.

From a physical standpoint, the heroin addict in withdrawal will experience diarrhoea, flu-like symptoms of sneezing, running nose and eyes, and alternate bouts of shivering and sweating. Waves of gooseflesh give rise to the term 'cold turkey' that is used to describe abrupt withdrawal. There are abdominal cramps, muscle spasms, and pains in bones and muscles, especially in the back and legs. The mental symptoms are concisely summarised by Tom Field:

> Like the body, the mind is in overdrive, turning over and over on itself. This, together with the physical edginess, makes sleep at night very light and broken ... In some way the deprivation increases physical sensitivity, it also produces a severe emotional vulnerability, coupled with anxiety and loss of self-confidence. Boredom is usual, in that the racing mind makes it almost impossible to concentrate and destroys both the interest and the drive to do anything.
>
> Deprivation sometimes causes an intense depression ... Perhaps the worst suffering caused by deprivation is the result of knowing that heroin, the cure for the sickness, is there, if only some way can be found to obtain it.
>
> 'You tell yourself that you know you can't get any but you can't help thinking about it all the same. Just thinking "if only" winds you up so much more than you would be normally. You go on and on thinking until you find a way that you think just might work. And suddenly you're so excited. You see the possibility of release from the agony. So you go out and do whatever you have to do to get it'.
>
> It is this way in which an addict's mind works that so often drives him to commit crimes. The mind harps on the subject, which both makes the suffering worse and minimises the difficulty or immorality of the action necessary to find the money to buy heroin. It is, therefore, a generally accepted fact that heroin illness is significantly more bearable when the addict knows he cannot get any heroin. (Field, 1985, pp. 62–3)

How long does it take to become physically dependent on heroin? The degree of dependence in practical terms is, as Field (1985) puts it, a matter of money.

> In general, the addict never has enough money. The more he has, the more heroin he can buy and take per day, the more his tolerance builds and, so, the more he needs to take and the more money he needs. And, the greater his daily dosage, the iller he will feel without it, and so, the greater his drive will be to get it. (p. 60)

But how long before withdrawal becomes a possibility? This depends partly on the definition of withdrawal. There are as yet no useful biochemical or physiological criteria for this, so its presence or otherwise is a matter of subjective judgement. With some drugs like marijuana or cocaine argument still continues about whether the vague changes that follow abrupt cessation of use are properly withdrawal or not. With the opiates, the withdrawal, when full-blown, is rather clearcut; however, there is still considerable subjectivity about where the lower limit is to be set.

Problems of definition aside, development of physical dependence depends critically on dose and frequency of administration. Therapeutic use of morphine—about 10 mg four times a day given orally—will give a mild withdrawal that may not be recognised as such by the patient after one or two weeks. Unfortunately, street users rarely know how much heroin they are actually using. Often they will state their intake in dollar deals rather than amounts: 'I'm using $100 a day.' A health care worker familiar with the street scene might know, for example, that in 1985 Sydney heroin was about 20 per cent pure, that a gram sold for $A300–350, and that gram deals tended to be further cut. This would suggest that an individual using '$100 a day' was consuming approximately 200–250 grams of powder, which contained between 10–40 mg of heroin (Reilly et al., 1985). The user seldom has even this vague information.

As a rule of thumb, under street conditions, 'between one and two months of daily usage may be taken as a rough guide, and two weeks of very heavy daily usage as a minimum' (Field, 1985, p. 53). Clearly, the 'one shot and you're hooked' myth is just that, at least from a physical standpoint. The psychological situation, as we shall see, may be a different matter.

If physical dependence does develop, just how bad *is* the withdrawal? From a pharmacological standpoint, this depends on the drug and the degree of adaptation that has occurred. It also depends on whether withdrawal is occurring under more or less natural conditions and on how long we choose to study the individual after the drug has been discontinued.

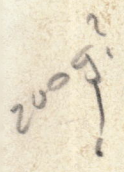

Just as the system needs time to adapt to the presence of a drug, it needs time to adjust to its absence. The rate of a drug's elimination from the body is therefore critical. If the body removes a drug quickly, the pressure to readjust would be expected to be more severe and more immediate than if the drug had a longer duration of action. This is in fact the case. Under natural conditions, the severity of the withdrawal is inversely proportional to the drug's rate of elimination. With short-acting drugs, withdrawal is relatively severe, though it lasts a shorter time. Thus, in the dependent individual symptoms of withdrawal from meperidine (Pethidine) occur within three hours after the last dose; they peak at about twelve hours and most obvious signs are gone in four days. Morphine or heroin withdrawal peaks two to three days after the last dose, and declines in seven to ten days. Withdrawal from long-acting opiates like methadone may need two days to become apparent to begin with, and the symptoms, while relatively mild, may take six to seven weeks to decline.

This difference in the severity of the withdrawal syndrome was one of the early reasons for methadone substitution. Cross-dependence occurs among related drugs, as well as cross-tolerance. This means that all opiates can substitute for one another to some extent, and one opiate can both suppress the withdrawal produced by another and maintain the physical dependence. The degree to which this substitution is possible depends more on pharmacological effects than chemical configuration. Thus, morphine, heroin and methadone—all relatively broad-spectrum drugs—can substitute for codeine and for each other. However, codeine, whose range of effects is much narrower, can substitute for morphine, heroin or methadone only partially. If a long-acting drug such as methadone is substituted over several days for heroin, abrupt cessation will result in a withdrawal syndrome characteristic of methadone rather than of heroin. Since addicts often express great fear of withdrawal, it was felt that the possibility of a milder syndrome might encourage at least some of them to give up their habits.

In fact, the situation is much more complex, both from a physiological and a psychological standpoint. It appears that the adaptations underlying physical dependence actually begin with the first dose of the drug and develop remarkably swiftly. Withdrawal from a one- or two-week therapeutic regime of morphine is barely noticeable. However, if the drug is not simply discontinued but rapidly displaced from its receptors by an antagonist like naloxone, withdrawal symptoms can be demonstrated after a mere two days' administration. Similarly, when methadone is displaced by naloxone, instead of being allowed to make its own slow way out of the system, withdrawal symptoms are immediate and severe. In fact, naloxone can precipitate a mild withdrawal syndrome in former addicts as long as a week after a single 40 mg dose of methadone (Jaffe and Martin, 1980). In other words, the severity of the withdrawal has little to do with the degree of adaptation that occurs to a drug's presence. Indeed, the whole opiate family seems to behave very similarly in this regard. What does matter is the time allowed the system to dismantle its compensatory mechanisms.

Determining the degree of physical dependence under natural conditions is quite difficult. Street addicts rarely know how much drug they actually use. Moreover, it is often to their advantage to exaggerate their dependence and the signs of withdrawal are well known and relatively easy to counterfeit. One can analyse body fluids for the presence of opiates but the assays are qualitative only—that is, they can indicate whether particular opiates were used within the last 24 hours, but not the extent of such use. Naloxone can also be used to precipitate withdrawal. Supporters of this technique argue that the method is objective and that it both minimises cheating and permits accurate estimates of the degree of dependence (Judson et al., 1980). Critics, however, point out that it causes unnecessary pain and discomfort to self-confessed addicts.

In practice, the most common technique is still trial-and-error: the patient is allowed to show signs of withdrawal and a test dose of methadone is administered. After eight hours, if signs have reappeared, another dose is given. If however the signs have been suppressed, withdrawal is allowed to begin again and the patient is tested with half the original methadone dose, then re-examined in another eight hours. This procedure is repeated until 24 hours have elapsed, and at that point the total amount of methadone required in 24 hours can be calculated. This then becomes the 'methadone substitution equivalent' (Sapira and Cherubin, 1975).

Obviously well informed addicts could cheat quite successfully in such situations. In addition to the deliberate cheaters, however, there is the problem of users who believe themselves to be addicts but who are not actually physically dependent. The development of physical dependence depends as much on regularity of use as on the amount actually used. In practice, the vast majority of addicts do not use heroin consistently on an ongoing basis. Less than half of the addicts who have been on the streets for more than a year will have used daily for that entire period (Johnson, 1978). They may voluntarily withdraw to reduce their tolerance, or the scene may be temporarily too much of a hassle, or they may have an important engagement such as a trial, at which an appearance of addiction would be undesirable. Or they may simply need a rest. During such times, physical dependence may virtually disappear, yet they will still think of themselves and describe themselves as addicts. In other cases, the users may never use enough drug to develop significant physical dependence. Senay (1986) estimates that between 25 per cent and 40 per cent of street addicts are not physically dependent. Nevertheless, such 'chippers' may wish to see themselves as addicts for reasons of their own, and will so describe themselves.

The withdrawal syndrome we have been discussing is what is termed 'primary' or 'early' abstinence. A substantial portion of the physical symptoms of this stage seem to depend on the activity of a part of the brainstem called the *locus coeruleus*. Opiates depress this area and it would therefore be expected to become hyperactive during withdrawal. The locus coeruleus is an important centre in the brain's fear−alarm system, and such hyperactivity would be consistent with the marked anxiety and agitation withdrawing addicts report. Fortunately for withdrawing addicts, other drugs beside the opiates can depress this region and one of them is clonidine. Clonidine is generally used as an antihypertensive agent, but in 1978 Gold and his colleagues reported that it could suppress or reverse the symptoms of opiate withdrawal. Subsequent work has shown that this reversal is by no means complete, but there seems no doubt that clonidine can make opiate withdrawal very much more comfortable.

Even if clonidine is not used, medical detoxification is usually accomplished by giving decreasing doses of a long-acting opiate like methadone. After a few weeks of this, the patient is usually opiate-free without having suffered any appreciable physical discomfort. Since a percentage of the methadone marketed for medical use finds its way into the streets, many addicts also detox themselves this way without formal medical help. Still others detox 'cold turkey'—without any pharmacological help at all. They simply tell their friends they have the flu, go to bed, and suffer in relative silence.

Medical supervision and assistance is certainly not essential for successful withdrawal. The addict's expectations, though, can be crucial. Rosenthal (1986) cites an experience of Ron Gornie, a medical social worker, with methadone-assisted detox:

> Although the patient knew he was being weaned from the drug, he was not told how much methadone he was being given each day, or how long the detox would last. For the last three weeks of the program, the individual was given a glass of Tang containing no methadone at all. He went through the detox perfectly happily. Then on the last day—when he had taken no opiate for three weeks—Gornie told him, 'that's it, you're done'. Recalls Gornie, 'He went into withdrawal right before my eyes'. (p. 170)

We will return to this phenomenon of 'conditioned abstinence' later.

Under natural conditions, then, the duration of early abstinence depends on the drug's rate of elimination and in the case of heroin most major symptoms should be gone within seven to ten days. At this point, however, the ex-addict is by no means normal. The first suggestion that the abstinence syndrome might be much more prolonged was made almost 50 years ago (Himmelsbach, 1942). However, the phenomenon of 'protracted abstinence' was first definitively demonstrated in rats in 1963 by Martin and his colleagues, and the work was later extended to human addicts (Martin, 1984).

A protracted abstinence syndrome follows withdrawal from both heroin and methadone and it seems safe to assume that it would occur with all opiates. The syndrome lasts a remarkably long time—at least 31 weeks after withdrawal, and perhaps longer. Blood pressure, pulse rate, body temperature and pupil diameter seem to be the main physiological variables affected. Behaviourally, the subject shows an increased propensity to sleep and there are negative changes in mood and feeling state. These changes resemble depression in some respects, but generally lack the feelings of guilt, hopelessness and inability to experience joy that are characteristic of the true psychopathological state. Rather, people undergoing protracted abstinence feel inefficient, inept, unpopular and unappreciated. They also feel chronically tired and inclined to be hypercritical.

All these changes are subtle and the individual usually remains within the normal range for each particular index. That is, while the changes are subjectively significant and enduring, they are not great enough to single out individuals in protracted abstinence as abnormal relative to the general population. It would be impossible to diagnose protracted abstinence in an unselected group by using these signs alone. Nevertheless, the significance of protracted abstinence is considerable. The ex-addict does not feel quite 'right', and the feeling goes on for a very long time. Add to this the knowledge that this feeling can be immediately relieved by a small dose of an opiate, and it is easy to understand why relapse rate after primary withdrawal is so high.

There is no question that physical withdrawal is unpleasant even if the degree of physical dependence is not very great. However, even in its classic form heroin withdrawal is not *that* serious, and in any case the majority of its symptoms can now be reduced if not eliminated by using clonidine or gradually reduced methadone. So why is it that so many addicts persist in using heroin under conditions which, so far as we can tell, give them every reason to wish to stop? And why do so many who have successfully withdrawn return to the drug?

Withdrawal symptoms, in fact, are the least of an addict's problems. The stubbornness of addiction depends far more importantly on two other factors. One is *psychological dependence*—the rearrangement of an individual's life priorities so that a desired object, person or activity moves toward the top of his or her needs hierarchy. The phenomenon will be discussed further in Chapter 7. Drug use is by no means the only activity that can lead to psychological dependence, nor does psychological dependence invariably occur whenever tolerance and physical dependence on a drug develop. Once psychological dependence enters the picture, though, the situation can no longer be explained in purely physical terms.

The other important factor has to do with *conditioning*. Cues like sight of the injection ritual can come to elicit the effects of opiates, very much as Pavlov conditioned salivation by pairing the ringing of a bell with presentation of food to his dog. The withdrawal response itself can be conditioned in the same way. Meyer and Mirin (1979) explain it this way:

> During his life on the street, an addict will often suffer a heroin deficit and feel the onset of withdrawal. Gradually the stimuli of the street—the sight of a 'works', a friend 'shooting up', the sights and sounds of the copping area—become paired with the beginnings of withdrawal. These stimuli, then, acquire the power to elicit the feelings, and even the physical symptoms, of withdrawal ... Thus, a former addict, abstinent for years in prison, or even under a maintenance dose of methadone, may suddenly experience all the symptoms of opiate withdrawal when he returns to his home area, reads about addiction, or experiences some feeling which had been paired with his earlier heroin use. He not only interprets his discomfort as a craving for heroin, but, in fact, he can relieve it by a heroin injection. (p. 48)

Presumably something like this happened to Ron Gornier's addict. Even though he had been opiate-free for three weeks or more, he needed the official statement 'That's it, you're done' to authenticate his drugless state—and to trigger his conditioned withdrawal.

Another form of conditioning is involved as well: reward-based or operant conditioning. Operant conditioning works on the commonsense notion that people will repeat those activities they find satisfying or are otherwise rewarded for. Its strength depends first of all on the frequency of reward, and the potential rewards of heroin are not difficult to imagine.

For many people, the pharmacological effects of heroin are rewarding in themselves. The rush, for example, is described as intensely pleasurable and a user may obtain this several times each day. At say three rewards a day, this quickly mounts up to a lot of reinforcement. Moreover, the time between the act of injection and the experience of the reward is very short and this is another thing that makes for strong conditioning. The pleasure inherent in the injection experience is not the only thing that might be rewarding either. For some addicts, the analgesic effects of heroin may relieve genuinely painful conditions that predated heroin use, or that have accumulated as a result of their unhealthy life on the street. Psychological pain is relieved equally readily. Yet the more heroin's ability to give peace and tranquillity is used to lessen feelings like helplessness, depression and frustration, the less will the user be able to cope with these feelings without it and the more traumatic and intractable they will seem.

There is a variety of non-pharmacological satisfactions as well. As Kaplan (1983) points out,

> Typically his friends are also addicts and he is embedded in their culture. Perhaps some have taught him the necessary street lore, even something so basic as how to use the drug, and perhaps he has taught others. We must remember that most of us, if presented with a package of heroin and a 'works' (an eye dropper, a needle, a spoon, and a piece of rubber tubing), would not know what to do with them—even if we had decided to use heroin.
>
> The addict's drug use permits him to enjoy his friends' company and esteem. Since his peer group consists of other addicts who share his perceptions about the worthwhile nature of heroin use, he will derive fellowship and psychological support from them ...
>
> He is likely to have acquired a whole set of beliefs and values respecting heroin use—including the views that people who don't use drugs are unbearably 'square' and that those who use drugs other than heroin are simply babies who are just playing around. To such addicts and their friends, only heroin users have the status that they desire and reward with approval.
>
> Such views may be reinforced, not diminished, by the evident disadvantages of the addict's life. Once he has suffered for his views, strong dissonance mechanisms come into play, which help convince him that his views must be correct—or else why would he have suffered so much for them? To support such an opinion, he will exaggerate to himself the advantages of his condition and downplay the disadvantages. (pp. 49–50)

It is not just the effects of heroin that are conditioned by these rewards; the whole of the complex drug use ritual is subject to operant conditioning as well. As a result, the addict attempting to stop using misses not only the effects of heroin but the process of obtaining and using the drug too. Here is what one user has to say:

> Once you decide to get off, it's very exciting. It really is. Getting some friends together and some money, copping, deciding where you're going to do it, getting the needles out and sterilizing them, cooking up the stuff, tying off, then the whole thing with the needle, booting, the rush, that's all part of it ... Sometimes I think that if I just shot water I'd enjoy it as much. (Powell, 1973)

And, in fact, some addicts do just that—they go through the motions of shooting up when no heroin is available, with or without anything in the syringe (Levine, 1974).

While frequency and immediacy of reward are very important, the scheduling of the reward may be even more so. It turns out that the most persistent behaviour occurs when it is followed by reward only some of the time, and the subject does not know in advance on which occasions this will happen. This is called *variable schedule* or *intermittent reinforcement*, and a little reflection will show that this is particularly likely to occur with street users of heroin. Both the purity of the drug, its availability and the user's ability to secure it can vary wildly. Addicts, in fact, live in a world of intermittent reinforcement.

Conditioning also exerts its strongest effects under circumstances that most closely resemble those in which the behaviour was rewarded. Chances are that rewards occurred most often in the addict's copping area, among his or her friends and in sight of particular landmarks. Use was probably also most rewarding when it removed the discomfort and depression that heralds incipient withdrawal. Unfortunately, both the street cues and feelings of discomfort are common in ex-addicts' lives. As they struggle to make a living and re-establish personal relationships, circumstances will often depress them. Such internal cues are likely to act most powerfully just when ex-addicts are least likely to have the willpower to abstain.

No wonder addiction is so durable. In the typical case, so many conditioned stimuli support the behaviour that even if the addict manages to detox and get rid of his or her physical dependence on the drug a host of environmental and internal cues will continue to trigger the old tendencies. An ex-addict would have to be very determined indeed to escape being 'hooked' once more. There is no need to invoke a loss of control arising from some obscure and entirely hypothetical 'disease' to explain this; the laws of conditioning are quite sufficient. Under the circumstances, the substantial numbers of former addicts who appear to have cured themselves should present no theoretical problems—but they should excite our admiration.

The negative side: harm and the question of recognition

'Harm' is a word with many meanings. Harm may be physical or mental and in each case it may be personal or social, that is, the effect may concern only the actor, or it may involve other people. Like all drugs, heroin carries some potential for each kind of harm. But whether harm will occur to begin with and the form it will take depends almost entirely on the *context* in which the drug is used.

While some of us are morally outraged by the concept of heroin use, as a society we are most concerned about its social consequences. We are worried about the relationship between heroin and crime. And we suspect that addicts, if left to their own devices, would impose a severe strain on the public purse either because their habit would cause physical disabilities that would make them socially unproductive, or because it would encourage them to choose to be so. We will take up the issue of criminality in Chapter 4. To jump ahead briefly, while there is support for the commonsense view that some addicts commit crimes to finance their habits, there is no evidence that addiction is the only or even the most important factor in an addict's criminality. And there is the undoubted fact that heroin would cost very little if it was legal.

The relationship of heroin use to social productivity raises both moral and practical questions. There is the philosophical issue of whether governments have the right to forbid the use of substances that cause widespread loss of productivity, and that certainly has not been resolved. Most of us take the view that the government should be able to insist only that we do not harm others, that we perform certain civic duties such as paying taxes and perhaps that we do not harm ourselves—at least in certain ways. We do not usually think that the government should require us to be productive too.

Nevertheless, historically governments have tried to do just that. Edward III of England, for instance, made bowling illegal—not because there was anything wrong with it, but because it distracted England's yeomen from practising archery, a matter of national importance. In more recent times, other governments have likewise tried to control things or activities conducive to idleness, though not necessarily consistently. Most countries today do not attempt to restrict most sports or television watching. Virtually all, however, take the view that they do have the right to interfere in the distribution of some drugs (but not others) that might cause an unwillingness or inability to work (Caplovitz, 1976).

Since an unambiguous resolution of the philosophical problem is unlikely, the real issue becomes the practical one of the extent to which heroin addicts' productivity or ability to hold employment would be impaired if the drug was freely available. The really astonishing fact is that we genuinely do not know.

Given the present illegality and therefore high cost of the drug, the obvious non-productivity of today's addicts cannot be used as a guide to what might be the case were things otherwise. Nor can we legitimately extrapolate from what was the case in other times, or is the case today in other cultures. There are simply too many differences. Thus, Berridge and Edwards (1981) concluded that between 1830 and

1860, the average resident of England—man, woman and child—consumed the equivalent of 127 therapeutic doses of opium each year: a very high level of use. Yet there is no persuasive evidence of widespread social incapacity. Opium users were clearly not lying about in the streets, or beating their wives, or filling the workhouses—that was the image of the wastrel drunkard—nor were the associated mortality levels too disastrous. But at that time opium was used orally and society was still predominantly rural, relatively crime-free by our standards, and based on free enterprise. The same might be said of the present-day hill tribes of Thailand, where opium is also freely available and average level of social harm seems relatively small (Suwanwela and Poshyachinda, 1980).

The ability of today's society to tolerate drug-caused impairment is in no sense comparable. We already demand more occupational skills than many non-addicts possess, and addiction becomes a serious additional handicap. Even if heroin was legal and inexpensive, an addict might not earn enough to support a large habit. And there might not be enough time to work. Addicts need heroin approximately every six hours and holding a steady job could be difficult for someone alternating between a dreamy euphoria shortly after an injection and a feeling of heroin deprivation before the next.

Nor do we have any reason to believe that addiction would be confined to those who are unemployable. If heroin was freely available, any increase in the productivity of today's addicts might well be cancelled by the lowered productivity of new addicts. The facts of the matter are that we have more questions on this issue than there are answers. We have no good evidence that prohibition of heroin on the grounds that it interferes with social productivity is justified. But neither do we have evidence that making it freely available would have no untoward consequences in this regard.

The situation is a little clearer if we consider personal harm resulting from heroin use. From the physical side, at least, there is no question that the majority of the health problems associated with heroin use arise from its illegality, not its toxicity. Morphine and heroin—in fact the opiates generally—are remarkably safe drugs. However, in this culture, the only group of users that are relatively unaffected by the difficulties occasioned by their illegality are the physician addicts. Physicians generally use far more drugs than other professionals and in the United States at least the incidence of opiate addiction among them is very much higher than in the general population. Various estimates place it at around one in every 100: some 4000 in the country as a whole. Yet these people rarely suffer negative physical consequences, though their psychological problems are often major. Physician addicts typically prefer the short-acting meperidine, though methadone and morphine are also commonly used. Heroin use is not common, but then, as we have seen, this is for most practical purposes morphine. Goode (1984) attributes the good physical health of physician addicts to four factors. First, they use standard doses and pure drugs. Their needles and injection techniques are sterile. They are aware of and compensate for nutritional deficiencies. And finally, physicians do not have to search for drugs, or for the money to maintain their habits. Some are reported to have been addicted for 40 and 50 years without complications.

Street addicts have none of these advantages. Their drug is impure and varies in potency, and it is largely because of this that addicts occasionally overdose. Other overdose deaths result from use of heroin in combination with other drugs, either deliberately or in ignorance, and still others are due to individual hypersensitivity reactions. A few are probably deliberate murders with 'hot shots' since heroin users often become liabilities to others.

The high price of heroin forces addicts to compromise both their nutrition and the conditions under which they live. The appetite-suppressant and analgesic effects of the drug mean that ill-health tends to be ignored until the problem is major. In any case, the illegality of addiction makes it more difficult for addicts to seek medical treatment for any ailment, whether caused by their habit or not. And most addicts inject their drugs intravenously—because it is cost-effective, because they want the rush, because that is what they were taught to do—for a whole host of reasons. Even sterile technique and pure drugs can cause damage. Three or four injections a day plus a certain number of misses will eventually leave their mark on delicate blood vessels, especially if needles are blunted or barbed, as happens when they are reused too often, or if technique is sloppy. The analogy of the self-injecting diabetic is not valid—insulin is injected subcutaneously, a much simpler and safer process. If in addition the drug is impure and/or the technique unsterile, the range of possible pathological sequelae is enormous and they can involve virtually every organ system in the body. The interested reader is referred to Sapira and Cherubin (1975) for an 'organ recital'. Still, the known health consequences of uncomplicated heroin use are sufficiently small to suggest that it might be made legitimately available to addicts, at least under particular circumstances. Unrestricted availability, though, is another matter. Since our knowledge of the long-term health consequences of heroin use is necessarily very incomplete, we cannot be sure that there would not be major health problems if there was free access to the drug. In this respect, heroin might turn out to be like nicotine. Tobacco use today is seen as a major cause of sickness and death. Yet these problems are slow to develop and the harm can only be demonstrated in large scale, long-term studies.

Like the physical harm, psychological problems resulting from heroin use seem mostly due to the illegal status of the drug. Acquiring heroin requires time as well as money. So the typical addict cannot hold a job long, except in quite unusual circumstances. Tom Field managed both habit and job for two years only, he feels, because he was lucky.

> Firstly, my addiction was comparatively small and, because I was prepared to put up with feeling ill from time to time, it stayed small. Secondly, much of the time I was living with my brother who was also addicted. As he was not working, he had time to waste buying the drug. Thirdly, I had the motivation. However, when I lost the motivation, when I became bored with the job and it lost its importance relative to heroin, then my life did fall apart. (1985, p. 65)

The loss of motivation for other activities is almost inevitable, and this does not stop with motivation to work or study. Friendship, love, anything that requires giving, come to cost too much in terms of time and effort. Heroin's 'affective analgesia' practically guarantees it: the addict does not care very much under the influence of the drug and when such concerns reassert themselves as intoxication wanes, another dose will ward them off again.

Any friendship and support systems the addict develops with other addicts are based on need, not trust—'because one cannot trust an addict, or rely on one. Your problems are never their problems' (Field, 1985, p. 67). With heroin costs high and problems pressing in on every side, morality also becomes too expensive and inconvenient. At the very least, an addict becomes an expert liar and manipulator.

Nevertheless, we cannot assume that all these problems would automatically disappear were heroin freely and cheaply available, any more than we can assume that there would be no health consequences of use under such circumstances. Once the honeymoon period is over, most users feel trapped by the need to order their lives artificially around the drug. Even the legitimately maintained user suffers all the frustrations, tragedies and misfortunes of ordinary experience and these too must be accommodated to the habit. For the street user, these are of course multiplied astronomically. Not surprisingly, users are prone to bouts of guilt and despair.

> I remember sitting at a table, in front of me an open packet of heroin, containing, I reckoned, enough to kill myself. I tried to think of a single reason not to do so. I couldn't. (Field, 1985, p. 76)

Perhaps the most destructive aspect of the whole thing is the static character of a life centred around a drug. As Field says, 'one comes out of addiction at the same mental age at which one entered it' (p. 93), and some of these developmental delays may be difficult if not impossible to make up. Another ex-addict, with five drug-free years behind her, puts it this way:

> I'm 29 years old. I wish that, by now, my career was all settled for me. That I had friends. You don't learn how to be a friend or what a relationship is when you're just getting high. And when you stop getting high, it's like being a baby and starting all over again from the beginning. When you're high, it's like being a robot. It's euphoric, but you could be anybody. All the people that are out there using drugs, the faces change, but they're all the same, they're all nobodies, because they're never going anywhere, they're never going to make anything of themselves . . .
>
> The main thing that bothers me is that the years that I lost while I was taking dope I will never get back. And you lose a lot of self-pride because of the things you end up doing, and it takes a long time to get that back. What I should have been doing all that time in my life was going to college, pursuing a career, and going out and doing the so-called normal things. What I was doing was hanging out on the street corner and getting high. And that was my whole life. You don't see a lot of things when you get high . . . If I hadn't gotten involved with drugs, maybe I would have had a career. Maybe I would have had more confidence in myself at this point in my life, because I don't have it now. I'd have some friends today, which I don't have now because after all those years, I really didn't have any friends left. (Goode, 1984, pp. 249–50)

Heroin use often becomes 'official' because of some crisis: loss of a job, financial disaster, an overdose or an arrest. The 29-year-old ex-addict gives an example of a typical situation:

> I was arrested because I was set up by two of these so-called friends. It was a federal offence—forging a money order or a check or something. I signed the check and went into a bank and my friends took off in my car when they saw the police, and I got busted, my second arrest. I was threatened by these people about saying anything about their involvement in it, but I ratted them out anyway, because they did the same thing to me. After I was arrested and taken to the police station, I wanted to call home. I wanted to tell my parents I'd be late—I was between apartments and living at home—that I was delayed somewhere. I didn't want them to know what had happened. So the police officer who was questioning me picked up the phone and dialed my parents' house, and my mother answered and he said, hello, this is officer

so-and-so, your daughter is under arrest, and he handed me the phone. Which they're really not suppposed to do. It's good that he did it, because my parents came down to the police station. When I was there by myself, I was being very rebellious and hard-headed and stupid. Because my parents came there, I ended up telling everything that had happened. And because my mother went to court with me, and I didn't have a previous record, and I was white, and middle-class—all that had to have something to do with it, I feel—and I wasn't belligerent in court, and I really did want help, they gave me probation. (Goode, 1984, p. 248)

By the time a crisis occurs, the problem is usually one of addiction rather than occasional use. People who care about the user, whether parents or simply friends, do him or her no favours by allowing matters to reach this point without trying to intervene.

How then does one recognise the signs of use? They are difficult to spot and will usually be open to other explanations. No single one, or even several together, can be taken as conclusive evidence. Nevertheless, they should alert one to the possibility of use.

Finding the substance itself or the paraphernalia for use is the most obvious sign. Heroin comes in many forms and its colour, texture and consistency vary with purity. The purest, or 'No. 4' heroin is colourless or white and it is a finely crystalline or fluffy powder. Less refined forms may occasionally be pink or bluish, but they are typically various shades of brown. As a rule, cruder forms are darker and increasingly granular, even lumpy. Heroin may come packaged in small plastic envelopes, but most street deals will be in small packets made of foil or paper, typically a heavy, non-absorbent or glossy type. The most characteristic feature is an intensely bitter taste.

Heroin may be sniffed. In this case, a razorblade is used to divide the powder into lines on a smooth surface, usually glass or a mirror, and the drug is sniffed up through a straw or a rolled-up paper tube inserted into a nostril. Traces of the drug will remain on all these objects.

Heroin may also be smoked. It is placed on a piece of kitchen foil, or the very fine foil from chewing gum or other commercial wrappers, and heated from beneath with a match or lighter. The heroin melts and gives off fumes, and it is the undulating movement of these over the surface of the foil that gives rise to the fanciful oriental term 'chasing the dragon'. The fumes are inhaled through a paper or foil tube held in the mouth and this tube is often crimped two or three times along its length. The underside of the foil will be blackened by the heat and the melting heroin will leave characteristic dark runnels along the upper surface.

Injection is the most complicated method and requires the most equipment. An 'outfit' (or 'fit', or 'works') will consist of a hypodermic syringe or, more usually, a needle affixed to an eyedropper, and a spoon, usually dessert size, with the handle bent back. This will be blackened underneath, since heat is needed to help dissolve the heroin in water. With brown heroin, heat alone is generally insufficient and a mild acid must be added, often lemon juice or vitamin C powder. Cotton balls or filters from filter-tip cigarettes are used to strain out impurities as the solution is drawn up into the syringe. Users typically save these, since they contain some heroin and can be boiled up for emergency use if heroin is unavailable. A tourniquet of some kind will also be needed, but this can be anything from a piece of rubber tubing to a stocking.

Users are unlikely to leave their implements in an obvious place and if they do, it may well be a plea for help. Nor are the implements always kept together. Many are ordinary household objects and mean nothing in their customary place. A lemon in the bathroom, however, may mean something. Bathrooms are frequent hiding places, since water is needed both to dissolve the drug and to clean out the apparatus, and they normally provide the privacy needed for the injection itself.

Smoking or sniffing heroin rarely leaves physical traces, though needle marks will always show if fresh enough. A series of injections along a vein will produce a long purple track and clumsy injections can cause gross bruises and discolourations. Long-term use of the same vein may leave permanent lumps or scars. Injection can be quite messy and it gets messier with each failed attempt as the addict becomes more desperate and flustered, and therefore more likely to fail again. Even with a successful injection some blood follows the withdrawal of the needle and unless this is staunched properly it may stain clothing. As the veins of the arm are most commonly used, such stains are most likely on sleeves—and a regular user usually wears long sleeves to cover tell-tale marks.

Other than injection marks, use leaves few clear signs. If the user is actually under the influence of the drug, the pupils will be contracted even in dim light. Addicts are usually aware of this and some attempt countermeasures, so this is not always a reliable sign. Pupils will dilate when an addict begins to go into withdrawal. Under the influence of the drug most addicts will tend to 'nod out'; this should be alerting if it occurs at inappropriate times and especially if it is accompanied by a tendency to scratch as though the body was itching. Beyond this, users tend to become pale and often lose weight dramatically. Such symptoms, and also signs of withdrawal, may be passed off as illnesses, usually colds or flu, since these are superficially similar. It is not the 'illnesses' themselves that hint at heroin use, but rather their abnormal frequency.

Behaviour changes are more significant than physical signs, but they are also much more difficult to pick up because they can develop quite gradually and may be fairly subtle. As Field points out:

> ... except after a large dose, a user remains capable of coherent, rational thought. It is rather his attitude that changes. Because the drug distances him from his surroundings, he tends to be less aware of other people's feelings and needs. He therefore tends to be less kind, less thoughtful and helpful, less tolerant, and in conversation more dogmatic and argumentative. If the user is your lover, the first sign you notice may be a diminution in sex. (1985, p. 89)

There may be a gradual withdrawal from contact with family and customary friends, together with an acquisition of new acquaintances:

> 'I noticed David seemed to have changed his friends. I said to him: "What's happened to Joe?" or "Don't you see Karen any more?" and he'd just shrug and say something like, "Oh, you know, Mum" or "I see them sometimes." I used to really like most of his friends. Instead, he started seeing people who looked shifty to me. He wouldn't introduce them to me if he could help it, which he'd always done before. And he stopped coming to talk to me. He always used to do that, like when I was doing the ironing or something. He'd come and chat and tell me what he was doing at college, that sort of thing. All I got from him now was "I'm going out now, Mum." It was as if a wall had come down between us.' (Field, 1985, p. 87)

Users may receive phone calls, often late at night, from people who will not leave a name. They may hold long conversations in obscure language—heroin has a slang of its own. They keep increasingly odd hours, they are late for appointments, they neglect to do things they said they would. So many things require explanation and however inventive and plausible these become, their very frequency should be alerting. Unfortunately significant people, especially parents, often prefer to accept even a far-fetched explanation rather than assume something more sinister—particularly if that is precisely what they are afraid of finding.

As the involvement with heroin grows, the user will need increasing amounts of money. For this, the most useful initial sources are close friends and especially immediate family. If these are relatively well-off and inclined to be generous, the user can extract quite surprising amounts of cash over a long period of time. Mothers and female relatives generally seem to be the most vulnerable. In due course, both good will and gullibility will fail. Some users then resort to tantrums, threats and various forms of extortion and again it is surprising how many relatives can be coerced and even terrorised into compliance.

Or the user may begin to steal from the household. In many cases, petty theft will have gone on even while family and friends were still willing to respond to pleas for gifts or loans. The mother of a Malaysian addict complained to me that she finally had to buy household staples like rice, oil and sugar in small daily quantities rather than in bulk lest her son sell them while she was at work. Most household appliances had already been sent to a sister for safekeeping and she was using a charcoal brazier for cooking. In our generally more affluent culture, thefts are likely to be less basic. Money and small, easily saleable objects are most likely to disappear. Medicines, too, are highly vulnerable, especially sedatives, tranquillisers and prescription analgesics. Or the user may organise a more major burglary that will appear to have been carried out by an outsider.

On the whole, then, heroin use is a matter for concern and would probably be so even if the drug was legal. As it is, its use entails enough potential problems that it should always be discussed if it is discovered or suspected. Discussion does not mean hysterical accusation, nor does it mean immediately pressuring the user to stop forthwith. Sufficient reasons to dissuade an occasional user are hard to marshall, especially if you drink or smoke yourself, no matter how moderately. Both alcohol and tobacco are physically more damaging than the opiates. The best argument is the real danger of addiction and even this will probably not be persuasive. While most users are well aware that addiction to heroin can develop, they are all firmly convinced that they personally will manage to avoid it.

So the real role of discussion is to bring the matter out into the open and to permit monitoring of the situation so that, should use escalate, further action might be taken. It also opens the way for the user to turn to you should he or she eventually feel that use is becoming a problem. At the same time, your own position needs to be made clear. If you disapprove, say so. This is a matter of basic self-protection. If you refuse to recognise that someone you know is using heroin, you lay yourself open to both exploitation and the emotional destruction an addict can wreak. The least you should do is forbid use in your home, especially if the addict is living with you. Permitting it is, after all, a criminal offence. If you do not live with the user, you can refuse to see him or her when they are 'stoned'. You won't lose much—under the influence of heroin, people are either dull or intolerable.

4
Heroin the commodity

The more power we give to heroin, the less power we have left to deal with it. Ultimately, we risk becoming so fixated by the aura of the drug itself that we forget to look at the factors in our society which have brought about its widespread use.
Simon Davies, 1986, p. 53

Heroin, like anything else, is a commodity and commodities, if left alone, will find their own price level depending on supply and demand.

If only government could keep its sticky fingers out of the situation (and ignore various pressure groups), heroin users would be able to finance their addiction for about the price of one or two loaves of bread a day ...

It is a trade between consenting individuals. The fact that the trade may be harmful to the user is not the business of government. Some people just like to travel in the fast lane.

Government prohibitions mean that instead of being able to support his habit for one or two dollars a day, he must find perhaps one or two hundred dollars a day. (R.D.S., Sydney)
Australian, 9 January 1985

The management of those who already use heroin is only tangentially relevant to the drug problem. They have already fallen from grace and we may treat them with sympathy or make public examples of them as current fashions dictate. The main thrust of our efforts is always to prevent use. We can try to do this by reducing demand through various educational strategies and, significantly, our efforts in this direction have been half-hearted at best. Or we can try to reduce supply, and this is where we have chosen to place the bulk of our resources. Much of the current effort is conceptualised in terms of a war and the essence of the battle plan in the drug war is that the enemy can be defeated if only the army is powerful enough. More and more money, time and expertise are being poured into drug enforcement, but the availability and use of illicit drugs continues undiminished. A major reason for this state of affairs is the almost total failure to consider the economic and geopolitical aspects of the situation.

Heroin, together with a wide range of drugs like alcohol, coffee, tobacco, cannabis and cocaine, alters mood and mental processes in a way that humans find desirable. Most psychoactive substances are subjected to legal control at some stage in their history and it is largely a historical accident that heroin, cocaine and cannabis are illegal today. Yet both coffee and tobacco were illegal in their day and alcohol continues to be so in some cultures. Penalties for use then, as now, were draconic, and in all cases they failed to change the patterns of use very much. None of these drugs has been successfully eradicated once it became established. Why not? If we want to achieve an end, it is patently absurd to pursue a policy that has never succeeded—and yet we seem to be doing just that.

There are, in fact, sound economic reasons why the appeal of these substances is so enduring. In the first place, all of them have been and continue to be traded in quantities so large that they are not merely big business but essential exports for the producing countries. Also, they are derived more or less directly from naturally occurring plant material. In the case of opium—and this is also true of coffee, tobacco, cocaine and to a lesser extent alcohol—mass production is more or less restricted to regions where terrain and climate suit the particular plant. Often enough, that same terrain and climate is inappropriate for most other crops. As a result, the local economies have been distorted and their survival is now tied to the continued export of the drug. So not only traders but also producers become 'dependent' on a particular product for their economic survival.

However, these commodities generate another kind of dependence. There is a wide range of experiences for which people will go to considerable trouble. In everyday language, people can become 'addicted' to them. Once so addicted, people will feel considerable psychological and even physical discomfort if the experience becomes unavailable. All the drugs mentioned can induce such desirable states in many people. Dealing with such commodities has some special features. The demand for them is what economists call 'highly inelastic', that is, no matter what the price, the customer needs to buy. Trading in such goods guarantees a secure and steady profit. If this can be combined with monopoly the result is super-profit, and such monopolies are hard to break. There is too much to be lost and vast sums of money, or naked power, may be employed to ensure their continued existence.

Mugford (1982) identifies three ways to achieve monopolies. One is the 'company town' strategy of controlling sales of all goods. A second and more common strategy is to tie the trade to the dominant social group. The last is currently the most relevant to the heroin trade: use of corruption to corner a market for an illegal product.

> Without legal sanction there would be only marginal profit in heroin. It is readily obtainable in Southeast Asia and any passing tourist could bring back a couple of kilos for sale without too much hassle. The market mechanism that maintains the very high profit of the heroin dealers is the fairly active attempts to restrict the trade. Most small independent operators are pursued and often caught. Some of the large importers are also put under pressure, and the street selling operation is also routinely harassed. We also know, however, that many of the largest smuggling operations run for substantial periods without harassment, some probably being virtually immune from prosecution.
>
> The relative immunity to prosecution is achieved via kickbacks and bribes. Only the most naive person would now believe that this does not occur in Australia. Police corruption is almost certainly widespread and serious. There is considerable recent evidence to suggest that this corruption is paralleled by active political corruption ...
>
> The overall result is a rather neat, if unpleasant, system. Differential harassment keeps down competition. Absence of competition leads to restricted supply and high prices. The high prices yield super profits. The super profits are used (amongst other things) to generate the funds to develop further corruption and to maintain existing 'connections'. (Mugford, 1982, pp. 64–5)

No wonder it has proved impossible to legislate drugs like heroin out of existence. Their very illegality contributes to their value as a commodity and it is difficult to argue with Mugford's final conclusion that if heroin use cannot be eliminated, then 'partial control is worse than no control, for its effect is to ensure corruption and super profits' (1982, p. 66). Our problem, then, is the fact that heroin is a commodity, the properties of which make inelasticity a general economic feature of its market. Where such properties are combined with monopoly the result is profit great enough to both attract continuing investment and, if necessary, to underwrite corruption to ensure its maintenance.

The international heroin market

The opium poppy is much more adaptable than, say, the coca bush, but it does best in well-drained soils and temperate to warm climates. Under ideal conditions two harvests can be expected each year. Flowers appear in about four months after planting and when the petals fall, the immature seed capsules are incised. The milky exudate which appears in the scores is gathered and dried to form brown raw opium.

Opium itself can be eaten, smoked or dissolved and drunk. A number of important medicinal substances are extracted from it, morphine and its derivative heroin being the most important for our purposes. The reason we have a heroin rather than a morphine problem has more to do with distribution than with user preference. Heroin is rapidly broken down to morphine once in the body, and most of its effects are in fact due to morphine. One kg of morphine converts to about 1.1 kg of heroin, but heroin is far more potent. In terms of effectiveness, 1 kg of heroin is equivalent to 3 kg of morphine, and the advantages of this for the illicit operator are obvious. Relative to morphine, heroin is eminently portable.

The manufacture of heroin from opium is fairly simple. It requires only basic chemical equipment, a few cheap and readily available reagents and a modicum of skill. A simple soaking, heating and filtering converts crude opium into a brown powder. Compressed into blocks, this is known as *morphine base* or sometimes *No. 1 heroin*. About 10 kg of opium are needed to make 1 kg of morphine base. Acetylation of the morphine base results in the powdery grey *No. 2 heroin* or *heroin base*. This is an intermediate step, insoluble in water and therefore unsuitable for injection. The two marketable products are *No. 3 heroin*, sometimes called 'smoking heroin', a granular, soluble salt that is usually grey or brown but may range from bluish to pink. This is probably the most commonly sold form, with a morphine content of around 30 per cent. Further refinement will produce *No. 4 heroin*, the purest form, usually a fluffy white powder. This can contain as much as 90 per cent morphine, though of course by the time it reaches the consumer it is usually massively diluted.

Opium products, especially codeine, are widely used in medicine and licit opium is grown in many places, including Australia. Until 1972, however, most of the world's legal opium—some 1 500–2 000 tons a year—came from government monopolies in India (70 per cent), Russia (15 per cent) and Turkey (9 per cent). The historical reasons for the development of an illicit market for opiates have been discussed in Chapter 2. As we saw, it began in Western countries around the turn of the century, and in the United States it gained a major impetus from legislation enacted between 1914 and the 1920s. Both alcohol and the opiates were prohibited at that time, and illicit suppliers found ready markets. American organised crime grew from local gangs to nationwide syndicates, and from the beginning the Mafia figured prominently in the illicit heroin trade. The reasons were rather prosaic. The production of heroin, while certainly not complicated, does require *some* technical skill, and until recently this was unavailable in the areas where opium is actually grown.

Of the three main legitimate producers, Turkey was the most vulnerable to the illicit trade. Indian poppy farmers were paid more per kilo the more they could produce. Such a system both encourages a high yield and rewards farmers for putting their entire crop into legal channels. In Turkey, however, legal opium sold for very much less, and at a fixed price. Since illicit buyers were prepared to pay up to three times more than the government, the temptation was great and substantial amounts of opium began to be grown strictly for the black market. This opium was turned into morphine base locally, but expertise for further conversion to heroin was lacking. The morphine base was therefore shipped to clandestine laboratories in Sicily and areas around Marseilles for the final processing. The entrepreneurs managing this complex enterprise were the long-established and well-organised crime 'families' of the Mafia, and they shipped the product on to cousins and in-laws (figuratively and literally) in New York and the northeastern United States for distribution and sale. This was the notorious 'French Connection'.

In Asia, the Chiu Chow syndicates took a parallel role. According to McCoy (1980), these began when a group of Swatow merchants won a government contract to sell opium in Shanghai's French Concession in the late 1800s. In the 1920s, they opened illicit laboratories in Shanghai and came to dominate an industry that supplied some 10 million Chinese addicts. In 1949, when the Red Army captured Shanghai, the syndicates fled to Hong Kong, taking their chemists with them. In the 1950s, they established new laboratories there, using morphine base produced in the Golden Triangle as their raw material. As government opium monopolies in Thailand, Malaysia and Vietnam closed in the 1950s and opiates were officially banned in response to international pressure, the syndicates expanded their operations to cover most of Southeast Asia. By the early 1970s they were in firm control of Asia's illicit drug trade. Hong Kong alone, at the time, had 100 000 addicts—some 2.6 per cent of its total population.

In the late-1960s and through the 1970s, the United States made some determined efforts to eradicate illegal opiate traffic, and its management of the 'problem' at this time has been described as a 'comedy of errors' (Ray, 1978). The immediate motivating force was the Vietnam War. When some 500 000 American soldiers appeared in Vietnam in the late 1960s, they presented an obvious potential market. The Chiu Chow syndicates despatched a number of their Hong Kong chemists to the area. Laboratories for No. 4 heroin production were established, pushers appeared in the army camps and by 1970 the GI heroin epidemic scandalised America.

As we have seen in Chapter 2, one result was President Nixon's declaration of a War on Drugs. Part of this 'war' included allocation of considerable sums—up to $12 million annually—to aid antinarcotics police in Southeast Asia. However, the United States was convinced of the paramount importance of the Turkey–Marseilles corridor to its domestic heroin supply, and the major offensive of the 'war' was therefore directed at Turkey and France.

The United States partially funded the successful elimination of the Marseilles laboratories by the French police. It also pressured the Turkish government to ban all opium production from 1972 on. In return for this action, it offered $35 million to reimburse the farmers for their financial loss and to help them develop new crops. Few actions could have been more short-sighted. The ban was on an important cash crop, and moreover on one that was closely woven into a traditional way of life. According to Halper (1975), at one point there were even suggestions that large numbers of families be evicted from their own property and directed into cottage industries elsewhere. This was never carried out, but the very suggestion illustrates the profound ignorance and arrogance of American policymakers with regard to peasant lifestyle.

Over and above this, though, the United States was asking for the ban during a worldwide shortage of legal opium. Legal use had exceeded production for some time, and the United States had released 200 tons of opium—half its strategic stockpile—to meet its own needs. America was thinking of growing its own poppies and it had actually encouraged India to grow more opium. To cap it all, the promised compensation was never fully paid, and very little of it seems to have reached the peasants. It is hardly surprising that all the poppy farmers and both Turkish political parties began to urge a return to poppy growing. The ban was abolished, despite American protests, in 1974.

What the two year ban on Turkish production and the disruption of the French Connection did, though, was force a major reorganisation of international heroin traffic. The process was complex, and it illustrates what McCoy (1980) has called the *'iron law of the international narcotics trade*: if an established heroin exporter is denied entry into an existing market he will create a new one, and if a major heroin dealer is denied access to an existing source he will seek and find an alternative source of supply' (p. 22).

The first effect was a temporary alliance between American heroin distributors and Southeast Asia's exporters. The former needed the product, and the latter were essentially trying to follow the GIs home as withdrawal of troops from Vietnam left them with surplus stocks. By 1973 Southeast Asian heroin accounted for approximately 30 per cent of total American consumption. However, it failed to take over the market; by 1975, it made up only about 9 per cent of all the heroin seized on the streets. The reasons are unclear. Some have argued that the main problem was lack of reliable connections, since Asians traditionally deal primarily with other Asians. McCoy (1980), however, maintains that the reasons were purely economic:

> The [U.S. Drug Enforcement Agency's] seizures and arrests imposed an informal but costly 'customs duty' on Chiu Chow heroin entering the U.S. and began to discourage further syndicate exports. Faced with the alternative of closing down their operations at a loss, the Chiu Chow syndicates, according to DEA's intelligence analysts, decided to develop new markets for No. 3 heroin in Europe and Australia where there were then realtively few addicts . . .
> Chiu Chow syndicates based in Malaysia opened up No. 3 laboratories in the Thai—Malaysia border area, supplementing ongoing No. 4 production on the Thai—Burma border, and made Kuala Lumpur a major terminus in the international traffic. Using commercial air passengers with concealed 'body-packs' as couriers and the large Chinese community in Amsterdam as their distribution point, the Chiu Chow syndicates began making regular shipments of No. 3 heroin to Europe in early 1972 . . .
> Once regarded as an 'American problem', heroin addiction began spreading rapidly in Europe. In the Netherlands, for example, the number of heroin addicts jumped from 100 in 1970 to 10 000 in 1975. Similarly in Sydney, police first observed a trickle of Southeast Asian heroin entering the city in 1968, a greatly increased flow in 1974—5, and an unprecedented flood in 1977 and 1978. (p. 347)

The gap left in the United States market by this redirection of Southeast Asian interests did not remain empty for long. By the time the street shortage resulting along the eastern seaboard in 1973—74 had raised prices to attractive levels, Mexico was ready to take up the slack. Heroin had been produced there for some time, and it accounted for some 39 per cent of American heroin in 1972. 'Mexican Brown' was distributed mostly in the west and southwest, while the eastern states were originally supplied primarily by the French Connection. With the eastern market temporarily vacant, plantations and laboratories in Sinaloa, Durango and Chihuahua increased production enormously and their share of the American market jumped to 90 per cent by 1975. And, as Ray (1978) points out, the Mexican Connection will be much tougher to deal with than the French Connection; there are 2000 miles of border between United States and Mexico, as well as miles of easily accessible coastline.

America's War on Drugs, then, has compounded the problem, not provided a solution.

The net result of the American effort during the 1970s has been to increase the complexity of the world heroin trade by expanding the number of markets and sources, making eventual suppression even more difficult. In the mid—1960s Hong Kong and Marseilles were the only major producers of heroin for the world market. A decade later producers included Marseilles, Hong Kong, western Mexico, Burma, Thailand and Malaya. In the mid—1960s the U.S. had the only major heroin market among the affluent nations, but a decade later major consumers included not only the U.S., with still more addicts, but Australia and Western Europe. With a larger number of markets and suppliers, the web of trafficking became far more complex and the capacity of syndicates to survive police suppression has increased greatly. (McCoy, 1980, pp. 348—9)

Nor is this the end of the story. Having begun to entrench itself as a major supplier to Europe, Southeast Asia was hit by severe droughts in 1979 and 1980. Opium production dropped from an estimated 500—600 tons in 1978 to less than 200 tons in 1890 (*Asiaweek*, 1983). At the same time, the Golden Crescent of Pakistan, Afghanistan and Iran was ready to enter the market.

The distribution centre for the Golden Crescent is Pakistan. Commercial cultivation of the poppy began there only in the 1960s and it remained legal until 1979, with the government buying up the entire crop for scientific, medical and other use. In 1979, several developments came to a head. There is evidence that money from the American Mafia had been supporting import of European expertise in refining, and Southeast Asian traffickers may have helped this along in the hope of developing a new route for their raw materials into European markets. However, the major incentive seems to have been provided by the Iranian revolution. Iran then had a very large addict population, and even today estimates put it at around one million people. The reforming revolutionary forces made the business much more hazardous. Traffickers and other key figures fled to nearby Pakistan, bringing with them money, connections and technical skills. And the weather was favourable. In 1978 the Golden Crescent produced a bumper crop of an estimated 1 600 tons of opium. Since Pakistan's addict population was relatively small, this meant a large surplus. At the same time, drought had hit the Golden Triangle, and enforcement there had become more sophisticated and effective. The time was clearly ripe to cut into the Golden Triangle's lion's share of the international market, and the traffickers of the Golden Crescent did so, with a vengeance. From an all but negligible contribution to world sales of heroin before 1979, estimates today of Pakistan's share of the international market range from just over 50 per cent to as high as 90 per cent (*Asiaweek*, 1983, p. 26).

In the meantime, Southeast Asian production recovered, with the Thai hill tribes harvesting three crops between November and February 1980−81. The yield was 600 tons of opium and production has remained at that level ever since. With the Golden Crescent now in the picture, this meant that most producers were holding huge stockpiles of opium. The result was predictable: any legitimate business concern would have behaved similarly.

To begin with, operations were made more efficient and middlemen were cut out wherever possible. In practice, the most significant result of this was the development of local refineries in virtually all opium-growing countries. Traditionally, the production of heroin required a series of transactions, with the price of the product rising as it travelled between the separate steps of the procedure. Integrating the various steps at the source reduced transport costs. It also offered access to cheap labor as well as the possibility of mutual defence and security arrangements. Production of heroin close to the actual opium fields began with the jungle laboratories of the Golden Triangle in the early 1970s. Other opium producers gradually followed suit, with a great upsurge of manufacturing incentive occurring at the end of the decade. By 1980, heroin laboratories had been established in Syria, Lebanon, Pakistan, Turkey and Afghanistan, and they continue to operate there.

One result of this streamlining of production has been a significant drop in the cost of heroin. Lewis (1984) estimates that one kilo purchased today for £3 000−4 000 on the Northwest Frontier might have cost £40 000 to £55 000 in Marseilles or Palermo in 1980. This in turn led directly to yet another development: there is now increasing incentive for small-volume, freelance traffickers to enter the business. It is obviously cheaper and easier to negotiate for a single kilo near the Khyber Pass where there is little or no threat of police intervention and the suppliers may even offer to expedite export arrangements.

The presence of this new type of trafficker does more than just increase the spread of heroin: it makes the enforcement of existing drug laws quite complicated. In 1978, the United Nations Secretariat commented as follows:

> Not so long ago, perhaps no more than a few years ago, it seemed relatively easy to distinguish between the trafficker and the 'victim' abuser: the trafficker was a member of an organised professional gang that obtained the raw material from illicit cultivation or from leakage from licit cultivation and arranged for the transformation of the raw material into a finished product that was transported and sold to the 'victim' . . .
>
> But during the past few years this pattern has been complicated by many changes in the way of life of large segments of the world population. Masses of people are on the move throughout the

> world ... A proportion of all these migrants found first that they could obtain drugs for themselves at relatively cheap prices and then that they could make a profit by bringing back some hashish or opium or heroin ...
> It is now almost impossible to make a clear distinction between clases of traffickers and categories of trafficking offences since a very large proportion of the semi-professional traffickers are themselves consumers. (p. 45)

The current drop in the price of heroin is not just the result of more efficient production. Those in the heroin business have seldom felt the need to pass on much of the profit from an increased volume of trading to their customers. Rather, real price-cutting wars are going on as major traffickers struggle for control of the lucrative trade. The current situation on the Thai−Burma border is typical. In this area, the two major drug trafficking forces are the Shan United Army (SUA) and the Shan United Revolutionary Army (SURA), both ostensibly committed to Shan independence from Burma. Both bodies operate and provide protection for a network of mobile heroin refineries. In late 1983, *Asiaweek* reported that rivalry between the SUA and the SURA was affecting street heroin price in Southeast Asia:

> The SUA has been attempting to keep prices up to recoup some of its losses brought on by recent reversals, but SURA refineries are selling cheap, thereby forcing the SUA to lower its prices as well. The spiral of price cutting, coupled with the sheer volume of raw opium being bought up by both organisations, has meant that a kilo of No. 4 heroin, selling a year ago at around $7 000, can now be purchased for around $3 900. Just where the border price war is leading is uncertain, but drug enforcement insiders monitoring events along the border foresee the possibility of either a spill-over into armed conflict between Shan pocket-armies or, alternatively, the sort of deal that would stabilise prices and possibly allow for closer cooperation between SUA and SURA forces. Most expect a deal as the more likely outcome. (p. 22)

The major Asian traffickers are also seeking to expand their markets, and as Western countries increase surveillance of their borders, many are turning to the smaller but more readily accessible profits to be made within Third World countries themselves. Most of these now have major drug problems and control measures have not been conspicuously successful.

Tiny, relatively easily managed Singapore has had more success than most. The republic's Central Narcotics Bureau managed to cripple its major drug syndicates by the late 1970s, and in 1977 it launched 'Operation Ferret', aimed at seeking out addicts and small-time dealers.

These were incarcerated in special rehabilitation centres for treatment. The results were not spectacular. As Rajah (1981) remarked,

> compassion for the weak is not always rewarded by the weak becoming strong ... not all drug takers who were released from the centres repented and redeemed themselves. In fact, most of them in the initial stages quickly took to drugs again and were promptly back in the Rehabilitation Centres. The introduction of aftercare helped ... [This] resulted in the relapse rate dropping from 69.8% in 1977 to the present 40%. (p. 102)

Still, many of this 40 per cent came back not once but three times. Since the minimum stay in Singapore's programs is one and a half years, this means that for some addicts three to four and a half years of mandatory treatment are not enough. In 1981, out of the 2 500 persons in the centres, 600—approximately 24 per cent—were classified as such 'hard core' addicts. This population has been increasing by three to four per cent yearly, and they are now being handled in special government programs that are even longer and more intensive. The whole exercise, of course, has been enormously costly.

Malaysia, by contrast, has not achieved even this level of success. The country is a transit route for international traffic from the Golden Triangle outward, but a substantial amount of the product goes no further. *Dadah* is the local term for any illicit drug, but in practice this means heroin, morphine and to a lesser extent opium. Between 1970 and 1980, 55 395 dadah dependents were identified; in 1985, there were 101 000 *registered* addicts in the country, and estimates of the total addict population generally agreed on about half a million. This does not include mere users—these figures refer to *addicts*. At present, the total population of Malaysia is slightly over 15 million.

Understandably, the country regards dadah as its No. 1 enemy, well ahead of all others including communism. Indeed, dadah is considered to be a matter of national security and an Anti-Dadah Task Force is housed within the National Security Council. This means that suspected addicts, even those who surrender to the authorities voluntarily, may be (and usually are) committed to prison for security reasons. At present, the period of commitment is two years, renewable; some form of rehabilitation may be attempted during this time. Major drug offences carry the death penalty, and since 1983 possession of over 15 grams of heroin, morphine or a mixture of the two makes the death sentence mandatory. The government also sponsors massive, ongoing media and education campaigns and vast sums are being spent on interception and detection. But the dadah problem gives every indication of continuing to increase.

The domestic market

The illicit heroin market has much in common with any other sort of market. It has its importers, distributors, wholesalers, retailers and, of course, buyers, all subject to various market forces. It is criminal because its product is illicit, not because its operation is inherently predatory. It involves the class of crime sometimes called 'victimless' or 'consensual', and it shares that category with gambling, prostitution and certain currently disapproved forms of sexual activity.

The extent of the profits to be made in the drug trade are sometimes exaggerated, but they are impressive by any standards. A kilo of heroin purchased for £4 000 on the Pakistan–Afghan border, separated into ounces, may sell for as much as £42 000 in London (Lewis, 1984). The impact of the illicit heroin economy may be perceived most dramatically in the boom of local economies geared to the traffic. The explosive economic expansion of cities like Palermo (Sicily) and Chiang Mai (Thailand) is a case in point.

The distribution industry: heroin on the streets

'Street dealing' is a misnomer. Overt trading is very uncommon and restricted to very specific areas in a few large cities. A cynic might infer that one reason for the continued operation of such open-air markets is their value as tourist attractions, much as the poppy fields of northern Thailand feature in local travel brochures. Some pubs, clubs and housing complexes also carry on a semi-public trade. However, most drug transactions occur behind discreetly closed doors.

Neither is the drug trade some vast, highly organised monopoly. This popular image is an outgrowth of the myth of the totally enslaved user who will do anything for a fix, and it is perpetuated by regular media references to various Mr Bigs. The market is in fact highly competitive at all levels. The users, as we shall see, are by no means enslaved. There is a great difference between the drug that may be preferred and the one that is actually consumed. The point at which the asking price affects a user's response of course varies widely, but there will always be a limit beyond which that individual cannot or will not go. There is ample evidence that users may abstain, seek treatment or substitute other drugs rather than pay monopoly prices. They also do a considerable amount of shopping around or, in the argot of Preble and Casey's (1969) informants, 'chasing the bag'.

> In a community with a high incidence of heroin use there will be two, three, or four competing bags on the street; that is, bags which have come down through different distributorship lines. Because of the low quality of the heroin, users want to get the

best one available on a given day. The number of times it has been cut and the ingredients that were used to cut it are the main considerations. The dealer who has the best bag on the street at a given time will sell his merchandise fast and do a big volume of business ...

It is common practice for a new dealer to come on the street with a good bag and keep it that way until he has most of the customers. Then he will start to adulterate the heroin, knowing that his reputation will carry him for a few days; by that time he has made a good extra profit. When he starts losing customers in large number, he can build the bag up again. Users are constantly experimenting with the products of different dealers, comparing notes with other users, and attempting to buy the best bag that is around ... A report on the street that a heroin user died of an overdose of heroin results in a customer rush on his dealer for the same bag. (pp. 11–12)

Competition at the wholesale level is naturally smaller than at the retail end, but it is there even in New York City, which probably has the most highly structured drug market anywhere.

It is essential to remember throughout this discussion that our information on the intimate workings of illicit markets is necessarily ephemeral. Much of it comes from 'participant observation' of people actively involved in the trade and this can be a very sensitive task. Since most of the behaviour is illegal, outside observers are potential threats. Researchers cannot guarantee immunity to their informants and, conversely, they themselves may be seen by the authorities as approving the illicit activities. Nor does their scholarly status ensure protection from some of their own subjects. Thus, when Lewis and his colleagues studied the British heroin market in 1985, they made no attempt to interview bulk suppliers above the multi-ounce level. Their reason is a masterpiece of understatement: 'It was felt,' they wrote, 'that such people would have no interest in speaking to us and that the element of risk involved for fieldworkers was too great' (p. 284).

The reliability of the information is not the only problem either. The structure of drug markets varies dramatically from place to place and it is impossible to extrapolate from one system to another. Since each market also evolves through time, it is even difficult to predict the future activity of a given system from its own past performance. Nevertheless, some very broad generalisations are possible. To illustrate these, we will examine the New York City system. It is certainly the best studied, but there is also good reason to believe that it is far from typical and the reader should bear this in mind. Preble and Casey (1969) studied the New York City heroin economy in the late 1960s, so the prices they quote are very different from those of today. Nevertheless, the ratios between them have remained remarkably constant, and may still be used as guidelines. Here are their findings:

A United States importer, through a courier, can buy a kilogram of 80% heroin in Europe for $5 000. The quality is represented to him in terms of how many cuts it will hold ... The importer, who usually never sees the heroin, sells down the line to a highly trusted customer through intermediaries. If it is a syndicate operation, he would only sell to high level, coded men, known as *captains*. These men are major distributors, referred to as *kilo connections* and, generally, as *the people* ...

The *kilo connection* pays $20 000 for the original kilogram ... and gives it a one and one cut (known as *hitting it*), that is, he makes two kilos out of one by adding the common adulterants of milk sugar, mannite (a product from the ash tree and used as a mild laxative) and quinine. The proportions of ingredients used for the cutting varies with the preference of the cutter ... After the cut, the kilo connection sells down the line in kilos, half kilos, and quarter kilos, depending upon the resources of his customers. He will get approximately $10 000 per half kilo for the now adulterated heroin ...

Assuming that the connection buys directly from a kilo connection, he will probably give the heroin a one and one cut (make two units of each one), divide the total aggregate into ounces, and sell down the line at $700 per ounce ...

The next man is known as a *dealer in weight*, and is probably the most important figure in the line of distribution. He stands midway between the top and the bottom, and is the first one coming down the line who takes substantial risk of being apprehended by law enforcement officers. He is also the first one who may be a heroin user himself, but usually he is not ... This man usually specialises in *cut ounces*. He may give a two and one cut (make three units of each one) to the good ounce from the connection and sell the resulting quantity for $500 per ounce. The aggregate weight is again reduced, and now the unit is called a *piece* instead of an ounce.

The next customer is known as a *street dealer*. He buys the *piece* for $500, gives it a one and one cut and makes *bundles*, which consist of 25 $5 bags each. He can usually get seven bundles from each piece, and he sells each bundle for $80 ... This man may or may not be a heroin user.

The next distributor is known as a *juggler*, who is the seller from whom the average street addict buys. He is always a user. He buys bundles for $80 each and sells the 25 bags at about $5 each, making just enough profit to support his own habit, day by day. He may or may not make a small cut, known as *tapping the bags*. He is referred to as someone who is 'always high and always short', that is, he always has enough heroin for his own use and is always looking for a few dollars to get enough capital to cop again. (pp. 9–11)

Naturally there are variations on this general theme. As in the marketing of any product; a quantity purchase can be made at a lower price, and a dealer who turns over a wholesaler's product rapidly will receive higher benefits. And all the way down the line, the good customer is the key to success: someone who buys regularly, does not ask for credit or try to bargain, and who can be trusted.

Today's illegal drug trade is a very big business. In 1982, Pileggi estimated that in New York City alone the importation and distribution of illicit drugs amounted to a $45 billion-a-year cash business. At that figure, it surpassed the city's $24.5 billion retail trade, the $14.6 billion manufacturing industry and the $13.9 billion revenues of hotels, advertising and service businesses. The drug trade also employed a substantial staff. According to Pileggi (1982):

> the business is run by about 10 000 middle-to-high level importers and distributors. Among them, they employ between 100 000 and 300 000 part-time workers with an array of special skills: fast-talking street hawkers, nimble-fingered heroin baggers, bank-connected money-changers, and broad-backed musclemen who tote eighty-pound bales of marijuana from ship to shore. In addition, thousands of part-time couriers carry millions in contraband hidden in their suitcases or stomachs. Hundreds of lawyers advise and defend the dealers ...
>
> Though the drug business doesn't rank among the city's largest employers—there are 594 868 workers in the wholesale and retail trades, and 496 760 in the manufacturing of durable and nondurable goods, for example—it does top the garment industry (141 804 workers) and construction (83 936 workers).
>
> What's more, the drug business seems to be recession-proof. While consumer spending in general is weak, spending on drugs is up, and, in particular, dealers are enjoying a heroin and cocaine boom. The customers are there, [and] the profits incredible ...
> At this point, heroin is worth more than gold. Last week, gold was selling for $435 an ounce, while that much heroin cost $10 000. (pp. 39–40)

Even allowing for journalistic hyperbole and the fact that the American market is almost certainly the largest in the world, the drug trade is clearly an industry to be reckoned with, both in terms of revenue and employment capacity. The profits are of course tax-free, the employees non-union, and the paperwork almost non-existent.

The degree and kind of risk involved in the trade varies. From a law enforcement standpoint, all authorities agree that the organisers and financiers who mount the smuggling operations face very little risk. Those who are caught are generally mere 'mules' who are paid specifically to undertake these very risks. Since they are usually not very knowledgeable about the overall operation, they can tell the police little. Their employers therefore face only the loss of the heroin seized and the need to pay future 'mules' higher wages. In real terms, this is still a small outlay compared to the profits of successful smuggling.

The closer one moves to the actual interaction between dealer and user—customer, the greater the risks of apprehension become. A consumer with even a small habit requires almost daily contact with a dealer, who in turn must make regular contacts with a higher-level distributor. The pattern of contacts for any user is relatively predictable and this makes his or her supplier very visible, particularly since in the interests of security the supplier must deal only with regular or vouched-for customers.

Risk of apprehension, however, is not the only problem facing the dealer. At all levels, but again most obviously at the lower ones, dealers must cope with predatory crime within the industry itself. The dealers become fair game for the numerous thieves and musclemen that abound in just those areas where heroin is most available, and they can hardly complain to the police that their stock was stolen. Even if money is stolen rather than drugs, the disadvantages of attracting police attention and having to answer embarassing questions about the source of this wealth are generally enough to deter complaints. Of course, the heroin seller can lessen risk by hiring protection. However, this not only increases costs but poses the danger that the protectors may decide that they can handle the enterprise themselves.

In many ways, the consumer is equally vulnerable to predation. Buying heroin is not quite the same as buying marijuana. As Zinberg (1972) commented, 'If you are not familiar with a heroin-using group, you have to go cold to one of the roughest parts of town and search around. Your chances of getting gypped, beaten up, or "ripped off" are excellent.' And addicts may also prey on each other. Referring to a fellow addict who had cheated him, one victim said, 'he beat me today, I'll beat him tomorrow.' Another addict who specializes in robbing other addicts said, 'I beat them every chance I get, which is all the time.' Another informant summed up the attitude between partners this way: 'I'm looking out for myself—I might be sick tomorrow; anyway, he's got something working for him that I don't know about' (Preble and Casey, 1969, p. 8).

In return for their substantial cash outlay and the considerable personal risks they take, users get remarkably little. From Preble and Casey's analysis of dilution procedures, it should be obvious that the amount of heroin in a street bag is very small.

> A generous estimate of the aggregate weight of a $5 bag is 90 milligrams, including the adulterants . . . the amount of heroin would be about 3 milligrams . . . This is the average analgesic dose that is used in those countries such as England where heroin

can be prescribed in medical practice. It is a minimal amount, being considered safe for someone who does not use opiates. It is equivalent to about 10 milligrams of either morphine or methadone ... The average dosage of methadone used in opiate maintenance treatment is 100 milligrams—about 10 times the amount in the street bag. One informant said of the effects of a street bag today: 'All it does is turn your stomach over so that you can go out and hustle, and you had better do it fast.' (Preble and Casey, 1969, pp. 14–5)

These are American figures, and in terms of purity, even today when prices have fallen dramatically and street heroin tends to be purer, the United States is still at the bottom of the range. Its street heroin is seldom more than 10 per cent pure. By contrast, Australian street heroin is currently around 27 per cent pure and Lewis and his colleagues (1985) set British retail purity 'in the region of 45–55 per cent.' But even in Britain and Australia distribution level purity still varies wildly. A substantial proportion of the samples analysed by the NSW Analytical Laboratories contain no psychoactive drugs at all (Cook and Flaherty, 1978). And even those that do contain active drugs are sold as bags or foils, not by weight. The customer simply gets a pre-wrapped package. As a rule of thumb, this contains approximately one-tenth of a gram, but opportunities for deception are clearly considerable. Basically, the customer has no guarantee of either weight or content.

Traditionally, both the British and the Australian drug markets have been less violent than those of the United States. They also tended to be less organised, with deliveries being both more direct and more casual. These differences are no longer so apparent. Violence has increased across the board, and not just in the drug trade. And the organisation of the market has become much more fluid. With heroin increasingly being manufactured close to its organic source in the poppy-growing areas, almost anyone with the inclination and a relatively small amount of capital can set up as a small-time entrepreneur. Such people may make a quick profit and then move out of the market—though not necessarily into legitimate pursuits—to be replaced by someone else before the police have time to build up their case. Even if they are caught, very little is accomplished. Such part-time operators are in the business too briefly for the imprisonment of even a significant number of them to have much effect on the overall market.

This is not to say that organised crime has withdrawn from the drug trade. Its contributions are probably as great or greater than ever. However, it has increasing competition from amateurs, and this does not make matters easier for anyone except perhaps the user.

The redistribution industry: drugs and crime

Most people assume a necessary link between drug use and crime and the media constantly reinforce the connection. Periodically, both police and government sources produce statistics which claim to prove the connection, usually with the goal of increasing enforcement activity and further tightening controls. Such official statistics are notoriously unreliable, for a whole host of reasons.

One of these is failure to define *drug, use* and *crime* adequately. Both governments and the public focus overwhelmingly on illegal drugs and, for the public at any rate, 'drug' currently has the special meaning of 'heroin'. This is unfortunate, since today's heroin users are predominantly polydrug users, and the several drugs they may use do have very different effects. Alcohol, for instance, is clearly linked with crimes of violence, but the relationship of these to heroin use is much less clear. What are we to conclude if our users take both drugs?

'Use', too, is a vague concept. There is a clear difference between an experimental user and a person who is physically dependent on a drug, but 'use' has very different connotations for different drugs. Users of cannabis are almost always assumed to be just users; users of heroin, equally, are almost always assumed to be 'addicts' and this word automatically generates further assumptions, including that of the addict's criminality.

Finally, which particular 'crimes' are we talking about? The majority of drug-related offences are 'drug-defined' crimes, that is, they are violations of drug laws. Mere possession of heroin is a crime and so is selling the drug. There is also a group of crimes related to the illicit distribution network—bribery, assaults, hijacks and so on—and again these are linked to heroin use only because heroin is illegal. Some studies include such drug-defined crimes in their drugs-and-crime statistics, some do not, and the result is considerable confusion. The average citizen who is concerned about the relationship between drug use and crime is really thinking about the link between *heroin use and income-generating crime against persons or property*, and he or she is particularly worried that these crimes will be violent ones.

That such a relationship should exist makes a certain amount of intuitive sense—provided that we accept some preconceptions. It is true that heroin, because of its illegal status, is very expensive. It is also true that a person with a large habit would need heroin several times a day and that securing an adequate supply would take a considerable amount of time and energy even if money was not a problem. So it seems reasonable to conclude that street addicts cannot hold jobs and, even if they could, that they would probably not earn enough to afford their addiction. This is certainly true for many street addicts. Nevertheless, it is also certainly an exaggeration.

Much of the misunderstanding comes from an unquestioning acceptance of estimates of the money addicts need to maintain their habits. Some very questionable assumptions underlie them. One is that addicts, once addicted, maintain a steady level of intake. In reality, while many develop very large habits at some point in their careers, most do not continue to use at this rate for long. The usual calculations, moreover, accept the once-an-addict-always-an-addict myth, and multiply the average daily habit by the total time elapsed since the onset of addiction. This, of course, fails to take account of most addicts' frequent periods of reduced use or abstinence.

A far more serious problem is that many addicts inflate their average use considerably. There are several reasons for this. Since the questioner often has some official standing, it may be to their advantage to try to impress him or her with the seriousness of their problems and their need for preferential treatment. Other reasons have to do with the way in which addicts view their own heroin use. Many consider a large habit to be a status symbol and are therefore inclined to exaggerate. According to one addict, 'When they ask me the size of my habit, they're really asking me whether I'm a real man or a pipsqueak.' In a number of places, experience with and ability to handle drugs has formed a new ranking system among young people who need to affirm their maturity and competence, and some quite bizzare situations can arise. Being the biggest freak in a culture of freaks is not always easy. Smith (1969), for instance, cites the following statement from a 'speed freak':

> 'I know I scared an intern half to death once. He said that a person who took 500 milligrams would croak, so I shot a flat gram right in front of him; he turned every color of the rainbow just watching me. I fixed two spoons [slightly more than a gram] in Marin County, I'm a legend in Marin County. They're always talking about the guy who shot two spoons'.
>
> The same individual recalled a speed-shooting contest, which he frankly admitted was a self-destructive act;
>
> 'This was a down to the death dope-shooting contest. One of the two of us was supposed to die when the thing was over. He'd shoot a half gram and I'd shoot a gram, and he'd shoot one and a half, and I'd shoot two grams, and he'd shoot two and a half and I'd have to shoot three. Nobody would back out, we'd die before we'd back out.' (p. 82)

The fact of the matter is that some users do use at very high rates periodically, but they report these rates as their average consumption. Others simply exaggerate their actual use and report levels they feel are appropriately impressive.

Addict exaggeration aside, though, the way in which most of this information is collected is likely to be seriously biased toward singling out the high-dose, heavily involved user. The bulk of our data on the drugs—crime link comes from users who are either in prison or in various treatment programs. Prisoner samples necessarily contain persons who run a high risk of detection. This visibility may result from very heavy involvement in crime, or from lack of skill. Or it may simply reflect increasing vulnerability because of previous encounters with the authorities. Once a person has been arrested, the probability of further arrests soars. Similarly, once a person is known to be a heroin user, he or she will be much more closely scrutinised by enforcement agencies and thus more liable to eventual arrest.

There are similar problems with treatment agency samples. Relatively few addicts enrol in treatment programs voluntarily, and those who do are in trouble. Gould (1974) for instance argued that addicts are most likely to seek treatment precisely when the size of their habits or other circumstances mandate increasing involvement with crime. Given that places in treatment centres are limited, it is obviously in the addicts' interests to exaggerate the seriousness of this involvement to enhance their chances of acceptance. Once in, of course, there is a need to de-emphasise criminal activity and this may spuriously increase the apparent effectiveness of the program. In any case, a very substantial number seek treatment only *after* arrest in order to impress the sentencing judge, and many also arrive in treatment as a direct result of a court order or as part of probation.

Both prison and treatment agency samples are therefore very select groups, heavily biased toward addicts with the largest habits, greatest number of problems and highest probability of criminality. A few recent studies have attempted to overcome such sampling problems by analysing the drugging habits of active street users, but these too are a special group. They literally live off the streets, and they are more intricately involved than most with the drug distribution network. According to Goldman (1981), the bulk of their funds comes from dealing rather than property crime. And no study so far has satisfactorily reached addicts from the middle and upper classes or the professions. In other words, the addict typically available to our investigations is the *casualty*—someone who probably had relatively few legitimate skills to begin with and who for a variety of reasons can no longer cope, at least for the time being. The actual criminality of such people is likely to be higher than average, and both it and their involvement with heroin will certainly be highly visible.

The danger of drawing inferences about the general heroin-using population from such samples is best illustrated by a few examples. In 1971, Singer took the estimated number of addicts in New York City, a daily average habit cost, the rate of theft reported by his addict sample and the assumption that stolen property sold to a fence generally realises only about a quarter of its value. From this, he calculated that New York City addicts would have to steal some $4–5 billion each year to pay for their heroin. The total property stolen in a year in New York City actually amounts to some $330 million. In other words, Singer's calculations suggest that addicts alone should have perpetrated about three times as many thefts as were actually recorded.

Dobinson and Ward's (1985) survey of a population of imprisoned addicts in NSW suggests that the situation in Australia is rather similar. The prisoners reported that their average weekly consumption of heroin prior to arrest was 7 grams of street-pure heroin, with a median expenditure of $A2 000 per week. The majority were young, socially-disadvantaged males, so it seems unlikely that more than a few could generate in excess of $100 000 per year by any means, legal or otherwise. So either they used far less than the stated amount, or they paid less for what they used. This conclusion is strengthened by some other facts. The majority of these addicts (78.2 per cent) stated that property crime was their main source of income. The average number of armed robberies committed annually by each member of this group was eight, and the average number of burglaries was 143. Now in the same year (1982), there were 1 896 accepted reports of armed robbery and 83 162 of break, enter and stealing in NSW. Dobinson and Ward therefore speculate that 237 individuals like those in their sample could have accounted for all the robberies and 581 for all the burglaries respectively. Yet the estimated number of 'hard core' addicts in NSW at about that time was at least 10 000 (*Woodward Report*, 1980).

The assumption that addicts must steal the full price of their habits is as great a fallacy as the assumption that the size of their habits is constant over time. Many middle-class addicts do not commit any crimes other than drug-defined ones, though they may victimise parents and relatives and perhaps eventually the welfare system. Even street addicts typically supplement their illicit incomes through welfare, help from family and even legitimate casual employment.

Probably the single most neglected source of income is drug dealing or associated activities. While the profits at the top of the heroin distribution pyramid are taken by non-addicts, those from street dealing are earned mostly by addict pushers, and they are considerable. In New York City and surrounding communities, profit margins from retail drug sales range between 100 and 200 per cent. From this it follows that half or more of the money spent on heroin could be obtained through the sale of heroin. As Gould (1974) noted, if all heroin users used the same amount, then hypothetically half the drug users could finance their drug use by selling to the other half. In practice, this does not follow directly, however, since some of those who sell drugs support themselves as well as their drug habit through income from drug sales. Computing the price of a heroin habit and assuming that an addict must steal all this amount therefore involves a kind of double counting. The street price of heroin includes the sizeable profit at the retail level, which goes to feed the habits of the many addicts who sell the drug as well as use it. Nor is all the heroin used paid for in cash. Both Goldstein (1981) and Wardlaw (1978) have pointed out that rooms, meals, cash, alcohol and drugs are often obtained either as gifts or as payment for various services and favours rendered in the drug business. Goldstein, for example, estimates that 26 per cent of the heroin and 14 per cent of the cocaine used on the street is obtained without any cash outlay.

Table 4.1 presents some figures gleaned from several studies on addicts' various means of support. Note the relationship between the results obtained and the nature of the sample. Less than half of the active addicts on the street support themselves through property crime. Predictably, crime figures largely in the prison sample, and it is much less prominent though still significant in the two samples entering treatment programs. People who lack legitimate means of support and those who turn to theft to support their use are overrepresented in both prison and treatment populations, but even in these biased samples a substantial proportion support their habits entirely through legitimate or quasi-legitimate means.

Table 4.1 Means of support among several groups of addicts

	Addicts entering medical clinics (US)[1]	Addicts entering methadone maintenance (US)[2]	Addicts in prison (AUST)[3]	Active street addicts (US)[4]
Welfare	4.0	18.4	2.6	⎫
Spouse or parents	4.0	16.1	3.9	⎬ 29.0
Job, other legal means	15.0	31.0	5.1	⎭
Dealing	21.0	⎫	9.0	⎫
Pimping, prostitution, other	5.0	⎬ 31.0	1.3	⎬ 38.0
Property crime	39.0	⎭	78.2	⎭

1 Newmeyer, 1972
2 Schut et al, 1972
3 Dobinson & Ward, 1985
4 Hughes et al, 1971

All the same, the number of addicts who do engage in crime is significant and, whatever their proportion, these people can still account for a lot of theft. In Dobinson and Ward's (1985) study, for example, ten of the 89 prisoner addicts interviewed had been involved in 271 minor break, enter and steal offences—but 200 of these were committed by a single respondent. Similarly, ten were charged with 147 offences of receiving stolen property, but 80 of these were the responsibility of a single individual.

The question, then, is not whether addicts engage in crime—clearly many do. The real issue is what proportion do so, how this proportion compares with the number of non-drug users who also turn to crime and, in the case of criminal addicts, what the correlation between drug use and crime really means.

Before we examine this issue, one important question needs to be asked: does drug use precede or follow criminal behaviour? From a policy standpoint, each situation leads to quite distinct control strategies. As Dobinson and Ward (1985) point out, if the heroin addict is first and foremost a criminal, law enforcement methods would be the most appropriate approach to the prevention of illegal use and its associated crime. On the other hand, if drug use causes the criminal activities, crime becomes just a symptom of the addictive state, and treatment of the user would be a more appropriate strategy.

Like almost everything else about drug use, its relation to crime depends on the historical period being studied. Prior to 1950, the majority of addicts seemed to be non-criminal before addiction, and until at least the 1970s it was also possible to state with some confidence that heroin users were less likely to be involved in such crimes as homicide, rape, kidnapping and aggravated assault than non-drug users (Eckerman et al., 1971). Increasingly, however, drug offenders have criminal records that predate their first use of drugs, sometimes by many years. Summaries of the relevant data may be found in Wardlaw (1982) and Dobinson and Ward (1985). In general, it appears that at least a half and perhaps as many as three quarters of the heroin addicts who come to official notice today have criminal records that predate their drug use. They also seem more likely to commit crimes against the person than was once the case. A simple explanation for these changes is sure to be inadequate. Nevertheless, there have been some thought-provoking suggestions.

With respect to the apparent increase in violent crimes, we need to note, first of all, that society as a whole is becoming more violent. Violent crimes have been increasing at a faster rate than non-violent ones since 1960, and the crimes committed by addicts may simply reflect this general trend. Moreover, the relatively uncomplicated heroin use of the past has been largely replaced by polydrug use.

Heroin is now often used in combination with alcohol, barbiturates and amphetamines and all these drugs are fairly clearly linked to assaultiveness and violence. What may be most important, though, is analysis of the particular violent crimes addicts commit. Preble and Casey (1969) have argued that like their non-addict colleagues, addict criminals tend to specialise in certain forms of crime. Which these will be depends partly on such factors as personality, skill and experience, but for the addict criminal the overriding factor is always financial gain. Thus, Preble and Casey (1969) found that 40.9 per cent of arrests among addicts were for burglary, compared to 19.7 per cent of all arrests. Felonious assaults constituted 5.6 per cent among the addicts, compared to 27.9 per cent of all arrests. What this shows, they conclude, 'is not that heroin users avoid crimes of violence as compared to non-addicts, but that they avoid crimes not involving financial gain' (p. 18). Wardlaw (1982) has reached an essentially similar conclusion: addicts are prepared to engage in violent crime to the extent that it has a pecuniary return.

Two aspects of the modern addiction scene may help explain the increased tendency for criminality to precede drug use. Both, incidentally, would also be relevant to the apparent increase of violence in drug-related crime. The first is that addicts in general have become younger. Like all young people, young addicts will tend to have fewer marketable skills and to be more active and more impulsive than older addicts. The probable effects of this on the overall pattern of their criminal behaviour are obvious. As Chambers (1974) has suggested, younger addicts are likely to be 'criminal opportunists'—that is, they will be attracted by whatever criminal opportunity presents itself.

Another feature that has gradually emerged over the last several decades is the centralisation of drug use as a subcultural activity. This new drug subculture, however, has intimate interconnections with the more general criminal subculture. So heroin use may now be simply another deviance that occurs in an already criminally-inclined population. Whatever may have been the case in the past, the current relationship between heroin and crime might be merely coincidental. Thus, Kaplan (1983) argues that rather than causing crime, heroin may have been adopted by a number of deviant groups as something to set them apart from the rest of society and emphasise their negation of, and superiority to, the dominant society's values. It binds group members more closely to each other and ensures the resentment and hostility of the group toward the law enforcement apparatus.

Still, while such a 'subcultural' view can provide a highly plausible explanation why individuals begin to commit crime and/or use heroin, it cannot readily explain why the criminal activities of users appear to fluctuate with their drug-taking behaviour. There is evidence that criminality decreases during non-addiction periods, and it has even been possible to establish some sort of relationship between the purchase price of heroin and changing crime rates. Brown and Silverman (1974), for instance, applied market analysis techniques to information about heroin prices and available crime statistics and from this developed a formula to predict crime patterns. They calculated that a 10 per cent increase in the price of heroin would lead to a 3.6 per cent increase in robberies, a 1.8 per cent increase in burglaries, a 2 per cent increase in petty larceny, 2.5 per cent increase in auto theft and a 1.7 per cent increase in taxicab robberies. When these predictions were compared with actual data from a number of American cities, the results were ambiguous, but on the whole they suggested that heroin price and crime were positively related.

Where does all this leave us? There does seem to be some evidence to support the commonsense view that the cost of heroin is an important determinant of criminality in some heroin addicts. However, it is also clear that both drug use and criminal behaviour are exceedingly complex phenomena which would not lend themselves to simplistic analysis even if available data were sufficiently trustworthy—and we have seen that they are not.

The majority of those conclusions that do have reasonable empirical support in fact run counter to the commonsense view. There is, for instance, no solid evidence that heroin users commit crimes of violence as a direct consequence of the pharmacological action of this drug.

Moreover, the population of heroin users is composed of individuals with widely varying habit sizes and individuals show considerable variation over time. At any one time, persons falling into the 'addict' stereotype are probably in a minority, so aggregate estimates of habit sizes and analyses based on this are inappropriate.

A significant percentage of the income needed to support large habits is generated within the drug distribution network itself, and a large number of heavy users also obtain substantial financial support from family, welfare and employment. Probably not more than 30 to 40 per cent of income expended on drugs is obtained from revenue-producing non-drug crime, and of this percentage, not all will derive from property crime. Substantial amounts are also obtained from illegal gambling and prostitution.

Finally, although there is evidence that heroin users commit proportionately more property crime than non-users, it is impossible to determine how this affects the extent of property crime as a whole.

On the whole, such facts as we do have suggest that while the association between drugs and crime is real enough, its *strength* is grossly exaggerated. Contrary to the rationales for many of our current enforcement policies, therefore, eradication of heroin use would probably *not* result in a massive downturn in crime. Gould (1974) reaches the same conclusion by applying classical economic principles of supply and demand to criminal markets, particularly that black market upon which stolen goods are sold for cash.

As increasing dependence forces drug users to steal and sell more goods, he argues, the price of stolen goods will drop and theft will become less profitable. In such a situation, any individual thief will either have to steal more to maintain the same income, or turn to other income sources. Now unlike addicts, non-addict thieves are not compelled to escalate their activities when drug prices rise. Gould therefore hypothesises that as theft becomes less profitable, non-addicts will leave the field sooner and in greater numbers than addicts.

> Addiction, then, would not increase theft in direct proportion to the number of addicts who steal, but would change the composition of the labor force of thieves ... In balance, drug addicts may out-hustle non-addicts in the marketplace of theft and by doing so drive prices down and expand total amounts of thefts, but in the long run a new balance of supply and demand should be reached which may not lead to much more theft than there was when addicts were not in the market. (p. 65)

If our drug policies are to be based on rational empirical foundations, they must take these complexities into account. To date, the necessary analyses have rarely been performed. Policies have generally assumed that there are simple and direct links between what are in fact complex social, economic and psychophysiological phenomena. It is currently fashionable, for instance, to press for the removal of all legal controls as the solution to an obviously unsatisfactory situation—yet this is no less simplistic than the counter-argument that the answer lies in more stringent law enforcement. *Every* policy has costs as well as benefits. A suggestion that the criminal activities of addicts may actually be beneficial sounds fantastic. Nevertheless, a case can be made even for this. Preble and Casey (1969), for instance, point out that:

> The distribution and sales of goods and property stolen by heroin users has become a major economic institution in low income neighbourhoods. Most of the consumers are otherwise ordinary, legitimate members of the community. Housewives will wait on the stoop for specialists in stealing meat (known as *cattle rustlers*) to come by, so that they can get a ham or roast at a 60% discount. Owners of small grocery stores buy cartons of cigarettes stolen from the neighbourhood supermarket. The owner of an automobile places an order with a heroin user for tires, and the next day he has the tires—with the wheels. At the Easter holidays there is a great demand for clothes, with slum streets looking like the streets of the Garment District ...

> The heroin user is an important figure in the economic life of the slums. In order to support a $20 a day habit, he has to steal goods and property worth from $50 to $100. Usually he steals outside his neighbourhood ... and he brings his merchandise back to the neighbourhood for sale at high discounts. This results, to some extent, in a redistribution of real income from the richer to the poorer neighbourhoods. Although non-addict residents in the slums may deplore the presence of heroin users, they appreciate and compete for their services as discount salesmen. (pp. 19–20)

Doubtless the redistribution industry would continue without addicts—but it might be substantially reduced, with a resulting cost-of-living increase for some legitimate members of the community!

Legalising heroin would eliminate some of the present costs of drug addiction, but it would also generate costs of its own. These, as we shall see, are likely to be far more serious than minor cost-of-living increases in low income neighbourhoods. Most costs and benefits can be measured in real, objective terms—dollars, for instance. In the end, the solution to the heroin problem may have to wait until we learn to do our sums more honestly and carefully.

5
Controlling the heroin market

Heroin kills kids, mothers and others stupid enough to use it and all our laws have been inadequate to save them ...
Where am I to find an honest public official when the profits of 1 kg of heroin equal 40 average policemen's yearly salary or 60 times the cost of having an honest cop murdered? The very fabric of Australian society is threatened as never before ...
It is only the basic morality instilled into millions of Australians by their forefathers that leaves the stuff in the hands of the scum who now market it. (P.J.G., Rasmussen, Qld)
Australian, *3 January 1985*

I doubt it is possible to get a team of Jesuit investigators to be incorruptible, and you have to face this. (B. Swanton, Australian Institute of Criminology)
Sydney Morning Herald, *23 October 1984*

The background of the conferences that shaped today's international drug laws has been discussed in Chapter 2. The countries most concerned were Britain and the United States and the form that the early legislation took reflected their domestic concerns about drugs closely. At that time—the late 1800s and early 1900s—'drugs' of course meant opium and its derivatives, although cocaine and Indian Hemp (cannabis) were added to the list by the Geneva Convention of 1925. After World War I, the League of Nations took over international narcotics control. There followed a proliferation of treaties, amendments and secretariat functions, and when the United Nations inherited this hodgepodge in 1945 it quickly added several other treaties and protocols. By the mid–1950s, it was obvious that the obligations, rights and privileges of both signatory nations and control agencies were becoming confused if not actually obscure, and the United Nations General Assembly asked that the complex machinery of drug control be simplified. The result was the 'Single' Convention, which was ready for ratification in 1961. Virtually all nations had signed this treaty by 1980.

The Single Convention is a complex document containing some 50 articles that form part of the actual treaty, as well as some more general 'resolutions' concerning, among other things, the need for record keeping and for the provision of treatment to addicts. In essence, the Single Convention rules that the use of certain substances is permitted only under specifically defined conditions, and that all other use constitutes abuse and is to be prevented. The substances in question are opium, its derivatives and synthetic forms, coca derivatives and cannabis. There is also a provision that the World Health Organisation (WHO) can add to this list drugs which it considers to be liable to abuse and without mitigating therapeutic advantages.

Signatories to the treaty are obliged to take steps to deal with licit and illicit drug trade, but the actual measures to be taken are subject to the constitutional limitations of the parties, where such exist, or to their domestic law. In other words, the Convention may specify a penalty of 'deprivation of liberty', but it is up to each country to decide whether this is to be imprisonment or something else, and for how long. In practice, drug-related legislation of the parties to the Convention varies widely.

Signatories to the Single Convention make the following commitments:

1 to provide information to the United Nations about their domestic medical and scientific requirements for the restricted drugs, about their illegal traffic, their domestic drug laws and similar related matters;
2 to give 'special attention' to the provision of facilities for the treatment and rehabilitation of addicts;
3 to limit the quantities of any drug manufactured or imported to those necessary for medical or scientific purposes, to export drugs to other countries only for legitimate purposes and to do so in accordance with the recipient countries' laws; and
4 to take legal action against drug offenders. Article 36 of the Convention states:

> Subject to its constitutional limitations, each Party shall adopt such measures as will ensure that cultivation, production, manufacture, extraction, preparation, possession, offering, offering for sale, distribution, purchase, sale, delivery on any terms whatsoever, brokerage, dispatch, dispatch in transit, transport, importation and exportation of drugs contrary to the provisions of this Convention, and any other action which in the opinion of such Party may be contrary to the provisions of this Convention, shall be punishable offences when commited

intentionally, and that serious offences shall be liable to adequate punishment particularly by imprisonment or other penalties of deprivation of liberty.

It is this paragraph that brings up the question of policy with respect to actual drug users. Is use of drugs, and possession of drugs for personal use, to be penalised? The list of activities to be considered punishable offences does not include the 'use' of drugs. Parties to the Single Convention are therefore not obliged to include penalties for use, as such, in their domestic legislation. On the other hand, 'possession' is included in the list, and there is ongoing controversy whether this is to be interpreted only as possession with intent to sell or otherwise distribute, or whether it also includes possession for private, personal use. It has been argued, particularly by law enforcement agencies, that prosecution and conviction of traffickers would be much easier if *all* forms of possession were proscribed, but the fact remains that the Single Convention, as it stands, leaves the issue open. The majority of signatories have attempted to resolve this by specifying the maximum amount of a drug that can be considered as being for personal use. Note, also, that Article 36 distinguishes between 'offences' and 'serious offences', and the interpretation of this is again left to the discretion of national legislators. Some of the effects of various attempts to comply with Article 36 are discussed further below.

The Single Convention established two agencies to oversee the implementation and operation of the treaty. The first, the United Nations International Narcotic Control Board (INCB), was formed to monitor and regulate the legal production, storage and requirements for the restricted drugs. It is not an enforcement agency, and it can only try to negotiate cutbacks if supply seems to be outstripping demand in a particular country. The strongest sanction it can apply, and that only after prolonged unsuccessful remonstration with the culprit, is to recommend to the other signatory countries that they stop trading in drugs with the country concerned. In practice, its most valuable function seems to be in keeping records about where legal opiates come from and where they go.

The second controlling agency is the United Nations Commission on Narcotic Drugs (CND). Its major role is to update and revise international agreements on restricted drugs. During the postwar period, many countries experienced a sharp increase in problems with use of non-opiate drugs. There were several amphetamine epidemics, and in the 1960s a variety of mind-altering drugs like LSD and PCP made their appearance. The CND began to work on this problem, and in 1971 it put forward the Convention on Psychotropic Substances.

This established four schedules of drugs liable to abuse. The drugs ranged from hallucinogens through barbiturates and amphetamines to major tranquillisers. They were ranked jointly on abuse potential and therapeutic usefulness, and complex control and record-keeping measures were set up. These in general followed the lines of the Single Convention: they assumed that suppression of availability is the best preventive policy, and that 'rigorous measures are necessary to restrict the use of such substances to legitimate purposes.' However, for the first time, substantial attention was also given to drug users and how to deal with them. Where the Single Convention merely suggested that parties give 'special attention' to the matter, Article 20 of the Convention on Psychotropic Substances is much more explicit. This states that:

1 The Parties shall take all practicable measures for the prevention of abuse of psychotropic substances and for the early identification, treatment, education, after-care, rehabilitation and social reintegration of the persons involved, and shall coordinate their efforts to these ends.
2 The Parties shall as far as possible promote the training of personnel in the treatment, after-care, rehabilitation and social reintegration of abusers of psychotropic substances.
3 The Parties shall assist persons whose work so requires to gain an understanding of the problems of abuse of psychotropic substances and of its prevention, and shall also promote such understanding among the general public if there is a risk that abuse of such substances will become widespread.

Moreover, for the first time, alternative means for dealing with offenders were formally acknowledged. Article 22, 'Penal Provisions', states:

Notwithstanding the preceding sub-paragraph, when abusers of psychotropic substances have committed such offences, the Parties may provide, either as an alternative to conviction or punishment or in addition to punishment, that such abusers undergo measures of treatment, education, after-care, rehabilitation and social reintegration ...

As we shall see in Chapter 8, an increasing number of countries are introducing various forms of 'diversionary' programs for drug offenders. What they may be expected to achieve is still unclear.

The Convention on Psychotropic Substances proved unpopular from the start. Predictably, representatives of pharmaceutical industries argued that such international controls were not needed and that the drugs proposed for control were not harmful. Countries with large pharmaceutical industries like Switzerland and Britain agreed, and neither country is a signatory to date.

The United States vacillated for years, on the ostensible grounds that adoption of such a treaty would freeze its own laws, and that enacting the new laws would mean amending the Constitution, a laborious process. Nevertheless, cynical observers saw other possibilities. There were pointed suggestions of richer countries victimising poorer ones by selling them psychoactive substances which they could ill afford, and which were likely to cause problems into the bargain (Smart et al., 1981). A number of countries also questioned, and rightly, the sincerity of a government which asks for international help with its own drug problems, but is unwilling to commit itself to help other countries with theirs. Whether to avoid loss of face or because its domestic deliberations were finally complete, the United States did sign in 1980, but its delay meant that many other nations have also refused to sign. Even now, many hold out—Canada, for instance, on the not unreasonable grounds that it already has adequate control over the drugs covered by the Convention, and ratification of this treaty would inolve it in enormous additional paperwork for no discernible additional benefit.

Indeed, we can reasonably ask what any country achieves by signing an international drug control treaty. The poorer countries, especially those that produce the raw materials or in which drugs are illicitly manufactured, may obtain considerable economic benefits. Foreign funds for heroin control are often labelled military or economic aid and various trade concessions may also be offered in return for co-operation in the drug war.

For more developed countries, the benefits are less obvious. The treaties permit them to restrict imports of particular drugs, but this could be managed through national controls. Most developed countries have long had treatment facilities for addicts, so the treaties cannot be said to have initiated their development. The insistence on stringent record-keeping may help control diversion of legitimate pharmaceuticals into the illicit market but, again, most countries had something along these lines before the treaties were ratified.

Perhaps Smart (1983) is correct: the main value of an international treaty may be that 'its ratification indicates our intention to take the drug problem seriously, both nationally and internationally' (p. 153), and the mechanisms established by the CND and the INCB do provide both worldwide information on drug use trends, and a forum for discussing issues of general policy. In the last analysis, though, this is not much to have achieved. And, as we shall see, the costs have been great.

International heroin controls

Two major activities are involved here: the prevention or at least regulation of heroin production, and the prevention of its entry into those countries that do not produce it.

The cultivation of the poppy is a rather public matter. It takes place in the open and the plants are visible for a considerable period before opium can be harvested. One would think that once the fields were discovered, it should be relatively easy to destroy the illegal ones—especially now that we have the Multispectral Opium Poppy Sensor (Swank, 1977) and similar technological marvels. In practice, it is effectively impossible.

The poppy-growing countries are sovereign nations and their willingness to allow American or any other planes to spray defoliants on their own people is likely to be limited at best. Doing so over their objections would have repercussions that are, at the international level, unthinkable. In any case, many of the opium-producing countries probably could not effectively prevent poppy growing even if they were willing to cooperate. The farmers most involved tend to be politically marginal members of ethnic minorities who may be in open rebellion against their formal rulers, and who at no time confer much legitimacy on them. For such people, the poppy is often the only crop that is a consistent money-maker. It produces a high yield on land unsuitable for crops and it can be grown successfully without fertilisers or much irrigation. It can be harvested without machinery, and while its harvesting is labour-intensive, labour is usually available in plenty. The poppy itself has many uses: the leaves and seeds may be eaten, its oil is used for cooking and the rest of the plant for fodder or fuel. Opium itself, once extracted, is a low bulk, high priced, non-perishable commodity. It can of course be used as medicine, but it can also be hoarded as a nest egg for potential dowries and other eventualities.

In this sense, the poppy has been part of the peasant economy in eastern Turkey for 3000 years. A comparable symbiotic relationship with it prevails in the Golden Triangle. Here, poppy cultivation and harvesting do not conflict with the rice crop and in years when the latter fails, hoarded opium is typically the first asset liquidated to pay for substitute consumables. In either country, middlemen are prepared to pay cash to the growers directly, and they are also prepared to lend money and seed against the next opium crop in a context where there are no agricultural banking services. The reality is that farmers can double or treble their profits by growing opium rather than other crops and, understandably, attacks on opium growing tend to be seen as attacks upon living standards and upon a way of life.

In any case there is, at the individual level, what Lewis (1984) calls the 'gulf of mutual incomprehension'. The difference between the world-views of the teetotal Afghan cannabis smoker, the drinking Westerner and the Lahu opium smoker is so profound that they are unlikely to see trafficking in their own drug of preference as anything more than a technical infraction of irrational and misguided laws.

Nor is personal profit and pleasure the only issue. Profits from the sale of the crop can buy guns and supplies for insurgent groups. Clear correlations can be seen between the extent of opium processing and armed insurrection. International resolutions, crop replacement programs and lectures on drug use prevention have little or no relation to the self-perceived needs of the growers or to their way of life. Nor is it in the immediate economic interests of traders or corruptible officials to comply with abstract legislation.

Local governments, then, would face a formidable task in bringing such intransigent groups to heel. In some cases, it is not in their interests to do so for still other reasons. The Thais, for example, have historically encouraged the development of a buffer region in the north against their Burmese neighbours and, more recently, against leftist insurgents operating from Burma and Laos. That role has, since 1949, been filled by the border warlords who control the opium trade and Thailand therefore tends to move against them rather half-heartedly.

Similar geopolitical considerations affect the government of Pakistan which is, in principle, opposed to the opiate traffic for both religious and medical reasons. Opium is grown around the Afghan border, and in those areas it tends to be the only cash crop. However, the tribal territories of the Northwest Frontier provinces are still largely autonomous. These people, the Pathans, are traders of great repute and efficiency in firearms, opium, heroin, cannabis and other forms of contraband and they police their own trading rigorously. They are also loyal solely to tribal organisations, and would be expected to put up a stiff resistance in the event of a Soviet–Afghan incursion. A sustained poppy growing eradication campaign by Pakistan would therefore not only alienate a fiercely independent and vengeful people, but in a very real sense destabilise the Afghan border region. The result is that Pakistan, like Thailand, prefers to retain the goodwill of its tribal peoples—it is essential to the integrity of its border and helps limit the possibility of internal rebellion.

Other opium producers have somewhat different interests in maintaining the opium trade. The governments of Mexico, Turkey and Iran are not currently dependent on trafficking bands or tribal groups for border security. If they tried to eradicate the poppy, they would certainly have problems with difficult terrain, local hostility of growers and traders, and there would probably be armed resistance. However, their main problem would be loss of direct and indirect profits. In these countries, the cash flow from the opium and heroin trade finances large black markets in otherwise unobtainable goods and services, and it is a major source of foreign currency. In 1976, for example, heroin sales allegedly accounted for 6 per cent of Mexico's gross national product, and for a while the economies of six northern Mexican states were based essentially on opium (Halper, 1975). Combatting official corruption in such a context is bound to be a losing battle. Bribery is a way of life.

In any case, there is reason to believe that Western countries are not entirely committed to their avowed determination to eradicate opium growing either. A pattern of primary producers suffering from distorted economies has been a constant feature of the economic and political relations between advanced capitalist countries and the Third World. Altering this pattern would entail altering the entire economic order, to the general detriment of the developed nations, and the West has been quite reluctant to do this. Thus, when Turkey suggested the granting of quotas on American sugar and mineral water markets to facilitate a switch from opium production to other crops, the proposal was summarily dismissed (Lamour and Lamberti, 1974). Continuing international demand for opium and its derivatives seems guaranteed. Under the circumstances, as long as the West refuses to provide real economic incentives to the Third World to change its agricultural system, there is no reason to believe that opium production will decline in the foreseeable future.

On the balance, the international repercussions of total suppression of the heroin trade would be so serious as to render this course of action politically impossible. Nor is it even realistic to contemplate it. The poppy can be grown in a great many places and the world's total illicit market is but a fraction of the world's potential production. It has been calculated that America's entire illegal market—currently around 10 tons of heroin—could be satisfied by the production of 25 square miles of land (Kaplan, 1983). Any one of a dozen countries, including parts of the United States itself, could readily meet the need, and history suggests that not one but several would quickly rise to the challenge.

Failing effective suppression of production, the next major strategy would be the prevention of smuggling. That current policing at national boundaries is somewhat effective is shown by the sharp increase in the cost of the product once it has crossed the borders. Nevertheless this task, too, is effectively impossible.

While the United States uses some 10 tons of illicit heroin each year, it is estimated that 100 million tons of legitimate freight move across its borders at the same time, not to mention some 250 million legitimate border crossings by individuals. Ten tons of heroin spread across this would literally be a drop in a bucket and there is every reason to suppose that a sizeable proportion of that 10 tons bypasses border formalities altogether. Just how difficult it would be to stop drugs at a border is demonstrated by the famous Operation Intercept of 1969, which the United States mounted largely to demonstrate the depth of its concern about the drug problem to a disinterested Mexican government. During the three weeks of the operation, all persons and vehicles entering the United States from Mexico were searched. Traffic became hopelessly snarled, great economic dislocation ensued and Mexico not only protested vehemently but threatened retaliatory action.

At the moment, the United States Customs Department estimates that it seizes about 5 per cent of the heroin entering the country. It is difficult to believe that this percentage could be significantly increased without either causing intolerable inconvenience to those legitimately entering the United States or paying for a vast increase in technology and manpower. And, as we have already seen, the chances of netting a high-level dealer or significantly affecting the total market in this way are small indeed.

Domestic heroin controls

There are very good reasons why attempts to reduce heroin production abroad and to prevent its movement across national boundaries show such limited results. Substantial amounts of heroin enter most Western countries and it is unlikely that the various enforcement agencies could do much better at stemming the tide, even if they would. It appears, therefore, that the brunt of control must fall on domestic criminal law. We have, currently, a general policy of heroin prohibition. We have criminalised all aspects of supply from production to distribution and in doing so we may be contributing more to the maintenance of the problem than to its solution. It rapidly becomes obvious that many of the problems that apply to controlling the international market beset domestic enforcement as well.

The law and the user

All signatories of the Single Convention spell out punishments for both drug trafficking and drug use within their borders. The law thus bears directly upon the users, and not merely by making their chosen drug difficult to obtain and exorbitantly expensive. Being involved with the drug is itself a crime and arrests for use far outnumber those for trafficking. Enforcing such user-oriented policies is very costly, and we may reasonably ask what benefits are expected in return for our investment.

A major problem with implementing use offence laws is actually defining 'users'. As our analysis of the domestic market suggests, it is often very difficult to distinguish between use and trafficking at the street level: many users are also traffickers. From a legal standpoint, this should present no difficulty—provided that evidence of trafficking could be actually demonstrated. No one has any doubt that selling proscribed drugs is a criminal offence, so the trafficker-user is clearly a criminal by virtue of the trafficking. But what about the user who only wants to use, without any intention to sell? Article 36 of the Single Convention makes purchasing a proscribed drug and offence, but suppose the drug is a gift—does accepting it make the receiver a criminal? And what about the state of being a user, of wanting the drug?

The present legal situation with regard to users is quite unsatisfactory. The crime for which they are prosecuted is not 'addiction'. As we shall see, addiction is difficult to define, and in any case it is not an all-or-nothing condition. Moreover, our criminal system works best when the accused have free will (and are therefore responsible for their actions), and when they are not fundamentally different from average human beings (see Chapter 7). Again there is controversy. Public and professionals alike are divided about whether these conditions hold for addicts. Many claim that while addicts initially choose to use their drug, it soon takes control of them. And many feel that addicts are somehow fundamentally—perhaps biochemically—different. In the event, addiction as such has never been a crime in Britain, and while it was effectively so in the America after the *Harrison Act*, the United States Supreme Court declared in 1962 that treating it as a crime was unconstitutional. Nevertheless, in practice unsanctioned use of proscribed drugs remains a crime everywhere.

The term 'use' does not actually appear in the law either. Laws against using would be extremely difficult to enforce. Observation of the actual act by an enforcement officer is fairly unlikely, and while analysis of body fluids would readily reveal the presence of opiates it is currently impossible to seize persons at home or on the street and subject them to such tests on the mere suspicion that they might be users. Most legal systems get around these difficulties by criminalising 'possession' of the drug, and it is the amount possessed that makes the difference between a user and a trafficker in the eyes of the law. The actual amounts that render a possessor liable to prosecution as a trafficker can vary substantially from place to place. Depending on the country, users may also be criminalised through a variety of ancillary offences such as possession of drug paraphernalia, or 'loitering for the purpose of narcotic use'.

In all, arrests for heroin use offences far outnumber those for heroin trafficking—for the United States, the ratio is 11:1—and the volume is substantial. About 130 000 cases are processed annually in America, and comparable statistics for Australia will be presented in Chapter 6. What do we hope to achieve with all this activity?

To some extent, punishment of users helps to limit supply, since many users are also dealers. The small-time seller may be impossible to apprehend in any other way. Nevertheless, the reduction in supply brought about in this way is likely to be marginal at best.

A deterrence argument can also be made; prosecution and punishment of users will stop their behaviour and will deter others from starting. Some neophyte users probably *are* deterred. For some addicts the intervention of the criminal law may also be the last straw which, added to all their other hassles, tips the balance and drives them into giving up the drug, with or without formal treatment. For the majority of users and addicts, however, it is abundantly clear that with minimal care their chances of evading the law are excellent.

If supply reduction and deterrence were our main objects, enforcement of use offences would hardly be worth the effort. In fact, the real purpose of these laws is rather different, and it rests on one or other of two assumptions about users. Both confuse *use* with *addiction*, a persistent but critically important misconception that is discussed further in Chapter 7.

The first assumption is that heroin users are a danger to society and that the law must therefore isolate them, by imprisonment, to protect respectable citizens. Few people today openly put the argument that users are a danger to public morals, though that argument is clearly very much alive. The ostensible rationale is usually the need to protect public health, especially that of youth. Heroin users, according to this argument, have a communicable disease that can 'infect' healthy people and they should therefore be quarantined to prevent the disease from spreading. Unfortunately, heroin addicts neither die nor recover from their disease very quickly. Most continue their addiction, off and on, for a substantial period, and they would have to be isolated for quite a long time for the quarantine to be effective.

Other arguments for isolating users rest on the crimes they allegedly commit. A major difficulty here is to demonstrate an invariable relationship between heroin use and crime. An increasing percentage of people involved with heroin today are moderate, controlled users, most of whom—along with some addicts—do not pose any special risk of property crime. In any case, since we cannot keep most criminals locked up for very long, it becomes important to ask what we hope to achieve by this in the shorter term.

Does imprisonment alter drug use upon release? The existing evidence is depressing. A very large proportion of cases that pass through the courts are recidivists. These figures are probably somewhat inflated, because once a person is 'known' to the police probability of re-arrest becomes much higher. Still, the deterrent effects of prosecution and conviction seem to be rather small.

Moreover, it appears that jail can teach users some things we would prefer they did not learn. Schlosser (1984) for instance quotes the Chair of the NSW Prison Officers' Association as declaring: 'Of course junkies don't improve in jail, they only learn more about breaking the law, it's not even a deterrent—junkies have no tomorrow, they're not aware of repercussions' (p.1).

Similarly, an anonymous addict maintains that 'You get the contacts in jail, learn where to buy firearms and how to shorten them—it's like going to university—it's the college of crime.'

And Laurie (1971) presents the following thought-provoking vignette from the American drug scene:

> My good friend's mother found his paraphernalia ... She went to my father, and my father took me for a ride. He was very understanding. I finally broke down, admitted I was using drugs, said I never would again. And of course, I no sooner left him than I made a phone call to my friend ... and that night we got loaded ...
> Somebody's mother called the police and they busted in an appartment where we were sitting, fixing, and it hit the newspapers ... The high school was rocked. Right off the ground. The worst thing they'd had was hub-cap stealing. So—the arrest, go to jail, and of course in jail meeting a lot of people, making new connections, friends, where to get drugs later, how to go about it, new ways of making money, and—you know, don't pretend you're naive, pretend you're pretty slick, because that's the scene here ... Thought about my old friend and wished he was around so I could show him what I knew now as a result of my nine months at Lex[ington]. I could really put him down. He wasn't hip any more ... (p. 53)

It appears, then, that jail terms are, if anything, counterproductive for drug users. Yet to date, the legal system does little more than detain those sentenced. Dobinson and Ward (1985) for instance, found that the penal institutions of New South Wales held a substantial number of individuals with drug use histories. However they also found that there were virtually no rehabilitation services, and that where they did exist they were provided by voluntary bodies or other departmental agencies, not by the Department of Corrective Services.

The second assumption underlying the criminalisation of use springs directly from the 'disease' model of addiction (see Chapter 7). According to this model, heroin users are sick people who because of the nature of their illness will not accept treatment voluntarily. We must therefore hospitalise them in prison-like institutions—for therapeutic rather than punitive reasons. In theory, such involuntary institutionalisation has fewer repercussions than imprisonment. The stigma of a criminal record is eliminated and the addict is to be released as soon as cured. But, as Wexler (1973) points out, there is stigma of a different kind, and since we cannot guarantee to cure addiction, the reality is that addicts can be confined as long as their therapists wish. In practice, civil commitment of addicts to such treatment is very uncommon in Western countries, although it is the rule in a number of Asian nations. The situation that exists in Singapore and Malaysia has been touched on in Chapter 4. As far as can be determined, the outcome of such measures, in terms of permanent rehabilitation of users, is unimpressive. And the cost of the process is enormous.

In Western countries, however, it is now fairly common to give convicted users a 'choice' between imprisonment or some other form of punishment and undergoing a course of treatment. The line between punishment and treatment is never entirely clear: each has some of the qualities of the other. When the aim of punishment is preventing the repetition of a crime, it may be seen as a kind of treatment. Conversely, to the extent that treatment prevents people from doing what they find pleasurable or profitable, it acts as a kind of punishment. However we choose to view it, the fact remains that courts are increasingly 'diverting' convicted users into a variety of non-penal programs. Since this process is officially considered to be a form of treatment, we will dicuss it more fully in Chapter 8, together with other treatment options. Suffice it to say here, that diversionary programs will probably not provide the answer either. So far, there is no convincing evidence that coercing convicted users into treatment is a particularly useful alternative to more traditional criminal procedures.

The law and the trafficker

The criminal law uses much the same means to deal with both drug traffickers and drug users. There are two principal strategies. One is an attempt to isolate the active criminal from the rest of society. The other tries to deter would-be criminals from involving themselves in the undesirable activity. As we have seen, neither strategy works very well with drug users. Success with drug traffickers is even less impressive.

Isolation works on the principle that if we apprehend a sufficiently large number of key people, the criminal activity will be much reduced or may even cease. Unfortunately, no special skills are needed to go into the heroin business, and for each heroin dealer arrested, there are usually several able to fill the gap.

Deterrence works only if the risk of apprehension is adequately high. The severity of the penalty—something that many people feel ought to be increased in the case of drug offences—is a very secondary consideration. The sentences currently specified would probably be sufficient if those in the business thought their chances of being caught were substantial.

Moreover, the risks of apprehension must be weighed against the probable gains from the activity. Profits at the higher levels of the drug trade are very large, and at the lowest levels the personal, physical need for heroin will make many addict–dealers that much harder to deter. For a variety of reasons, police are consistently urged to concentrate on high-level traffickers. This, however, is easier said than done. The more sophisticated police methods of detection become, the more careful the operators will be. They have an essentially unlimited amount of money and no legal constraints on the way this is deployed. The police, on the other hand, have limited resources and they are hampered by regulations that protect such rights of citizens as privacy and due process of law. In fact, discovering the identity of major drug traffickers may be fairly easy; building a provable case against them within the constraints of existing laws is another matter entirely.

What then are we to do? We could increase the resources available to all stages of the criminal process. A dramatic increase in funding might decrease trafficking, though there is no guarantee that this would happen. But such resources have to come from somewhere. Public health, education, welfare and housing all compete with the criminal justice system for funds, and in the long run improvements in these areas may be as important in lowering drug-related activities as more effective law enforcement.

We could also choose to give up some of our present rights as citizens. We could permit stop-and-search procedures, or wire tapping, and spare the police the necessity of getting warrants for many of their activities. We might conceivably go so far as to take their word about the criminal activities of heroin sellers, without demanding that objective evidence of guilt be presented in court.

Any of these strategies would increase deterrence and, theoretically, the efficiency of enforcement agencies in their war against heroin. They have all been proposed by politicians and members of the general public, as well as by enforcement experts. At the same time, they have also been vehemently condemned. For the time being, at any rate, supporters of traditional civil liberties seem to have prevailed. Police powers, while wider in the drug enforcement area than in many others, are still sharply limited in Western countries, and the escape of a certain percentage of heroin traffickers is part of the price we pay for this privilege.

This is not to say that enforcement of domestic drug laws has no benefits. The police do seize significant amounts of street heroin and they do put a certain number of suppliers out of business, at least temporarily. This reduces the total amount of heroin accessible to the average consumer. However, not all potential customers have equal access to the drug to begin with. Differential enforcement literally structures the market.

What happens is this. In areas where heroin has not gained a foothold, police generally can prevent a retail market from developing. Such areas tend to be middle-class neighbourhoods, but many lower-class areas are also relatively heroin-free. It seems to be more a question of local tradition than class or earning power as such. In such areas, police also tend to have comparatively generous resources in relation to the volume of criminal activity they must contend with, and they can therefore devote more attention to drug suppliers. Sellers are also much more visible. There are fewer of them, they are unable to fade into any addict subculture, and their presence often calls forth both citizen cooperation and demands for police action. Without local dealers, citizens tend to abstain and by and large, drug-free areas tend to remain drug-free. It is possible, therefore, to contain heroin use and trafficking in areas where it is not really a problem.

A quite different situation obtains in areas where heroin *is* a problem. These are typically the low-income, minority areas of cities, and containment of drug use there is virtually impossible. The high rate of other crime—often either more serious or more urgent than heroin trafficking—requires a great deal of the police force's time and effort, and heroin use is already so high that huge police resources would be required to lessen it appreciably. Traffickers are difficult to distinguish from the general population, and their many customers have a vested interest in protecting them from the law. The judiciary system, too, is usually so overburdened that it lacks the resources to deploy against violent crime, let alone against mere drug offenders. The result is that both heroin use and trafficking rapidly come to be regarded as something the law is unlikely to take very seriously. In other words, the nature of the system again tends to perpetuate the existing pattern of heroin use and availability.

The final picture is something like this. Even though large amounts of heroin are produced in the world's poppy-growing areas and it is almost impossible to interfere greatly with smuggling across national borders, heroin is effectively unavailable to substantial segments of the population of most Western countries. But we have every reason to believe that those segments have a very low probability of using heroin in the first place. So we find ourselves in the unsatisfactory position of being able to manage what is essentially a non-problem, while we are unable to deal with truly problematic heroin use at any price we could realistically afford to pay. Moreover, the benefit, if we choose to see it that way, of keeping heroin away from those segments of the population that are now drug-free is obtained at enormous cost. And the resources that are diverted into enforcement activities are are only a small part of the price we pay.

One cost that emerges directly from our efforts to restrict the availability of desirable drugs deserves special mention by way of an example. By making drugs like heroin illegal we encourage the development of legal alternatives, and 'designer drugs' are rapidly becoming a problem. Until a particular substance is classified as 'controlled' by law, it remains legal to make, sell and use it. A slight modification of the molecular structure of a restricted drug is all that is needed. Heroin is, after all, just such a modification of morphine.

Some of these drug modifications can be carried out by any backyard chemist, others require considerable technical sophistication, but both sorts of entrepreneurs have entered the market. 'China White', which made its appearance in California in 1979 and is now killing two heroin users each month in that state alone, is a variant of the synthetic opiate-like drug fentanyl. The 'new heroin', which arrived in 1982, is an analogue of meperidine. In the latter case, users can pay a high price for sloppy chemistry. If 'new heroin' is carelessly made, the drug can contain enough of a particular by-product, MPTP, to produce what seems to be a kind of Parkinson's disease. This is a condition that generally occurs only in the elderly and it is associated with destruction of nerve cells in certain areas of the brain. Behaviourally, the symptoms include paralysis, impaired speech and tremors, and it was precisely the appearance of such symptoms in a group of people much too young to have classical Parkinson's disease that brought 'new heroin' to public attention.

Designer drugs are not a new problem in the United States—they have been around since at least the mid−1960s, though of course not all are heroin analogues. There is a brisk market for various synthetic cocaines, for example. But their production increases in step with both enforcement and the addition of new compounds to the restricted drug lists. The connection seems somehow to have escaped the authorities. In 1984, Congress gave the Drug Enforcement Administration (DEA) a new weapon to combat designer drugs—emergency scheduling powers. Normally it takes six months to a year to schedule a new drug, but the new powers allow the DEA 'to ban designer drugs with the stroke of a pen and a year to justify the action' (Shafer, 1986, p. 73). This is madness. The only conceivable result is proliferation of further designer drugs. For every drug the government prohibits, the underground chemists will simply generate another.

Designer drugs notwithstanding, probably the greatest cost of drug law enforcement has been the resulting high price of heroin. We are facing the inevitable economic consequences of attempting to decrease supply without correspondingly decreasing demand. If we make it illegal to traffic in commodities for which there is an inelastic demand, the actual effect is to secure a kind of monopoly profit to the entrepreneur who is willing to break the law. In a very real sense, partial control is worse than no control and, as we have seen, partial control is the best we can do.

> For a moment, let's look at the problem through the eyes of the trafficker. In simple business terms, prohibition of the importation of drugs is really giving him a policy of preferential treatment, an exclusive market. We know that normal imported commodities, which must be imported because they are not produced in Australia, are very expensive to the consumer. Thus, in relation to narcotics and cannabis, we have an ideal situation for the importer. Production is prohibited in the consumer country, as is importation. The importer/trafficker need only create a market or some demand and he is in business.
>
> The more the traffickers are pursued by law enforcement groups, the more sophisticated will their operations be. Money will buy the technology, the informers inside law enforcement groups, and even politicians. Contributions to that fund will come from the victims: they will have to pay higher prices. Any suggestion of manufacturing and retailing the product in Australia will be absolutely resisted. The community would not have it—this would be tantamount to opening the flood gates to drug use. For the trafficker, this is music to his ears—as long as the community advocates prohibition he will remain in business. He, like the community, but from other motives, will fight legalisation. It would take the bottom out of the market. (Stolz, 1982, p. 17)

We also provide strong incentives for the very persons who are supposed to enforce the drug laws to enter the business. As long as profits in heroin dealing remain so high and the means of law enforcement do not change, there will continue to be no way to guarantee the honesty of all the officers enforcing heroin laws. Corruption of this kind does more than merely reduce the efficiency of heroin prohibition. Itts effects on public attitudes toward the police are devastating.

The possibility that our efforts at controlling the heroin market by legal means have been less than inspired has not escaped a wide variety of commentators. Whitlock (1977) gave the following evidence before the Senate Standing Committee on Social Welfare:

> One point needs to be established: unless we can say precisely and honestly why we wish to place restrictions on some drugs and not others, we will have little impact on persons who can legitimately point to the inconsistencies in our attitudes and flaws in our arguments. It simply is not good enough to seek shelter behind international agreements if the effects of signing these Conventions merely add to our problems. Blindly following the U.S.A. initiative in the matter of drug control does not appear to have brought any benefits in its train, either in Australia or elsewhere ... We would be wise to use our critical intelligence in this matter, rather than follow a course of action which after some 100 years has resulted in enormous social and health problems, notably in the U.S.A. which has been most prominent in persuading the rest of the world to accept its policies. The moralistic and criminal law approaches to drug control have not been fruitful. Whether we can devise anything better in their place is another matter but to persist with manifestly ineffective measures is hardly a rational approach to the subject. (pp. 1887–8)

Mugford (1982), speaking to a group of experts on drug trade and crime, had this to say:

> Many, or perhaps most, readers or listeners will have apoplexy at the thought of legalising marijuana, cocaine, heroin and so on. They will say my 'realistic' solution is the realism of mammon, the devil, or worse ... To those purists who have some idea of producing a better alternative (or eradication of drug use) I have only one thing to say: the pursuit of your policies is, has been, and will be, a dismal failure. In the self-righteous pursuit of an end you cannot achieve, you *create* the very problems you seek to destroy. You—as much as the 'evil drug pusher' whose profits you *guarantee and increase*—have to answer for the grim results of 'drug abuse' today. (pp. 67–8)

Meanwhile, back on the 1986 international scene, the United Nations General Assembly asked the CND to prepare yet another Convention Against Illicit Traffic in Narcotic and Psychotropic Drugs. There appeared to be increased problems with illicit drug production, traffic, demand, use and so on. The CND commented:

> The adverse effects of that traffic now extend from threats to the health and well-being of individuals, to the subversion of public order, the spread of corruption and criminal conspiracy, and in parts of some regions, threats to national security and the

> structure of society ... Many national enforcement agencies were now at a considerable disadvantage in terms of human, financial and other resources, as compared with trafficking groups, which were progressively increasing both their professionalism and their illegally acquired resources ... (Rexed, 1986, p. M4)

The drafting of the new convention has begun and it is to be presented to the General Assembly at its 40th session. It appears that history is about to repeat itself. More legislation rather than less is likely to be the official response.

6
How much heroin?

Unfortunately, much of our data is anecdotal. Recognizing the extreme limitations of this form of medical reporting, we nevertheless realize that it does have some epistemological values. Thus, a single case report is referred to as an anecdote. More than one anecdote reported by the same author constitutes a retrospectively collected series. Therefore, a prospective series is a collection of anecdotes which the author chose to report in advance of observation. Two prospective series of anecdotes, collected simultaneously, when fortified by hypothesis consists of a controlled study, which is tantamount to truth.
            Joseph Sapira and Charles Cherubin, 1975, p. ix

The Rev Ted Noffs of the Wayside Chapel in Kings Cross has buried 150 people who lost out to heroin ... 'What we are dealing with is a drug war,' he said. 'We have a genocide among our young.
'So poorly are we organised nationally that there is not even any statistical analysis of the problem ...
'But really, what has to be done is that there has to be an emergence of a philosophy. A philosophy about what we as a nation are going to do about people using and dying from drugs ...
'I know what's going to happen at the summit,' he said. 'All the medical authorities will be there, all the legal authorities will be there, all the heads of government bodies will be there and nothing will be done because those people are not on the front line and they all have their vested interests to protect'.
            Sydney Morning Herald, 3 January 1985

How many people actually use heroin, who are they and what are the results of such use? Sensational media reports regularly suggest the presence of tens of thousands of addicts in a given area, and indicate that their numbers are increasing at a 'terrifying' or 'alarming' rate. Sometimes the figures are attributed to some 'acknowledged expert', or it may be claimed that they originate from an 'informed source' or someone representing an official organisation. In no case are the bases of the estimate ever stated. This is not surprising: *there are in fact no reliable methods of estimate.* Where the media are culpable is not so much in reporting these figures, but in failing to report them for what they are—guesstimates at best, and wild guesses most of the time.

The experience of the Australian Royal Commission of Inquiry into Drugs (1980), known as the *Williams Report,* may be taken as a case in point. The Commission commented at length on the deficiencies of the statistical information available to it. Even in areas where data at first appeared to be reliable, more thorough investigation revealed major shortcomings.

> It must be said that there were times during its sittings and in later assessments of evidence when the Commision felt fully justified in agreeing with the old adage that there are 'lies, damned lies and statistics.' It must also be said immediately that the Commission detected the intentional misuse of statistics inferred by this quotation only on a very limited number of occasions. Far more common in the Commission's experience, and perhaps even more disturbing, was the unintentional misuse of statistical data. In such cases the uninformed reader is convinced of the relevance of a particular argument unsoundly based on data which are intrinsically deficient. In addition the proponents of the argument are lulled into a false sense of security believing that the available statistics and their interpretation of them are appropriate to the situation and in no need of improvement . . .
>
> Well-intentioned studies undertaken by various interested bodies on subjects such as drug use patterns within given community groups produced results which frequently and confidently were presented to the Commission as accurate representations of the real situation. On closer scrutiny by the Commission's Statistical Officer it became clear that in many cases these reports were at best somewhat misleading and at worst absolutely worthless due to significant errors in sample survey design, misinterpretations and faulty presentations of the basic survey output . . .
>
> Even [the] more sophisticated surveys produced results of limited value since commonality in methodology and presentation was seldom evident and consequently between-survey comparison of results usually quite impossible. The Commission's misgivings on the adequacy of Australian population survey work in drug-related areas were intensified by the realisation that many of these endeavours had been wholly or partially supported by government funds. (*Williams Report*, 1980, pp. D61−2)

By way of an illustration, the Commission cited the case of an on-the-spot interview-type study conducted throughout one state as a community awareness service:

> Although the researchers indicated that their results were open to challenge on the basis of weaknesses in the sampling technique employed, they asserted that 'the basic thrust of the figures' could not be overlooked. In the Statistical Officer's opinion, however, the approach adopted was so inadequate that, in fact, 'the basic thrust of the figures' should have been completely disregarded. In effect this meant that the results were completely worthless, and that a probably not insubstantial amount of money and the time of a large body of well-intentioned volunteers had been wasted because of a failure to adhere to even the most rudimentary principles of sample survey design. (*Williams Report*, 1980, p. D63)

The Commission concluded that 'not only was statistical information in Australia in a totally inadequate state, but that this fact was well known' (p. D61). Nor was this Commission the first to point to these problems. The reports of the Senate Select Committee on Drug Trafficking and Drug Abuse (1971), the Western Australian Honorary Royal Commission Inquiring into the Treatment of Alcohol and Drug Dependence (1973), the Senate Standing Committee on Social Welfare (1977), the Tasmanian Select Committee on Victimless Crime (1978) and the South Australian Royal Commission into the Non-medical Use of Drugs (1979) all said the same thing, and so have similar bodies from other countries.

That being the case, one can reasonably ask why this unsatisfactory state of affairs is permitted to continue. There are two basic reasons. First, epidemiological research in the area of drug use is genuinely difficult. Second, there are too many mutually incompatible vested interests.

In his testimony before the Williams Commission, Dr G. Milner proposed three types of drug use statistics: the actual, the known and the declared. He defined *actual* statistics as 'accurate', and this is a practical impossibility. The drug scene changes, often very rapidly. Even if we could completely describe the situation at a particular point in time, this information could serve as no more than a guideline. That leaves us with known and declared statistics. The *known* statistics, according to Dr Milner, refer to 'doing the best we can'. *Declared* statistics are those published by individuals or agencies with particular interests. Thus, what is published may or may not be the same as what is 'known', depending on the nature of the interest and the extent to which the reporting individual or agency is committed to it.

'Known' statistics and doing the best we can

Assessing patterns of drug use is admittedly complex. Suppose we wish to measure the prevalence of drug use. 'Prevalence', according to Mant and Thomas (1978), 'can be defined as the number of *active cases* of a *given phenomenon* present in a *defined population* during a *specific period of time*' (p. 173). Several problems immediately arise.

First, what constitutes a case? Do we count addicts, current users or people who have 'ever used'? Can we even differentiate these kinds of users? Will frequency of use be a factor, and how will terms like 'occasional' or 'heavy' use be defined? Are we interested in all use, or only non-medical use? If we choose non-medical use, will we count only use supplied from illicit sources, or will misuse of legitimate medication qualify? Are people in jail or in treatment 'active cases'? How will we validate our case identification? Drug use is typically a 'condition' rather than an objectively identifiable physiological state. Biochemical analysis might reveal the presence or absence of a drug in a person's system, but this depends very much on dose, frequency and recency of use, the pharmacology of the drug and the sensitivity of the assay. For practical purposes, drug use is a social construct, a matter of behaviour. Under the circumstances, how valid is a subjectively reported case?

Second, which drug are we in fact studying? If we set out to study the use of heroin, how are we to deal with the fact that the majority of those who use it also use other drugs? Even 20 years ago, 'relatively few offenders had abused one drug only, and although many individuals had named their drug of choice, their stated desire for a new experience had resulted in their having imbibed or injected any drug new to them and/or mixture of drugs readily accessible to them' (LeFevre, 1971, p. 396). Today, polydrug use is typical and some of the drugs used together with heroin may be legally obtained opiates like methadone. Which drug is responsible for which result?

Third, which population will we study and how will we go about it? 'Use' means very different things for different groups of people. For some, it is a normative behaviour, with non-users being the exceptions. In other situations, use is unusual, uncommon and even deviant. Who should be studied? Once a population is selected, a suitable sample must be chosen. The researchers may then conduct a survey, or they may rely on analysis of existing records. Either method presents difficulties.

Conducting surveys

In conducting surveys, the usual procedure is to work with a randomly selected sample representative of the general population. Setting up a suitable sample of this sort is difficult at best. Choosing subjects from phone books or electoral rolls in itself makes certain assumptions about the persons sampled, as does calling at dwellings.

When the potential sample is finally assembled, it will prove impossible to locate some people, and others will refuse to be interviewed, for any of a wide variety of reasons. In the household survey of drug use conducted by Heine and Mant (1978), for example, refusers fell into three groups. The first consisted of migrant families who were worried about being questioned by government representatives on any issue. The second group had difficulty in understanding what was involved and were generally suspicious of the motives behind the survey. These were often elderly persons. The last group were generally young, and they gave very diverse reasons for not wishing to participate. Some simply said they were not interested or too busy, both perfectly valid reasons.

Clearly, social and cultural parameters can alter responsiveness to surveys generally. But when the survey concerns a behaviour which is illegal and which, if admitted, could lead to prosecution of the respondents, problems of cooperation can become considerable. It seems reasonable to suppose that some of those who refused to participate in Heine and Mant's drug use survey were the very people the researchers were interested in.

Where sensitive material is being surveyed, a personal interview tends to be less acceptable than an anonymous, self-administered questionnaire. With questionnaires, however, there is no way to tell whether respondents really understood the questions, or interpreted them consistently. Neither is there opportunity to probe if a respondent is reluctant, or to pursue potentially important leads further.

Both interviews and questionnaires, though, share two problems. One is the practical one that respondents will be prepared to give only so much time to the exercise. There is thus a real limit on the amount of data they will permit the researcher to collect and every question counts. This means that a wide-ranging, free-form inquiry cannot be made. Questions must be fairly directive, and herein lies the second problem.

The questions that go into the item pool are of course reflections of the investigator's theoretical view of things and they will shape the outcome, sometimes to a dangerous extent. In a sense, therefore, every survey discovers what it set out to find. If the investigator strongly believes that drug use is a result of, say, social disadvantage, he or she will frame the interview or questions accordingly. Given the protean nature of drug use, it would be surprising indeed if at least some support was not provided for almost any theoretical position.

This is particularly a problem if the theoretical variables being studied are rather abstract. It is one thing to ask questions about a person's level of education; it is quite another to develop ones that measure his or her level of anomie, or alienation or, for that matter, depression or psychological adjustment.

All interviews and questionnaires, then, have built-in biases based on the theoretical orientation of the investigator. Other biases may come from the population itself. So far we have been discussing surveys that attempt to sample the general population as a whole. This approach is useful only if we have reason to believe that the behaviour in which we are interested is common enough to appear reliably in samples that are manageably small. It also assumes that the behaviour is sufficiently well accepted in the community to permit respondents to be reasonably honest in their answers. These assumptions probably hold for questions about the use of prescription drugs. They may also hold fairly well for social drugs like alcohol and nicotine, and possibly even for cannabis. However, neither holds for heroin.

The use of illicit opiates in an unselected population appears to be very low. If there is to be a database of any size, therefore, heroin users must be actively *sought*. This means either tapping the captive populations of users who seek help or are apprehended, or penetrating the drug scene itself. Neither of these samples can be assumed to be at all representative of heroin users in general. The first group represents the casualties of the drug scene, and we have already touched on some difficulties in extrapolating from such samples. In the second case, there is likely to be a considerable degree of selection bias. Consider the following example. When they surveyed use in an Australian drug subculture in 1973, Krupinski and Stoller gained entry to the scene through university graduates or senior students who had drug-using friends. These friends then referred the interviewers on to other users, a technique known as 'chain' or 'snowball' sampling. What happened, though, was that two-fifths of the users eventually contacted turned out to be current university students, and the proportion who had had some contact with tertiary studies exceeded 60 per cent. In the same study, using general population sampling, drug use was found to be particularly prevalent among school leavers and working youth. So the data on the drug subculture were not really comparable: they represented only a specific subgroup of its total membership.

The situation is more equivocal with respect to the respondents' honesty. In surveys of the general population, both under- and over-reporting can occur for a variety of reasons. In a large survey of NSW high school students, for instance, Homel and his colleagues cautioned that 'estimates of the level of use of certain of the more esoteric substances—e.g. hallucinogens, narcotics and stimulants—may be a little inflated by bravado of "smart" replies' (1984, p. 11). Some effort to estimate the level of honesty is therefore desirable. On the whole, if the survey seems serious, if it is conducted in an appropriately neutral manner—that is, neither threatening nor challenging—and if the assurance of anonymity appears genuine, most of the participants will probably be reasonably honest. However, there is no excuse for not including some inconsistency checks. A number of formal questionnaires have built-in lie scales, and these might be used. Or various spot checks might be made. For instance, users of street drugs would be expected to have some knowledge of the drug subculture argot.

The reliability of information supplied by populations of drug users and especially drug addicts has been the subject of some debate. Dishonesty is part of the popular addict stereotype. Ausubel (1968) for example castigated 'radio commentators, newspaper columnists and special-feature writers' for foisting 'tons of mischief' on the American public during the 1950–1957 teenage drug epidemic. 'Lacking easy access to reliable and scientific data, these persons turned to drug addicts themselves in their desperate effort to meet the public demand for information. What they obtained and passed on to a credulous public was a highly biased and dangerously distorted interpretation of drug addiction' (p. 5). Ausubel had no hesitation in passing on data emanating from his own studies, though. Presumably addicts were more honest with him.

The fact of the matter is that we must depend on the subjective testimony of users and addicts. Only they can provide certain types of information, and this information has been sought far too rarely—presumably because researchers are swayed by their subjects' 'known' untrustworthiness. Addicts vary in this regard, as do all humans. Some are honest, some are not. Lindesmith (1968) recalls that his chief addict contact, Broadway Jones, 'sometimes warned me that my new subject could not be trusted, and that I should keep one hand on my billfold and the other on my watch when I was with him. In other instances, the subject was characterised as an 'honest thief' who could be trusted implicitly to steal only from strangers and whom I could safely take into my home ... None of these ever pilfered anything; on the contrary, a number of them offered to provide us with stolen goods' (p. 6).

It is Lindesmith, in fact, who has provided one of the more level-headed assessments of the situation:

> It has often been said that the testimony of addicts is virtually worthless because of the secrecy surrounding addiction and the tendency of drug users to distort and falsify. I have found that this view is incorrect. The addict lies and distorts not because he has any indiscriminate urge to do so but in order to obtain certain definite and practical results. If it is clear to him that he has

nothing to gain by lying and nothing to lose by telling the truth, he is as straightforward and honest as anyone else. Of course, he will rationalise and offer excuses, but in this sense he is no different from non-addicts.

It is true that there are certain areas in which the addict has very strong inhibitions against giving the unvarnished truth . . . A drug user is particularly cautious about information concerning the sources of his supply, and if he is engaged in theft or other illegal activity, he will be very reluctant to describe this activity . . . The drug user has no special tendency to falsify concerning the nature of his habit . . . On the whole, once friendly contact is made, drug users are probably above average in cooperativeness, because many of them believe that they ought to be studied and better understood. (pp. 11−2)

There is no reason, therefore, to assume that addicts will be any less (or any more) honest than anyone else. Much depends on what questions are asked, who is asking and what the flavour of the situation is. Certainly surveys of addicts, like all others, should have built-in consistency checks. But it seems unnecessary to treat them as special cases in this regard.

The majority of surveys of drug use conducted in Australia have used schoolchildren, and the only time series is that carried out in NSW on Year 10 students (age 15−17) at approximately three-year intervals since 1971. These data show that alcohol, tobacco, analgesics and cannabis are used far more than other drugs. The use of these has increased in recent years, while the use of stimulants and sedatives (never very high) has decreased. The use of opiates in this population has always been rare—in the 1980 and 1983 samples, less than 1 per cent (Commonwealth Department of Health, 1986). The value of these data as estimates of illicit drug use is probably quite limited. There is reason to believe that people who become regular opiate users tend to drop out of school, and the cost of even minimal heroin use would be beyond the reach of all but a handful of schoolchildren. Also, other data, albeit from other countries, tend to suggest that heroin use generally begins after young people leave school, not before.

The few adult surveys that have been done have either sampled areas where drug use was believed to be considerably higher than the norm, or have directly involved the drug-using subculture. The only Australian study that gives any picture of what adult users are actually like and how they carry on their drug use is Krupinski and Stoller's (1973) survey of Melbourne youth. Beside a large sample of secondary schoolchildren, this study also sampled tertiary students and a group of working youth under 23 years of age. As might be expected, opiate use was very low. Of the almost 4 000 respondents, only 36 had used drugs intravenously on more than two occasions and of these 36, only eight had used opiates on five or more occasions.

However, this study also included a sample of users contacted through helping agencies, and another obtained through personal contacts with the drug subculture. Altogether, 697 people in these special samples were interviewed. Of these, the researchers felt that 58 (8.5 per cent) could be classified as 'narcotics addicts' in terms of their physical and psychological dependence on the drugs. One in two of the opiate users reported having had withdrawals at some time, but 45.4 per cent said that they had not used in the last three months. The most frequent reason given for this was that they had simply lost interest (20.2 per cent). Adverse effects were the reason for 15.5 per cent. Problems with availability, fear of apprehension, and substitution of other drugs were all relatively unimportant—4.3 per cent, 2.2 per cent and 0.7 per cent respectively—and 2.5 per cent said that they had ceased all drug use.

In this study, the majority of those using drugs were polydrug users and their method of use depended on which subsample they came from. As Table 5.1 shows, intravenous users—those most likely to have problems—were disproportionately more frequent among subjects drawn from helping agencies. Interestingly, 41 per cent of those using opiates intravenously gave as their reason the simple fact that that was the way the drug had been first offered to them. Only slightly more (44 per cent) said they used intravenously because they preferred this method to oral use. Conformity with friends' practices and economy were given as reasons by only 7 per cent.

Perhaps the most interesting finding was that more than 50 per cent of all respondents claimed that they never spent any money on drugs and that they were generally given supplies by friends. Expenditure on drugs in the previous year was zero for 17 per cent, less than $50

Table 6.1 Use as a function of type of population

Type of use	% Subjects from agencies dealing with drug problems	% Subjects interviewed 'in the field'	% Comparable subjects from survey of Melbourne youth
Marijuana	2.7	32.7	30.0
Multi-oral	26.5	50.3	57.8
Intravenous	70.8	17.0	12.1

Based on Table 4, Krupinski & Stoller, 1973, p. 21

for 28 per cent and $50–200 for 37 per cent. Only 7 per cent reported spending more than $500. These, of course, are 1973 dollars in a 1973 scene. However, the figures are still surprisingly low when placed against the criminal dope fiend stereotype. The point made earlier about the importance of the data collector's theoretical viewpoint and the specific sample studied is particularly well illustrated by the fact that in 1970, three years before the Krupinski and Stoller study, the Narcotics Section of the Australian Central Intelligence Bureau concluded that 63 per cent of drugs were bought from pedlars (Technical Information Bulletin, 1971). This represented an almost three-fold increase since 1969, and by 1973 the percentage would be expected to have increased further. What is found obviously depends on who is looking.

A few more pieces of information may be gleaned from Krupinski and Stoller's conclusions:

> Our survey has shown that illicit drug users come predominantly from a middle-class background, although working-class children were far from being immune to illicit drug taking ... When they turned to illicit drugs, they were more likely to become intravenous users than their middle-class counterparts. Ethnic groups ... reported significantly less drug use than Australians and British immigrants.
> Psychological problems prior to illicit drug use did not distinguish users from non-users, nor could these be regarded as responsible for the intensity of drug use among users ... However, after drug use the incidence of psychiatric problems doubled in the multi-oral group and trebled in the intravenous group ... There is no doubt that social functioning of drug users diminished with the intensity of drug use. While marijuana users continued with their education, the intravenous users had the highest rates of drop-outs, and they remained unemployed or casually employed in the community. They were more often also in conflict with the law, not only for drug-related offences ...
> Our survey did not support the notion that rebellion against society was a significant reason for turning to illicit drugs. Only a minute percentage of our respondents named rebellion as a reason for their behaviour. More importantly, the political involvement of our interviewees was insignificant, and the proportion of those politically involved decreased in proportion to increased intensity of drug use. Melbourne youth rejected the notion of alienation, and there were no differences in this regard between users and non-users ... The main reason for experimenting with drugs was curiosity, followed by availability and conformity. However, those who did not stop at experimentation, but became drug users, did it for other reasons. The marijuana users looked for excitement, mental stimulation or relaxation, whilst the

intravenous users tried to solve their intrapersonal problems. (1973, pp. 109–10)

On the whole, surveys of drug use give us little enough to work with beyond two important facts. First, regular illicit drug users are rare, and those who use opiates especially so. And second, where such people have been described specifically—and large-scale studies are virtually non-existent—they don't much fit the popular stereotypes.

Extrapolating from records

This assumes, first and foremost, that relevant records exist, and even today there are enormous gaps. For instance, in Australia, 'no adequate data collection system is at present available, even at State or Territory level, to cover treatment services either in terms of the resources applied, the clients who present, the problems presented, or the outcomes' (Commonwealth Department of Health, 1986, p. 24). For a variety of reasons, among them confidentiality, many treatment services refuse to divulge records, and this can be defensible. However, the number that do not keep records of any usable kind to begin with is very large.

If records do exist, very serious questions need to be raised about both their validity and their completeness. With respect to validity, consider the data on recent attendance in Australian methadone programs. By definition, a person in a methadone program is assumed to be dependent on opiates. As Table 6.2 shows, approximate attendance has more than doubled overall, and NSW shows a threefold increase. Does this mean that there is a new epidemic of heroin use? Perhaps—but what is quite certain is that in that period there was an epidemic of political concern with heroin. In Australia, 1985 was the Year of the Summit, and it saw the launching of the National Campaign Against Drug Abuse. The flavour of this stirring time has been vividly captured by Saunders (1985):

> The level of activity in the first few months of this year . . . was little short of frenetic . . . New policies were drawn up seemingly overnight, budgets devised in an afternoon. One had the impression of a steamroller careering madly downhill. Now the steamroller has slowed down we can survey the scene. The central issue is heroin addiction and the steamroller itself seems to be spurting methadone in all directions. (p. 155)

Despite the overwhelming conclusion by several pre-summit meetings of experts that 'alcohol and tobacco are the major drugs of use and abuse, and they should be a major focus of attention in the forthcoming national action', the Premiers' Conference concluded firmly that 'the

Table 6.2 Persons in methadone programs (withdrawal & maintenance) in Australia, 1985–86

State	February 1985	March 1986
NSW	840	2 400
Victoria	150	215
Queensland	700	950
Western Australia	240	350
South Australia	120	285
A.C.T.	24	55
Approximate total	2 000	4 250

Commonwealth Department of Health, 1985, 1986

Campaign will focus particularly on illegal drugs'. In NSW especially, this translated into a focus on heroin and, more specifically, on solving this problem by providing greatly expanded methadone programs. Perhaps the addicts now crowding into these programs were there all the time, and only now are receiving the care they were denied previously. This issue is examined further in Chapter 8. However, the main point for the time being is that the figures in Table 6.2 reflect the changing availability of a particular form of treatment, and they can offer no information either about the appropriateness of that treatment or the number of addicts requiring treatment at any given time.

Validity of available records is one issue. Their completeness and representativeness is quite another. In Britain, for example, compulsory notification of addicts by physicians has been in force since 1967. However, notification still depends on users coming to the attention of physicians prepared to notify them. Australia has no addict notification requirement, though some relevant health and law enforcement data are collected. The health statistics most relevant to estimates of the extent of heroin use include data on incidence of serum hepatitis, drug-related morbidity, and drug-related deaths.

Serum hepatitis is a notifiable disease in all states. This is a disease of the liver and it occurs as a complication of intravenous injection or transfusion. (Infectious hepatitis, also a notifiable disease, has no specific association with drug use). Serum hepatitis is a particular risk if the injection or transfusion is frequent, if the recipient is debilitated and/or if the procedure is unsterile. It is therefore a hazard of intravenous drug use. Over the last two decades, there has been a general increase in reports of serum hepatitis in all states, and this is sometimes taken to indicate a rise in illicit opiate use.

There are several problems with this. First, it is the procedure that is the problem; the nature of the drug has little to do with it. Thus, the opiates used need not be illicit, and drugs other than opiates can cause it. Moreover, drugs need not be involved at all—serum hepatitis is also a hazard of hemodialysis, and Mant and Thomas (1978) have pointed out that in Australia, at any rate, an increase in hemodialysis for people with kidney failure has coincided in time with what appears to be an increase in illicit drug use.

Second, the disease may not be notified—the sufferer may not consult a doctor, the doctor may fail to diagnose the disease, or may choose not to notify it although he or she is supposed to do so. Conversely, the same person may be notified more than once—either by different practitioners for the same episode, or for another episode in the same year or in subsequent years.

Relatively few statistics on *drug-related morbidity* are available. In 1981, for example, data was collected on drug-related admissions to public and private hospitals in NSW, Queensland and Western Australia. Some of the results are shown in Table 6.3. Over 80 per cent of the drug-related admissions involved alcohol; between 1.5 per cent and 4 per cent involved opiates. These figures are probably underestimates. Some of the people who experienced problems with drugs were not treated at all and others would have been patients of private doctors. At the same time, these data refer to discharges from hospitals, not to individual persons. As was the case with serum hepatitis, the same person could have been counted several times. Since suicide attempts, for example, are often repeated, this undoubtedly inflates the figures.

Table 6.3 Drug-related admissions to public and private hospitals in Australia 1981

	NSW	STATE Qld.	W.A.
Alcohol	13 980	3 619	2 976
Tobacco	6	2	2
Opiates	622	73	47
Marijuana & hallucinogens	74	26	4
Other drugs	645	313	114
Unspecified	1 482	255	111
Total drug admissions	16 809	4 288	3 254
Total opiates as % of admissions	1.6	0.9	1.1

Commonwealth Department of Health, 1986

In any case, drug-related problems cover a wide range of troubles—everything from adverse effects of medicinal agents through accidental poisoning to attempted suicide. If we pull out only those data that seem due to deliberate misuse of drugs (as opposed to accidental or suicidal overdoses), figures collected in 1983 suggest that opiates are involved in about 3.5 per cent of the cases. By contrast, benzodiazepine tranquillisers account for 30 per cent (Commonwealth Department of Health, 1986).

Finally, we can consider *death due to drug use*. For opiates, the situation in 1983 and 1984 appears in Table 6.4. As Table 6.4 shows, there seems to have been a real increase in opiate-related deaths during this time. The 1983 figure itself in fact represents a 70 per cent increase since 1979. However, several points need clarification. The deaths are not confined to persons known to be drug-dependent and 'opiates' includes such legally available substances as methadone, morphine, dextromoramide and meperidine as well as illicit heroin. In this sense, the figures would overestimate the amount of illicit use.

On the other hand, some deaths due to drug overdose are not recognised or not recorded as such. For instance, there are suggestions that some physicians tend to ascribe drug-related deaths to other causes, perhaps out of consideration for relatives (NSW Government, 1978). Moreover, if the victim died in some very obvious way, say as a result of injuries sustained in a car accident, an autopsy would still be performed but there might be little reason for the coroner or pathologist to look for evidence of drug dependence. Some proportion of the substantial rise in opiate-related deaths in the last decade is undoubtedly due to the fact that more people are *looking* for evidence of them.

The incidence of heroin overdose is sometimes used to estimate prevalence of heroin use as such. The 'overdose-multiplier formula' was developed by M. Baden (Greene, 1975) and it was originally based

Table 6.4 Deaths due to drug use, Australia 1983–84

Cause of death	1983	1984
Drug dependence	112	125
Accidental poisoning	38	42
Suicide	41	56
Total opiate deaths	196	229
Total alcohol deaths	3 198	3 174
Total tobacco deaths	16 620	16 346
Total deaths, all drugs	20 533	20 232

Commonwealth Department of Health, 1985, 1986

on a comparison of names of people designated as overdose victims by the New York Medical Examiner with names appearing in the New York Narcotics Register. Since 0.5 per cent of overdose victims also turned up in the Narcotics Register, the annual prevalence of heroin use in New York City became the number of overdose victims multiplied by 200. Subsequent research suggested that the number of addicts designated as such at autopsy, rather than simple overdose deaths, was a better indicator, and the ratio became 1:100 rather than 1:200.

The most recent attempt to apply the overdose multiplier formula to NSW seems to have been that of the Woodward Commission (1980). Using it, the estimated number of heroin addicts in NSW in 1978 was calculated to be 7 466. The Commission's other attempts at estimates produced figures ranging from 9 257 (calculated using the 'indicator–dilution' method discussed below) to a 'sort of wild guess' by a senior detective attached to the NSW Drug Squad of 'somewhere between 5 000 and 20 000' (Woodward Commission, 1980, p. 279).

The difficulty about using the overdose-multiplier formula has to do with the unique character of New York City. It is highly unlikely that many other countries or cities would replicate either its disease patterns or its mortality rates. It may be worthwhile attempting to restandardise the ratio for different localities, though. Currently, most estimates are based to some degree on figures provided by enforcement agencies, and these vary greatly with current practice. Death is at least unambiguous.

Enforcement-related records include data on drug-related criminal charges, seizures of illicit substances and chemical analyses of material seized. The last are probably the least useful from the standpoint of estimating the number of users.

It has been argued that the *purity of street samples* is a function of a drug's availability: the less available it is, the more it is likely to have been cut. This, however, presupposes the even more basic assumption that the more available a drug is, the more it will be used. This is reasonable, but only up to a point. Whenever drugs are discussed, someone is sure to bring up the idea that unrestricted availability will automatically produce runaway addiction, or at least runaway experimentation. Now milk is freely available, but a substantial percentage of people detest it. There is no reason to believe that the situation will be any different with heroin. In every society there is a maximum consumption level for all substances, and it is *not* 100 per cent use. We do not know where that saturation point is for heroin, but it is just conceivable that an increase in street level purity could mean that demand is levelling off. In NSW, the mean percent purity of street heroin seized by the police has shown a gradual but fairly steady increase from around 18 per cent in 1977 to some 27 per cent in 1983 (NSW Drug and Alcohol Authority, 1985). This could mean that increasing amounts are coming into the country to supply an increasing demand, or that enforcement agencies are less and less efficient, or that the stuff is not selling very well, either because people have been discouraged from buying, or saturation is approaching—or any combination of these possibilities.

Data on street purity are therefore difficult to relate to level of use at best. However, as they are now collected, they are also highly unreliable. The majority of samples that come in for analysis are submitted by the police for the purpose of securing prosecution in drug offence cases. A few come from health professionals and a small number are sent by concerned lay people such as school principals or anxious parents. From the standpoint of the police, a 'case' is defined as all the drug exhibits submitted in relation to a particular arrest. This may involve one or more defendants and the amount seized may vary from a single foil package to several kilograms of material. No distinction is made at this level between users and dealers, and several 'cases' may relate to the same offender.

Finally, not all drug offences result in a sample being submitted for analysis. It is not usually required, for instance, with a plea of guilty. So when official records show a progressive increase in the number of heroin samples submitted for analysis—from 163 in 1980 to 274 in 1981, 408 in 1982, 547 in 1983 and 398 in the first half of 1984 (NSW Drug and Alcohol Authority, 1985)—the only conclusion that can be drawn with confidence is that the State Analyst Laboratories have been working harder. As the Authority's report points out, the increases may reflect a real change in the availability of the drug, an increase in the level and/or success of police activity, or a change in police sample submission practices.

The *number of criminal charges* associated with drugs other than alcohol is shown in Table 6.5. From 1977 to 1981, the number of drug-related offences rose by almost 40 per cent. Almost all of this increase is accounted for by cannabis offences. The Commonwealth Department of Health commented that 'the significance of the increases is uncertain. It is impossible to determine how much is due to increases in the level and efficiency of law enforcement activities, how much to increases in number of users, and how much to an increase in trafficking.' (Commonwealth Department of Health, 1985, p. 21)

In any case, the charges laid relate to the use or supply of a drug, not to the kind of use, so they could not be used to estimate the number of addicts as such. Also, a single person could be counted more than once in either the same or a different year. Indeed, it is highly likely that a considerable amount of this goes on. Once a

Table 6.5 Criminal charges associated with some drugs

	1977	1978	1979	1980	1981
Cannabis	17 978	14 249	17 501	20 278	26 506
Narcotics	3 676	4 262	3 520	2 611	3 745
Total for all drugs	23 024	19 948	22 871	24 515	31 947

Australian Federal Police (Commonwealth Department of Health, 1986)

Table 6.6 Drugs seized by federal agencies

	1977	1978	1979	1980	1981	1982	1983	1984
Heroin	11.7	17.9	29.3	7.9	9.5	32.0	97.1	101.6
Cocaine	1.4	–	1.8	69.6	3.1	89.2	87.9	131.0
Cannabis oil	37.2	97.7	54.2	108.3	2.8	30.4	60.1	89.9
Cannabis other	704.0	7 648.0	554.1	581.0	1 728.9	2 499.7	1 665.4	6 822.9

Australian Federal Police (Commonwealth Department of Health, 1986)

person becomes known to the police, the probability of a rearrest becomes much higher.

Finally, *drug seizures* by federal agencies are shown in Table 6.6. Again, there is a general tendency toward increase, but again the figures cannot be taken as an accurate measure of the number of illegal drug users or the extent of illegal drug use. There may be omissions and duplications, and the amounts seized depend on the level and efficiency of law enforcement.

As if all this variability were not enough, there is reason to believe that the data may also be quite incomplete. Evidence presented to the Williams Commission (1980) by senior officers of the Australian Federal Police included some thought-provoking testimony. One officer indicated that 'the persons engaged in the processing of the data lacked qualifications appropriate to the task and did not have access to any specialised forms of training' (p. D76). Another commented that 'We have problems getting people to [complete and forward documents] ... and to do it properly' (p. D76). Yet another officer explained that there were significant omissions from that data because arresting authorities do not pass on complete information. 'Some two-thirds of charges laid have not had results of proceedings relayed to us ... I should qualify that by saying if we did receive all the operational information that would be of value, we would not have the staff to handle it' (p. D77).

The same witness provided the fact that of almost 9 000 seizures reported in 1976, quantities seized were not specified on 3 993 occasions, and he quoted a former head of a state Drug Squad as saying that 'if he knew of 60 per cent of the charges laid in his particular state, he thought he was doing well' (p. D77). Not surprisingly, the Commission concluded that 'the current national drug law enforcement statistics, which appear on the surface to offer a reasonable decision-making tool, must be judged to be totally inadequate' (p. D77).

Since each of the available data sources has limitations, how are we to estimate the extent of use? For a while, the *indicator—dilution method* (sometimes also called the capture-recapture method) was popular. Greene (1975) illustrates the technique this way:

> A lake contains an unknown number of fish represented by N. A sample of fish is caught, tagged ... and put back into the lake. This initial sample is designated $n1$. At some later time, a second sample ($n2$) of fish is caught. Among the fish in the second sample, a certain number (X) will be fish previously tagged in the first sample. If one assumes that the two samples are *completely independent of one another*, and that each sample is a *random selection* of all fish in the lake, the ratio of tagged fish in the second sample to all fish in the second sample (i.e., $X/n2$) should be the same ratio as all fish in the first sample to all fish in the lake ($n1/N$). (p. 7; emphasis added)

For our purposes, the lake is the population and the tagged fish are drug users. Tagging can be done in a variety of ways: treatment admissions, arrests, death records and so on. The two sampling occasions can use the same database or two different ones.

Thus, the first sampling ($n1$) might be persons arrested in one year for opiate offences and the second sampling ($n2$) might be those arrested in the following year. X becomes the number of $n1$ arrestees who reappear in the $n2$ sample and N, the prevalence of opiate use, would be calculated using the formula

$$N = n1 \times (n2/X)$$

Using 1976 and 1977 statistics for New South Wales, $n1$ (1976 arrests) = 748, $n2$ (1977 arrests) = 875, and X (number arrested in both years) = 77. Using the above formula, N (estimated prevalence of opiate use in 1977) therefore becomes 8 500.

Alternately, $n1$ and $n2$ can come from different sorts of records: $n1$ might be say arrests and $n2$ overdose deaths. X then becomes the number of persons who died of opiate overdose and who appeared on the previous year's arrest records. Again using 1976 and 1977 statistics for New South Wales, $n1$ (1976 arrests) = 748, $n2$ (overdose deaths in 1977) = 60, and X (people arrested in 1976 who died in 1977) = 5. N, the prevalence of use in 1977, becomes 8 976.

Note that the two estimates differ substantially. The South Australian Royal Commission (1978), which seems to have been the first Australian body to formally use this method, found an even larger spread. Their estimates for prevalence of use in South Australia in 1976 varied threefold: from 574 to 1 672, depending on the databases used in the calculations. Given the uncertainties about the completeness of the various records, such a range is perhaps no wider than might be expected. Unfortunately, Sandland (1984) has pointed out that the whole procedure is statistically invalid.

As Greene (1975) noted in his illustration, the two samples must be independent, and each must be a random and representative sample of all users. In addition, the procedure assumes that the number of users is constant in the time frames under consideration. While these conditions probably hold for fish in lakes, they cannot apply to heroin users. If we are using arrest/rearrest records, it is obvious that one arrest tends to increase the probability of subsequent ones. Moreover, people who are in one kind of trouble also tend to be involved in other kinds of trouble. The same users are therefore likely to figure in several sorts of records. The heroin users who get tagged are the casualties; we cannot assume they are representative. Finally, the heroin-using population is hardly constant. As some begin use, others die, enter custody and/or treatment, or simply give up using. But we cannot assume that the number leaving the scene in one way or another is the same as the number entering it—indeed, the reason we are doing these calculations in the first place is because we suspect that the absolute number of users may be increasing.

In other words, *none* of the necessary conditions for the valid use of the indicator−dilution method is met, and the calculated estimates are essentially worthless. In 1984, the NSW Drug and Alcohol Authority had this to say:

> In the previous annual report of the Authority, an estimate of the number of narcotic dependent persons was presented. The estimate was based on the indicator−dilution method ... Since then [the] Authority has received statistical advice ... which criticised the validity of the estimation procedure ... For this reason, no attempt to estimate the number of narcotic dependent persons in NSW will be made in this report. It may be noted, however, that there is little evidence of a dramatic increase in the number of heroin dependent persons in NSW. (p. 12)

In its 1985 report, the Authority again preferred to make no estimate of the prevalence of heroin use. In the same year, the Commonwealth Department of Health summed up its own annual report as follows:

> There is no reliable evidence to allow an estimate to be made of the number of illegal drug users in general, or users of any particular illegal drug (e.g. heroin). Nor can a firm estimate be made of the quantities of illegal drugs being used. (p. 10)

'Declared' statistics and vested interests

Bluntly, we have very little idea of what is really going on. It should be possible to monitor trends in drug use, drug-related problems and even business trends within the 'industry' itself. We certainly have the technology to do so. The relevance of our policies, appropriateness of our strategies and the effectiveness of our programs could then be properly evaluated and modified as needed. Yet to date no country seems to have been able to devise a satisfactory way to do this. In Australia, the Senate Standing Committee on Social Welfare (1977) commented on the lack of suitable data, and warned that this 'allows those with prejudices to advance their line undeterred by facts ... Often the use of statistics which do exist is either flagrantly dishonest or dangerously naive' (pp. 19–20). The *Williams Report* (1980) said it again, and, according to the Commonwealth Department of Health (1986), matters still have not changed very much. Why is this?

The anatomy of vested interests

It has become rather fashionable to suspect foul play by various (usually unnamed) official agencies. Such things do happen. Hawks (1985) for instance cites evidence of seemingly systematic government suppression of reports from reputable national and international sources on the problems associated with alcohol consumption. All these reports, he argues, suggest that consumption is now such that the deleterious personal and social consequences cannot be handled by present or projected statutory services unless there is an overall reduction in such problems.

> Why are we being protected from such conclusions, you might ask. Not because of their scientific reliability—this has not been seriously challenged. I can only conjecture it is because of the unwillingness of governments to entertain a significant decline in the revenue earned as a consequence of the present high levels of consumption of alcohol, and their responsiveness to the arguments presented by the alcohol industry. (Hawks, 1985, p. 212)

Heroin is illegal, so sales should not contribute to the national revenue. But what about personal revenue? McCoy (1980) has demonstrated that a degree of both police and political corruption is needed if a heroin distribution network is to survive. A person with a well-established habit requires almost daily contact with street-level dealers, who in turn must make regular contact with wholesale distributors. The pattern is too predictable and essentially too public to escape detection unless the police are at least partially neutralised.

Even with police protection, though, the probability of at least occasional arrest and indictment of major organised crime figures is significant. McCoy argues that to minimise the damage on such occasions, criminal syndicates also need access to the courts and ruling political parties. Political contacts can block a concerted police offensive. More important, though, once public pressure develops for an anti-drug campaign, there is urgent need to influence the political structure to ignore that public pressure. One of the most effective ways of diffusing the issue is to ensure that viable data are either lacking or contradictory, and then to appoint yet another commission, task force or other official inquiry to investigate the matter.

There can be no doubt that such corruption exists and that it serves to protect and perpetuate the *status quo*. Nevertheless, it is equally clear that all forms of police and political corruption involve a minority within the total establishment, particularly at its senior levels. The majority, either because of the type of work they do or through personal inclination have no direct involvement in corrupt practices. The prospect of the damage that revelation of even a small amount of corruption can do to a public career probably keeps an additional number somewhat reluctantly honest. This same factor, however, also ensures that once corrupted, a public official usually remains a lifetime servant of the vice entrepreneurs. Still, it is both inefficient and dangerous for a criminal syndicate to corrupt any more than the absolute minimum number of officers. This small number undoubtedly impairs both the law enforcement and policy-making capabilities of a society, and any disclosure of their activities erodes both public esteem and internal morale. But it is naive to assume that the apparent lack of real progress on the drug issue is due solely to the dilatoriness and obfuscation of corrupt police and politicians.

'Political will,' according to McCoy (1980), 'is paramount in any campaign to either reduce or eliminate the major vice trades, narcotics included' (p. 39). However, with the best will in the world, government bodies face almost insuperable problems in attempting to deal with drug use. Politicians, as Hackett (1986) puts it, must 'struggle with the art of the possible' (p. 272).

In the first place, governments must work within a particular political philosophy. Thus, when the *Baume Report* (1977) recommended sweeping changes in Australia's official attitude to legal drugs like alcohol and tobacco, the then government's philosophy of free enterprise restricted its ability to act on many of the recommendations. When community pressure for some sort of action became insupportable, it responded by channelling resources into such politically safe ventures as the National Drug Education Program.

There are also some facts of which politicians may be perfectly well aware, but which they cannot afford to see—literally. Thus, if Hawks (1985) is correct, a treatment response to alcohol problems is no longer feasible. 'The expense of such facilities if they were ever seriously contemplated would beggar the health budgets of even the most affluent countries. We are able to indulge the notion that the problem could be coped with if only there were sufficient facilities precisely because such facilities are not remotely attainable' (p. 212). Faced with such dilemmas, it is always possible to fall back on the need for more precise information before further expanding facilities one has no real ability to expand. In the same vein, Drew (1982) points out that a truly functional National Drug Education Program would require a supply of competent educators with special expertise in this area, and providing effective treatment services for persons with drug-related problems also presupposes a sufficient number of persons with special skills. Supplying either of these requires time and a large investment of coordinated effort, and this is not in line with community expectations of a quick response to a perceived need.

Nor is there likely to be the required amount of money. The fact that there is no consensus on the relative merits of different educational strategies could then be seen as an advantage. An obvious need for more information can avert or at least delay a potentially disastrous confrontation.

There are other facts the government simply chooses not to see, because that is what the community as a whole is doing. The government and the public service are both part of the community. Their policies reflect community thinking and community demand, and as such they will embody the attitudes of those who are used to, and able to, make their voice heard in some way. Governments must attempt to stay in power, so an action that would lose too many votes cannot be contemplated. In this regard, some community groups constrain government action more than others. State and federal bureaucracies are entrenched power bases and some professional groups such as doctors or law enforcement agents are also strongly placed to resist government intrusion. Any attempt to implement policies that threaten either will be met with great hostility and coherent defensive action. As Baume (1977) summed up, the surest way to have a recommendation ignored is to advocate the disbanding of jobs or areas of responsibility. Lest a holier-than-thou attitude creep in, readers should honestly consider what their own 'rational self-interest' reaction would be if their personal livelihood or their basic principles seemed to be threatened.

The curious thing about all such vested interest groups is that if one goes back far enough—and sometimes this is not very far back at all—one almost always finds a person or group whose motives, intentions and actions were unimpeachable and often wholly admirable. People become concerned and agitate about genuine issues. Prohibition began this way; so did the feminist movement, and gay liberation, and the movement to save the whales. And so did Alcoholics Anonymous. Yet, in all these cases, one almost inevitably finds that intolerance, dogmatism and manoeuvres that can only be described as questionable creep in. One of the better recent examples of this is the storm that greeted Sobell and Sobell's (1984a, 1984b) suggestion that some 'alcoholics' could return to controlled drinking. The whole affair is far from untangled, but it appears that the allegations made against them and their work, when not motivated by personal malice, seem to have drawn their inspiration from vested interests, including Alcoholics Anonymous in America. Having persuaded the public that the only way out of alcoholism was total and lifelong abstinence, these interests were reluctant to have this regime challenged. Very little Christian charity seems to have been shown in the process.

The nature of moral crusaders and their endeavours is explored further in Chapter 7. What concerns us here is the inevitable result of their 'institutionalisation'. However selfless the original motives, crusades have a way of generating increased self-interest and people come to support them for reasons that are less than pure. Many industries, for example, supported Prohibition because they felt it would provide them with a more manageable labour force. The crusaders themselves may develop what began as an amateur interest in a moral issue into a full-time job. Becker (1966) has examined this process in some detail. When a crusade succeeds, it leaves the crusaders without a vocation. Their interests then often generalise to other evils and they become professional discoverers of wrongs to be righted. This is particularly so if the crusade has produced a large organisation devoted to its cause, and some such institutionalisation is almost inevitable. Crusaders themselves are rarely concerned with mundane details like drawing up the new rules in suitably formal terminology. For this they usually enlist the help of various professionals, all of whom have personal interests which will tend to affect the legislation they prepare. Thus, much of the current debate on drug issues is medico−legal, because policy at the international level rests with the World Health Organisation. Were it in the hands of the Council of Churches, the regulations would doubtless be framed very differently, though not necessarily any more effectively.

It seems, therefore, that if a crusade is successful and new rules are established, institutionalisation is almost inevitable. What started out as a drive to convince the world of the moral necessity of a new rule finally becomes an organisation devoted to the enforcement of that rule. Such organisations must both prove their *raison d'etre* and ensure their future existence. On the one hand, they must show that their attempts at dealing with the problem are effective and worthwhile; on the other, they must demonstrate that the problem still exists. As Becker (1966) puts it, 'First, they say that by reason of their efforts the problem they deal with is approaching solution. But, in the same breath, they say the problem is perhaps worse than ever (through no fault of their own) and requires renewed and increased effort to keep it under control' (p. 157). Becker was referring specifically to law enforcement agencies. However, the same scenario is equally applicable to treatment centres and, for that matter, to research institutions.

The number of jobs created by what might be called the legitimate branch of the illicit drug industry is remarkable and the fund-raising efforts to date are impressive. In 1973, the Executive Director of the United States National Committee on Marijuana and Drug Abuse remarked that 'this year we have spent 796.3 million dollars and the budget estimates that have been submitted indicate that we will exceed the one billion dollar mark. When we do so, we become, for want of a better term, a drug abuse industrial complex' (Sonnenreich, 1975). That was more than a decade ago. In Australia, the taxes on alcoholic beverages nearly meet the cost of the doctors, social workers, psychologists, nurses and administrators whose main task is to treat the diseases and injuries caused by excessive drinking (Whitlock, 1982). The 1986 National Campaign Against Drug Abuse had a budget of $A60 million from the federal government alone. This did not include matching funds from individual states, and it did not include the cost of the vast machinery of government departments, enforcement, education and treatment oragnisations, both public and private, that were already in place. A growth industry indeed!

It is not surprising that governments have found it difficult to depart from entrenched policies. All the agencies and individuals concerned with the drug industry depend to a greater or lesser extent on being able to sell their ideas, programs or whatever better than their nearest rivals. There is mistrust and lack of cooperation at all levels, and people either withold information, or present it in variously skewed ways. In other words, they use declared rather than known statistics.

In fact, preoccupation with statistics really comes into its own during such interindividual and interagency power struggles. As Lindesmith (1968) has pointed out, emphasis on statistics is a particularly effective way to excuse laxity of research. Human behaviour, the reasoning goes, is too complex and too dynamic, and varies too much from culture to culture and from person to person, to be dealt with in any other way than in the aggregate or on the average. Such a position, of course, makes any theory unverifiable: the exceptions that would negate it are admitted in advance. If one is concerned only with some, many or most addicts, any number of theories becomes possible, each of them applicable to some addicts in some place at some time, and none of them applicable to all addicts anywhere. Under such circumstances no grounds exist for saying any such theory is wrong, that one is right and the others wrong, or that one is better than another. Acceptance of one above the others becomes a matter of personal taste or professional prejudice.

The result, as Brown and her colleagues (1986) describe it, is:

> ... facilitation of bitterness, despair and powerlessness in both clients and care workers, breakdown in effectiveness, tendency for empire building, pervasive insecurity with the maintenance and continuity of programs and funding failures which often lead to 'quick fix' programs. The professionals in general mistrust the media; the media in turn grasp at the sensational, the here and now and the trivial in the absence of cooperative policies. The politician is left poorly, ambiguously and irrationally informed. (p. 30)

The politician comes off rather too well in that analysis, and the agencies rather too badly. We earlier concluded that the general confusion of the official drug scene is not entirely due to government corruption. Neither, however, should the scramble for public monies lead us to conclude that what is really happening is that honourable, public-spirited and far-seeing politicians are being deliberately thwarted in their quest for the truth by the unscrupulous rulers of dozens of petty kingdoms. The embattled kingdoms are certainly there, and so are corrupt politicians. However, probably the most important reason for the lack of coherent policy is that political decisions, like those of most of us, are built around pragmatism, compromise, decency, expediency and ignorance, in more or less equal measure. Avoidance of drastic action is a very attractive strategy under the circumstances. The situation with hard data in the drug field being what it is, each rival theory can continue to press its claims with confidence. The politicians, for their part, can rest secure in the knowledge that none of them *have* to be supported until additional information can be gathered.

'We have met the enemy and they is . . .'

Every society makes rules for itself and it enforces them by defining certain behaviours as essential for group membership. These become what Levi-Strauss has called a society's 'totems'. Brown and her colleagues (1986) analysed the views on drug abuse submitted as part of the Australian National Campaign Against Drug Abuse in an attempt to assess popular feeling on the subject. They identified protection of the Australian community and of the family as the dominant national totems in this regard. Other important ones were an emphasis on education as a desirable strategy, an unwillingness to impose moral values and an active commitment to social equality as defined in pragmatic, materialist terms.

At the same time, conflicting totems of encouraging competition, in the sense that all people are entitled to do the best they can for themselves, and accepting a moral responsibility to treat and to punish were put forward by a substantial minority. Despite the emphasis on education as a preventive strategy and Australia's supposed 'child centred' orientation, protection of children was not given much emphasis. The more intellectualised submissions pointed out the virtues of community action and peer support, but at the level of practical involvement this seemed to translate mainly into the feeling that 'the clean, tidy nature of treatment as an option is aesthetically preferrable to the bleakness of a prison or the scruffiness of a community agency' (Brown et al., 1986, p. 193).

Social rules are even more importantly enforced by 'taboos'. Taboos are not simply rules against particular behaviour. They are a denial that such behaviour could even be considered. Incest and cannibalism are classic examples—behaviours which so threaten the family unit that they are regarded as unimaginable. Where laws are created to deal with infringements of the totems, tabooed behaviour tends to be actively denied and ignored. Heroin addiction remains 'so severely taboo that neighbouring families have no idea that they have a common problem, and parents deny even to themselves the evidence of their own eyes' (Brown et al., 1986, p. 7).

The crucial point is that these often inconsistent totems and taboos represent sincerely held societal values. No overt hypocrisy need be involved. People's understanding of the world and their mental picture of what an ideal person or society should look like is built up from earliest youth by interaction with significant individuals, communities and organisations. By young adulthood, it is no longer something that can be examined strictly analytically. Things simply *are* so; one's values are a matter of identity and feeling, not of rational deduction. 'The world in our heads allows us to make sense of the chaos in the universe but it also creates dogmatism and stops us from seeing that one man's totem is another's taboo.' (Brown et al., 1986, p. 47)

World views change with history. Mugford (1982) presents this example:

> Less than a century ago both Britain and America had numbers of nice, upright middle-class ladies who were members of the Women's Christian Temperance Union (WCTU). This group inveighed against the evils of demon drink. Lips that touched liquor would never touch theirs. Ironically (to us) what did touch their lips, in many cases on a regular basis, were bottles of patent medicine, laced not only with alcohol but, more importantly, with stiff doses of opium derivatives. Not to put too fine a point on it, many of these women were addicts.
>
> If I seem to poke fun at these ladies, to make them pathetic hypocrites, let me at once say that this is not my intent. Hypocrites a few of these people no doubt were, and many were somewhat self-righteous. Nonetheless, the vast bulk were sincere and concerned people. People who saw the evil consequences of unfettered alcohol consumption all around them, people disgusted by public drunkenness, alcohol-encouraged wife-beating and child abuse and the neglect of offspring by drunken parents . . .
>
> Rather, my purpose in discussing the opium-using WCTU member as an historical irony is to draw attention to the fact that today we have many equally decent and sincere people who are (rightly) horrified by the evil consequences of heroin abuse but think nothing of offering their dinner guests a pre-dinner Martini or scotch, opening some rather nice bottles of riesling and claret, and gradually progressing in the later evening to port, brandy and coffee.
>
> Are these people then hypocrites? In general, as with our WCTU ladies, the answer is no. They are properly concerned about a genuine problem. The point, however, is to realise that fashions and prejudices change . . . The first lesson of an historical approach . . . is to realise that the *status quo* has nothing particularly 'natural' about it. (pp. 61–2)

Our degree of concern with particular drugs and with their current legal or illegal status is therefore a matter of historical accident as much as anything else. And for every period, it will be possible to bring forward evidence that at least some of this concern is justified. A more critical problem, though, is that world views may also vary *within* a given period of time. There is no such thing as a single, monolithic society, and its many subgroups—ethnic, professional, religious, economic and so on—can and do hold different views on a great many issues. These views do more than define what is or is not a problem. They also specify acceptable solutions and the strategies that may legitimately be used to achieve such solutions.

Thus, a world view which sees the ideal society as some form of corporate state dictatorship would emphasise the role of the government as a preserver of moral values. Persons with such a world view tend to look to the government to provide guidelines about the legitimacy of particular forms of drug use; they are also inclined to accept legal control and compulsory treatment as appropriate and necessary measures.

By contrast, a world view that sees its ideal society as a socialist democracy would tend to underplay moral issues and to concern itself more with pragmatic human needs. Here legal controls on drug use would probably be more limited and there would be greater concern with providing voluntary access to treatment and support.

An anarchistic world view would place as few restrictions on human behaviour as possible. There would probably be no legal controls on drug use, but neither would there be sympathy for providing more than very limited treatment facilities or support mechanisms.

A number of other world views are possible, each specifying a particular ideal society, particular values, and, logically, different positions on drug use. Brown and her colleagues (1986) have identified no fewer than seven operating concurrently in present-day Australian society. The same contradictory mixture operates within political parties, and indeed within all interest groups of any but the smallest size. Under the circumstances, there *can* be no such thing as objective data, unemotionally interpreted. Drew (1982) argues this way:

> Subjective factors will always remain as an important element in putting meaning into our aims. Often, whether or not a given event is regarded as a benefit or harm, and how much value should be placed on each element in a cost-benefit equation, will be a matter of personal judgement. Because of this, any general aim ... will have considerably different meanings depending upon who is relating it to a real-life situation ...
>
> What emphasis will be given to palliative measures (directed against drugs) and what emphasis to corrective measures (directed to broader issues)? What balance will be drawn between attempts to protect the weak by regulation of behaviour and encouragement of responsible freedom of choice through education and exposure to risk? A choice must be made between attempting to develop the potential of the disadvantaged and regulating the expression of deviance. Decisions must be taken about the priorities to be accorded to economic issues (such as government income and industrial prosperity), and to more human considerations (such as the impact on health and welfare).
>
> These are deeply emotive issues, so it cannot be expected that

> decisions could be based on objective factors alone.
> Persons with privilege usually wish to retain that status and to believe that their behavior is normative. The use of corporate power to suppress problems is always an attractive policy option. As drug-related problems are closely interrelated with disadvantage and lack of privilege or power, the promotion of conformity and regulation of deviance are thus more attractive options than developing healthy, responsible non-conformity (self-responsibility) and investing significant resources in reducing the gap between the haves and have-nots of society. This is a strongly inbuilt social mechanism, not easily responsive to rational argument.
> It can hardly be surprising that most people, governments and commissions of enquiry elect to give a major priority to simple palliative, control-oriented policies which promise quick results, rather than to explore radical and long-term corrective options. (pp. 9–10)

Unfortunately, none of these 'quick fix' solutions can be effective, even in the short term, because they do not address 'the problem' as the community sees it. Much of the debate about drugs is not about drugs at all: rather, it provides what Goode (1984) has described as an 'occasion for ideological expression'. For Hackett (1986), similarly, the drug problem is:

> ... a mislabelled portmanteau: open it, and you find a need to discuss things not on the label. The drug problem turns out to be 'really' about things like unresolved attitudes to neurochemical by-passing of the human motivation to work, and about the fear that your children will become changelings. Deeply felt approval/disapproval judgements surge up around what we (and others) believe we ought to be doing. Right versus wrong. Good versus evil. Anger. Envy. Guilt. (p. 271)

'Drugs' are being used as a scapegoat for social problems and conflicts that are too difficult or too painful to tackle. The best drug use statistics in the world—and, as we have seen, the best are none too good—would not help policy makers solve these problems. The belief that the crucial policy questions about drugs can be resolved simply by carefully weighing the scientific, medical and statistical evidence accumulated by objective researchers is one of the commonest, most subtle, and also most destructive myths to bedevil this complex field.

So what is to be done? In such an emotive area, it is clearly unrealistic to talk about 'purely rational' policies, but it is still essential that decision making should take account of the best data available. More comprehensive and more validly derived statistics must be sought.

However, while some of the most obvious flaws of the present data collection procedures can be corrected, such data will always be 'declared' rather than 'known' statistics. That is, the material presented as objective scientific data will have inevitable ideological underpinnings. Someone, a real person with definite goals and prejudices, is doing the best he or she can. This does not invalidate the statistics—provided that the limitations are understood and actively taken into account.

At the same time, there needs to be a far greater emphasis on the evaluation of both the means and ends of policy decisions. All policies have costs as well as benefits, and there have been few situations indeed where even an attempt has been made to assess them critically. Thus, the very illegality of heroin inevitably increases the use of unsterile injection techniques and with this, the risk of both serum hepatitis and AIDS. In the second case, unsuspecting and perhaps utterly drug-free others will be exposed to a disease for which there is presently no cure. Similarly, the link between a drug's illegal status and the development of a whole network of criminal activities spanning users, dealers, corrupt professionals and uninvolved victims is also clear. Despite this, I have yet to see a convincing attempt to cast a balance sheet.

Consider a specific example. The National Campaign Against Drug Abuse produced, among other things, a policy on methadone as a preferred treatment for heroin addiction. There is no clear evidence generally, and certainly none in Australia, that this means of treatment is uniquely useful. Moreover, no consideration at all was given to what the potential results of such a policy might be. Addicts might be helped to a drug-free life. Or there might be no change in the level of addiction, or even an increase. Would we have, eventually, a situation in which large numbers of addicts were socially accepted? Or one in which social misfits were expected to live out their lives in passive dependence on some controlling authority? Simply, we do not know enough to predict what the methadone policy will do, and how it will affect either its targets or the larger community around them. What is worse, we have not tried to find out. That is not the way to build a viable policy.

If our community appears to lurch from crisis to crisis, as if by accident, we have only ourselves to blame. There is no point in blaming the government. In Pogo's immortal words, 'We have met the enemy and they is us.' But useful change is hard to come by. It needs commitment, skill, tolerance and an understanding of the process of change. Unrealistic calls for a rational policy will hardly be helpful in themselves. Drew (1982) argues that those who want change must participate constructively in the process by which change can be brought about. 'Persuasion is the key element. Only a small but vital part of this process relates to objective and quantifiable matters. The rest relates to the much more complex areas of individual emotion and group process' (p. 13). Only when the public's perception of the nature of the problem changes and some of the persistent misunderstandings and yearnings for simple solutions are dispelled will official policy be able to follow suit.

7
Heroin users and heroin addicts

The individual or agency which offers intervention to the dependent person inevitably bases the intervention upon philosophic premises relevant to the intervenor ...

RELIGIOUS: *Use is sinful. The answer lies in penance and prayer.*

LEGAL: *Abuse and its antisocial problems must be countered by stringent actions.*

ANALYTIC: *The roots of the ... problem lie in early unresolved problems. Lie on the couch.*

SOCIAL WORK: *No—the problem is in the present social faults. Let us convene a family counselling session.*

INSTITUTIONAL: *Let us place you in a safe place for a few months to facilitate change. Don't worry about the $200 per day cost. The fund will take care of most of that.*

ALTERNATIVE HABIT: *That chemical is bad for you. Have this one instead and as long as you keep coming back for it, we will keep you out of trouble.*

SOCIAL ENGINEERING: *This problem reflects faults in the workplace, the environment, the community, the level of availability. Let us initiate some legislative changes.*

MEDICAL BANDAID: *The symptoms in your nerves and stomach should settle with these tablets.*

ADDICTIVE PERSON: *Don't listen to what the so-called experts say. You are like us and we understand. Your personality, your metabolism, and your allergy to this drug. All you have to do is accept that you belong here.*

ADDICTIVE BEHAVIOR: *You have, like so many others in various ways, slipped into a habit which gave you temporary ease from*

> stress discomfort. *Now you are hooked on this habit. However, if you decide to change you can, and then become a completely normal and comfortable person.*
>
> *... The addicted person must be wooed in an acceptable way. And if we see him at a crisis point when he is susceptible, then we must be flexible enough to use the right bait. If we are overly concerned with our own philosophy and ego, we may turn off the customer. And however righteous we feel, we may have stuffed up his chance of finding a way out.*
>
> Pat O'Neill, 1985, p. 103

The mythology of drug use

What do we envisage when we hear that someone 'uses drugs'? The drug is heroin, of course—'the evil heroin, dispensed by the Mafia through the vilest of all criminals, the pusher' (Bell, 1974, p. 37). The user, moreover, has lost all sense of ethical and moral direction. Anything can be expected, however shocking and outrageous, if heroin is scarce. The user, in other words, is an addict. Naturally we do not personally know such people, though we may worry that our innocent children might run into them and be misled. Certainly we would never live next to one, share any of their ideals or buy them a drink. The user is one of 'them'.

In fact, the user looks very much like the next-door neighbour and the drug of choice is usually perfectly legal—alcohol, tobacco, coffee or aspirin. If it is illicit, it is least likely to be heroin and, even if it *is* heroin, the user is unlikely to be an addict. Clearly we need to take a closer look at our mythologies.

Myths about drugs and drug users

One of our most insidious myths is that we know what we mean by 'drug'. That, in reality, has been the subject of endless debate and I have discussed it at length elsewhere (Krivanek, 1988). For our purposes in this discussion, there can be no doubt that heroin is a genuine drug by any definition.

All the illicit 'drugs' about which we are currently upset are classified in this way because they supposedly have a *high addiction potential*, but addiction is actually not a property of drugs at all. Addiction is a property of the *user*. Drugs merely have particular effects. All of these are dose-dependent and most are strongly influenced by the user's physical and subjective state. In a very real sense, the effect a drug will have on a person depends on the effect he or she expects (or hopes or fears) it will have and this in turn depends on that person's sociocultural environment. Yet we persist with our myth that the danger somehow resides in the drug and that prohibiting its use will solve the 'problem'. The 'problem', incidentally, is whole droves of people becoming helpless victims of drug craving, with inevitable subversion or even dissolution of personal discipline, productivity and morality. No drug can produce these effects; every person, however, can choose to behave in this way, and drug use is only one of many behaviours that may be associated with the syndrome.

Just as drugs can be classified as legal and illegal depending on society's current degree of concern about them, drug use can be considered proper or improper. In every case, the distinction has very little to do with the actual drugs and their effects. What is more important is the adoption of a particular set of values. Terms like 'abuse' and 'misuse' are value judgements and they are impossible to define without reference to specific drugs under particular conditions. I had earlier defined misuse as the use of a substance 'when other alternatives are available, practical or warranted, or where use endangers either the user or others' (Krivanek, 1982, p. 82). This definition retains the value judgement that doing it with drugs ought not to be a first course of action, either in medicine or in everyday life. This does not mean that drugs should never be used, or even that they should be used only as a last resort. Simply, they should be evaluated as merely one of a number of possible alternatives, with the clear understanding that among their many effects some will be beneficial while others may be harmful. The concept of the 'magic bullet', a drug that has a single action only, is one of the most persistent myths about drug use. Closely allied to it is the idea that all users use drugs for the same reason. With illicit drugs, of course, the reason can only be reprehensible.

When a person misuses a drug within this definition, that is, where *use begins and continues when other alternatives are available, practical and warranted*, even if there is no immediate harm to the user or to others, it is reasonable to suppose that the drug effects or some aspects of the drug-using situation have become important to that person. The term 'psychological dependence' will be used to describe this state of affairs and the phenomenon will be discussed more fully below. For the moment, let us see it simply as an orientation toward and a tendency to repeat an activity that is personally rewarding. The intensity of a psychological dependence can vary from a mild involvement to behaviour that an observer would call irrational and even self-destructive. An 'addict' is someone who is involved with an activity to such an extent that it becomes the major focus of his or her existence. This is not an absolute state and no arbitrary line can be drawn between mere dependence and addiction.

Psychological dependence extreme enough to be called addiction can develop with any number of activities, from growing roses to pursuing a particular career goal. As a society, we are more upset by some forms of addiction than by others, and at the moment we are especially upset about addiction to some forms of drug use. One of our current myths is that certain substances, notably heroin, have the inherent and magical ability to produce addiction, and that they can, moreover, do so on first exposure. One shot and you are hooked. We do not generally make this error with, say, alcohol. But while all drinkers are not regarded as hopelessly hooked, users of heroin are generally assumed to be well on the road to physical and moral ruin. The development of addiction is seen as inevitable.

Confusing users with addicts has a number of serious consequences. Society has very definite ideas about what addicts look like, what they do, how this pattern changes in time and what the eventual outcome will be. Maintenance of such stereotypes is one of the ways in which the drug problem is compounded. They influence not only society as a whole but the behaviour of drug users as well. In a very real sense, they act as self-fulfilling prophecies, setting up expectations that users may consciously or unconsciously seek to meet or, sometimes, to prove incorrect.

Treating users like addicts also tends to aggravate their problems. For instance, reluctance to employ known users or their dismissal upon discovery literally puts them 'on the street'. Wender (1968) called this 'deviance-amplifying feedback'. The negative effects of accepting the sick role mandated by the overtly humanitarian disease or 'medical' model of addiction can also be major, and they will be discussed separately below.

Finally, cultural intolerance also preselects users. It stands to reason that individuals who use drugs strongly disapproved by their culture will be ones whose attitudes deviate markedly from the prevailing social norm. A drug habit may therefore be associated with problem behaviour not because of the drug's effects or the cultural perception it evokes, but simply because it tends to be adopted by 'problem' individuals in the first place. This of course merely confirms cultural beliefs about the dangerousness of the practice and tends to increase general disapproval. It also ensures that people in treatment or in corrective facilities are likely to be more disturbed and the condition as a whole to be less amenable to intervention.

In fact, for a very long time, the maintenance of the stereotype that users are addicts has permitted us to assume that addicts do not move in our circles and addiction is someone else's problem. The reality is that most of us use and misuse many substances. In addition, the stereotype also makes clear what ought to be done and who should do it. If they refuse to stop doing things that upset us, addicts are clearly criminals and we can invoke the force of the law. If they seem unable to do so, they are clearly sick and require medical care or at least psychological rehabilitation. Either way, average citizens—like us—need not, indeed cannot be involved.

Myths about ourselves

For most people, drug use is something addicts do and addicts are different. We could never be like *them*. In fact, our stereotypes and prejudices are showing. If we are referring to addicts' *addictions*, then the vast majority of us *are* like them. Everyone has not one but many psychological dependencies, and may be sufficiently involved with some of these to qualify as an addict. The focus of the addiction might be work, exercise or television watching.

If we are referring to their *drug* addiction, then the only difference between many people and addicts is the drug of choice. Substance use—whether of drugs, herbs or vitamins—to solve psychological and even social problems is today virtually ubiquitous. The purveyors of all these chemical problem solvers are legitimate multi-million-dollar industries and their volume of business increases yearly. Yet in spite of this, and in spite of a proliferation of medical technology and an enormous increase in the number of helping professionals of all types, people seem to be feeling worse. More working days are being lost through illness, more prescriptions are being issued and more patients are being admitted to hospital than ever before (Inglis, 1983). What has gone wrong?

Several issues are involved here. Many claim that people are having more problems, that modern life is too complex and too pressured for ordinary human beings. Actually the pace of modern life is probably not too different from that of earlier centuries. Rather, a number of things that were earlier accepted as facts of life have now been elevated to problem status. The new thing about the twentieth century is the existence of a vast industry for the creation of problems—'even if it be no more than letting you know that the kitchen mop you've always used has been a complete waste of time and energy' (Davies, 1986, p. 80).

However, we can also ask why people choose to solve so many of these problems through medication rather than by other means. One reason is that drugs are a commercial commodity. Pharmaceutical manufacturers wish to sell their wares and they use conventional marketing strategies to do this. Davies (1986) draws the following parallel:

> A. Grubby shirt collars look terrible! Get rid of the muck with 'X' laundry liquid; your husband will love you for it.

B. Tensions make your life a misery. They cause headaches. Use 'Y' to get you back on your feet. You'll smile again.

The commercial formula of *problem identification, problem ramification, problem solution and happy aftermath* works for both laundry liquid and drugs. We are not, as numerous inquiries have noted, encouraged to discover *why* we suffer tension, anxiety or headaches. We're simply informed that tension is bad and its symptoms must be eradicated. It seems we live in an age when *substances* can make life meaningful and prosperous. 'Feeling down?' ask the ads, 'then maybe you don't get enough fibre' or 'maybe you need more vitamins.' The relationship of substance intake to the state of mind and body is constantly reinforced. (p. 81)

But the situation is more complex than this. We need to understand how it is that people came to accept the objectively rather odd idea that a tablet can solve their interpersonal problems or help them through the day and, moreover, why they believe that taking the tablet according to a doctor's prescription is proper behaviour while buying the same tablet on the street is not. No single factor can explain this situation, but the changing role of medicine is central.

The transformation of medicine from an art into the major science it now claims to be is generally considered to have begun in the seventeenth century, when Giovanni Borelli advanced the theory that bodily ailments were analogous to problems with machines—grit in the works, insufficient lubrication, wear and tear. This 'mechanist' or 'organicist' theory was initially opposed by the 'vitalists', who claimed that diseases resulted from problems with one's life-force, but during the eighteenth century the mechanist theory gradually took over. Inglis (1983) traces the milestones of its progress through Claude Bernard, whose concept of homeostasis seemed to point to a built-in mechanism to counter disease and Charles Darwin, whose theory of evolution suggested that such adaptations could arise by chance. When Pasteur and Koch demonstrated that diseases like smallpox and tuberculosis resulted from infection by microorganisms, the case for organic causation of disease seemed unassailable. To be sure, Pasteur had insisted to his death that the 'terrain' was as important as the germ: pathogens, he argued, could only flourish where the host was accommodating. However, this was conveniently forgotten, and more and more diseases came to be attributed to single causes like bacteria, viruses or toxins. By the 1920s, Paul Ehrlich was predicting the discovery of 'magic bullets'—specific drugs for specific diseases.

Mechanism and materialism were of course not restricted to medicine. They gradually pervaded society as a whole with machine-oriented technology, a preoccupation with 'efficiency' and with production for its own sake. The needs of individuals increasingly came to be secondary to the maintenance of this so-called progress. Along with these trends came the growing conviction that new technology was always better than the old, and that any problems produced by the new technology could always be solved by more technology. In such a climate, few new techniques are thoroughly tested prior to wide adoption, and virtually none is audited once it is in place. 'Possible' is increasingly equated with 'justified' and even 'desirable' and 'necessary'.

Medicine, like all other institutions, took its cues from the spirit of the times. It became increasingly dependent on technology, more power- and profit-oriented, and it seized all its opportunities. Taylor (1979) argues that it reached the commanding position it enjoys today by exploiting a more or less accidental concatenation of events that occurred about the time of World War II. This period saw a concentrated infusion of technology into most fields of endeavour. In medicine itself, there were improvements in anesthetic and surgical techniques. Mass immunisation had begun shortly before this time, and the 1940s brought the introduction of penicillin, the antibiotics and the anti-tuberculosis drugs. Ehrlich's magic bullets had become a reality—diseases with specific organic causes now seemed to have specific treatments. All these new techniques were genuinely effective. However, the claim that they and the doctors who managed them were responsible for the decline in mortality that had occurred in the previous 150 years was fraudulent. The reality was that most infectious diseases had already been markedly reduced by improvements in nutrition, hygiene and sanitary engineering, especially the provision of safer water supplies. Nevertheless, the claim was made and the public believed it. By extension, it has come to be assumed that the standard of health we enjoy today is due entirely to the vigilance of medicine and to its marvellous technology. 'The corollary is that were it not for doctors, medicines and vaccines, we would die off like flies and the infectious scourges would return with a vengeance' (Taylor, 1979, p. 15). Professional health care is now seen as essential, and the belief that doctors possess knowledge and skills that are too esoteric to be freely shared with the laity earns them great respect. This attitude is regularly reinforced by folklore, popular fiction and television serials, all of which depict doctors as all-knowing and paternal. It is also regularly reinforced by some members of the profession. The patient, by and large, is expected to be appropriately submissive and even to show a degree of credulity. The giving and taking of drugs has become an important part of this mystique.

> To many, the handing over of a prescription by the doctor to the patient signifies that the doctor cares, that he has recognised that a problem does exist and has understood its nature, that the transaction is complete and that recovery from the dysfunction

can be expected ... in many cases the medicinal benefit is probably minimal but the psychological benefit of a caring gesture may be considerable. This 'caring gesture' has very strong placebo implications. (Senate Standing Committee on Social Welfare, 1981, p. 118)

The reality is that people have been increasingly 'patientised'. With infections largely controlled and the major illnesses still largely incurable, we might expect modern medical practice to consist of supportive care for the terminally ill and routine management of such accidents of living as indigestion, fractures and the like. And so it does. However, doctors have also begun to sell *prevention*, not in the sense of preventing the development of disease but rather in the form of regular medical check-ups. The idea is that these will detect early asymptomatic stages of various major illnesses.

Such screening can have positive results, but only in a few special situations where clear-cut, effective therapies are available. A minority can benefit, therefore, and for them these benefits can be enormous. However, they are offset by some very real drawbacks the procedure poses for the majority. Most people who submit themselves to this routine are in good health and theoretically there is no reason why they should not remain so. However, their very compliance with the ritual suggests that there has been a subtle but devastating change in their perception of what good health really means.

By presenting themselves for inspection, they are in effect saying either that they do not regard themselves as healthy or that, although they feel healthy, they fear that they might not be. They are in fact the 'worried well' (Garfield, 1976): people who have been convinced that health is not a subjective feeling of well-being, but rather an objective state that can be achieved only when every test for every disease is negative. For such people, minor aches and upsets are all possible harbingers of serious illness and therefore require professional attention. Only extensive tests with the latest technology will convince them that monstrous maladies are not gnawing silently at their insides. And since anxiety can have marked effects on physical health, the threat of an illness may cause more disability than the illness itself. We are well on the way to becoming 'a nation of healthy hypochondriacs, living gingerly, worrying ourselves half to death' (Thomas, 1975, p. 1245), in the face of the reality that most health-promoting measures can be understood and carried out by normal, average people without regular medical supervision.

There has been another negative spin-off from this wholesale patientisation: the medicalisation of an ever-increasing number of human problems. Some see this as yet another example of medical empire-building and this is partly true. Mostly, though, it is a question of interacting vicious circles that enmesh both doctors and patients.

People have been trained to believe that health care is an expert's job. At the same time, the traditional extended family where elder relatives are on hand to advise on such matters is fast disappearing. The increasing mobility of much of the population means that close neighbourhood ties are also less likely. This throws the whole onus of expert health advice, however minor, on the medical profession. Consider the case of a young couple who have recently moved to a new city. When a child becomes ill, they have no alternative but to turn to the local doctor who will reassure them, but who will probably also prescribe something 'just in case'. The prescription is expected, as part of the ritual. The child then speedily recovers, and in most cases would have done so without any treatment. However, the doctor who wrote the prescription is unlikely to point that out. The parents understandably assume that recovery was due to the treatment and that all similar illnesses will require similar intervention if recovery is to be uncomplicated. Their children will grow up with the same idea, and in their turn pass it on to the next generation. The result is that 'increasing numbers of the population are becoming addicted to professional medical attention for minor illnesses ... and so are being converted from normal people, able to look after their own and their family's minor ailments, into patients' (Taylor, 1979, p. 222). In the process, they are also becoming addicted to the idea that medication is an essential part of ordinary, healthy living.

With the help of the media, people are also increasingly discovering a whole host of hitherto unsuspected problems. Some are transient physical discomforts; others are essentially interpersonal. They dislike their jobs, their spouses or themselves; there are material worries; they feel they or their children do not match up to society's expectations. None of these is properly the province of medicine at all, yet so persuaded is society by the fantasy that medical technology can end all personal suffering and that for every difficulty there is an appropriate medicine that these 'illnesses' increasingly end up in doctors' offices. The pharmaceutical companies, of course, exploit this to their great profit (a favourite pharmaceutical advertisement suggests the product for 'the pain that comes from not fitting in'). So do some doctors. Most, however, genuinely try to cope and they are generally ill-equipped to do so. Straton (1981) explains that medical students are trained to regard diseases as definite entities responsive to appropriate procedures. Later, faced with vague symptoms like anxiety, they tend to label them as a disease to legitimise their treatment, and since they are not usually trained in alternative ways of handling psychosocial problems they automatically write prescriptions. The general public, meanwhile, has also come to expect 'miracle cures' from 'wonder drugs'. The expectation that drug therapy is the appropriate treatment is reinforcend by the doctor's prescription, and so the vicious circle continues.

Among the conditions that have been medicalised in this way are depression, attempted suicide, anxiety states of all kinds, behaviour and learning difficulties in children and, ironically, drug addiction. Medical monopoly in these areas has given the impression that the solution for such problems lies in some new technical innovation or a new drug rather than in the elimination of underlying social, environmental and economic causes. According to Taylor (1979), the consequences have been far-reaching:

> Even when social factors *are* recognised as antecedents of various medical and psychological conditions, it is usually considered that the problem lies in the maladaptation of the *individual* to the society in which he lives. The reverse, that is, that there is something drastically wrong with the society that humans are being asked to adapt to, receives scant attention. Rather, those individuals who suffer from these modern 'diseases' are labelled as 'susceptibles' ... Normal people are becoming patientised, social problems are being individualised and medicalised, and the individual is being blamed for maladaptation to society rather than the present social and economic system being held culpable for such maladaptation on a grand scale. (pp. 223−4)

Taylor's argument is true enough, if somewhat overstated. However, it presents only part of the story. An additional aspect is that it would be quite difficult for doctors to do otherwise, for several reasons. At a personal level, it would be very difficult for individual doctors to accept that much of what they do for their patients is irrelevant and sometimes even harmful. One has to be very eminent to admit such a thing, and one does not reach eminence by making such admissions. A more general problem is that many would not know how to do otherwise. The *status quo* is sustained by one of the most powerful commercial concerns in the world, the pharmaceutical industry. Not only does it spend billions annually promoting its wares, but because of its effective control of medical journals it can subtly channel both medical research and medical education. Doctors have become increasingly dependent on drugs as their foremost therapeutic weapon. Individually, they may deplore this; collectively, they have left themselves almost powerless to end it. Nor is the government likely to be of much help in demedicalising society. Interfering with the pharmaceutical industry would seriously affect the gross national product. In any case, the health services sector has developed vested interest groups and self-maintaining bureaucracies and all of these would resist any attempt to reallocate resources.

All the same, the most important force maintaining the current patientisation, medicalisation and reliance on pharmaceutical problem solving is the *public*. People much prefer things the way they are. They are upset about the cost of it all and about some of the ugly side effects, but they are happy with the model. They like the way drugs offer quick and effortless solutions and they like the way relabelling their problems as diseases removes the need to feel personally responsible, either for the problems or for their cure. Illness, provided it is a 'real' one, that is, attested by a doctor and implying medical treatment, carries considerable gains. One is relieved of blame and onerous duties, looked after and even cosseted, in direct proportion to the perceived seriousness of one's condition. There is much comfort in the role of the helpless victim. But that is not the whole story. The element of choice has also been much reduced by the commercial brainwashing that goes along with it. This may have begun with the media, but it is now ably seconded by parents who brainwash their children. We have become a profoundly dependent people. We are convinced that most human problems are diseases that medicine can cure with wonder drugs or that we can cure for ourselves with wonder drugs, licit or illicit. Most of us have lost the ability to care for ourselves without medical, technological and chemical props.

It is essential to realise that *the wholesale movement of drugs into the recreational forum would not have been possible without this conviction that needs and wants can be solved technologically, and without the aura of legitimacy medicine has given to drugging.* We continue, without much logic, to be upset by the recreational use of particular drugs like heroin—but drugging, as such, is commonplace and unexceptionable.

It is useful to see a person's potential for drug addiction as a complex function of susceptibility and exposure (Bejerot and Bejerot, 1978). Susceptibility is a function of individual physiology, psychology and life experiences, and as such changes constantly. Every person has a degree of susceptibility to addiction. Whether it will actually occur depends partly on the current level of susceptibility and partly on exposure. Exposure refers not only to the actual availability of drugs but also to such factors as peer group attitude toward drug use and people's perceived need for drugs. Again, all these change constantly. Exposure may increase or decrease susceptibility, but in general the greater the exposure, the smaller will be the critical susceptibility necessary for addiction to occur. What we must realise is that for a whole complex of reasons, ours is a medicated, intoxicated society in which the use of drugs is a normal and accepted part of living. This means that our exposure to drugs is great and, individually and collectively, our baseline liability to drug addiction is substantial.

Why heroin?

Self-admistration of drugs characteristically begins in adolescence or young adulthood, and just about every conceivable facet of human life and activity has been implicated in this process by one researcher or another. I have discussed these issues more fully elsewhere (Krivanek, 1988), but two general points may be made here.

First, adolescent drug use is *functional*. It is not the senseless by-product of a disordered brain, or even of a disordered society. There are reasons for drug use and they are compelling ones. Drug use always fills a perceived need..In theory, at least, a particular need can be filled in a number of different ways. To some extent, the final choice an individual makes reflects the richness of opportunities afforded by the particular environment. Some offer many possible avenues for need fulfilment, some fewer. More important, however, is the individual's *perception* of which avenues are available and likely to be effective. When a person chooses a drug solution, he or she does so because it seems the most effective and/or the least onerous way to do things at the time.

The way in which people perceive their world and their options within it is a function of their sociocultural environment on the one hand and their 'personality' on the other. The latter depends critically on their relationships with significant others. The most important seem to be interactions with the immediate family in early and middle childhood, although the family continues to have considerable influence throughout adolescence and young adulthood. Sociocultural environment and family background, then, form the most important determinants of drug use.

Second, it is clear that adolescent experimentation with substance use is neither statistically atypical nor developmentally abnormal. Nor are adolescents who use drugs deficient in coping skills. Indeed, Baumrind (1985) has demonstrated that it is the most competent adolescents who are also most likely to experiment with drugs. Experimentation with some drugs like nicotine and alcohol might even be regarded as a step toward acceptable adult behaviour. But heroin is illegal and, unlike the equally illegal cannabis, it seems to have no social support whatever, tacit or otherwise. So what makes people experiment with this drug?

For some, it is perhaps the very expense, illegality and perceived riskiness of heroin that makes it attractive. However, most of those who try heroin do not have a positive drive to do so. Rather, as Field (1985) argues, they acquiesce. 'The willingness to try heroin can amount to as little as an inability to say no ... Simply put, people try heroin because they do not have sufficient reason not to do so' (pp. 24–5). Burroughs (1953) said much the same thing: 'you become a narcotics addict because you do not have any strong motivation in any other direction. Junk wins by default.' Both men are ex-addicts, and presumably should know.

According to Field (1985), a barrier to trying heroin is anything that provides enjoyment, satisfaction or fulfilment, or anything that is placed at risk by the act of using. 'The less there is to be sacrificed, whether principles or time or money, the easier it is to succumb' (p. 29). It is sobering to note that many of the factors that might be expected to act as barriers seem to be in a decline. These include traditional morality, religion and respect for the law. An active interest in anything could be a barrier, and so could driving ambition—yet both are conspicuously lacking in much of today's population. We have become a culture of spectators, not doers. And we must also remember that recreational drug use is firmly established in this society, as is the use of drugs to solve a variety of problems. By the time they reach their teens, most young people today are thoroughly indoctrinated to expect that drugs can both give pleasure and reduce discomfort, and that it is basically all right to use them for these purposes. Since the mythology of heroin together with its very expense seems to promise sublime, orgasmic pleasure, why not?

Finally, there is chance. Field (1985) calls it the 'link between availability and willingness'. Certainly some people have no barriers against drugs and are always willing to try whatever is offered. Even so, it is possible never to have contact with heroin. When an addict's history is reviewed, it is often tempting to piece together a series of events that seem to form an inexorable progression with addiction as the inevitable climax. In reality, the development of a career in addiction is not too different from the development of any other career. For the majority, many of the early choices are pure chance. One is in a particular place at a particular time and certain things happen while others fail to do so. As with any other career, each choice tends to narrow subsequent options and increasingly forces more and more specific subsequent choices, but the fact remains that the early links in the chain are largely fortuitous.

It is important to remember that our attempts to unravel the causes of heroin experimentation are hampered by the fact that most experimenters are inaccessible to formal research. Such knowledge as we have comes largely from reminiscences by hard core users about their early involvement with the drug, and there is every reason to suppose that their views and perhaps their actual experiences are not particularly representative. However, a few tentative conclusions may be made.

One is that while most people find the effects of a therapeutic dose of opiates neutral or pleasant, the first experience with illicit heroin is often disagreeable. For one thing, many people dislike the idea of injection, particularly self-injection. More important, the effects of heroin are not all positive. Many first-time users, for instance, experience at least nausea if not vomiting and while tolerance to this effect develops fairly quickly, the initial sickness can be enough to dissuade a neophyte user from trying the drug again. Other people may experience gross consciousness changes, perhaps even blackouts. Both the nausea and the mental clouding are dose-dependent, and Field (1985) suggests that their marked tendency to occur in neophyte users is partly due to the fact that their first dose is usually relatively high. The dose for a neophyte is necessarily guesswork. If, as usually happens, the initiator is someone who has personal experience with heroin, his or her own customary dose will probably be used as a guide. If the initiator has built up any tolerance to the drug, it will be almost impossible to remember how much less he or she once needed. As a result, many first-time users receive rather large doses, and negative side effects are quite likely.

Under the circumstances, it is not surprising that a significant number of experimenters do not proceed beyond their first or second experience. Dole (1978) estimates that perhaps one person out of 50 exposed to heroin becomes heavily involved with the drug. Even those who do not become sick and who have no special objection to needles do not automatically go on to regular use. Heroin is simply not their thing. Some of the various reasons why people try and subsequently reject heroin are illustrated by comments collected by Davies from senior high school students in 1985. They are particularly interesting because they tap into that normally invisible group that does not come to official attention.

> *Brian* is a year 12 Parramatta student and is the second eldest of a family of five. He describes his parents, both professional people, as 'middle class' and as having a high income. Brian achieves well at school, is an excellent athlete and has an enviable sex life. He told me:
> 'I went to a party at a girlfriend's place and we all got a bit pissed. There were some kids there sharing a needle and they said to me it was heroin and would I like some and like I said I was a bit pissed and I agreed to it . . . I felt a bit funny but other than that it was a waste of time.'

> *Damien*, also a year 12 Parramatta student, is a very different sort of character to Brian. He's a moody and often angry youngster who has always found both school and sport an uphill battle. He too comes from a middle class family and is a lone child. He uses marijuana 'whenever it's around':
> 'The dope was bad, you know. It's always fuckin' bad and I'd

just had a session with this shit cow-food stuff that I'd just paid twenty bucks for and I said "fuck this shit" and threw the bong across the room ... then after that Dave just said "come with me" and we went into his bedroom and had some smack ... It was sort of OK but I prefer the real thing—you know, the grass.'

Anne, a Westmead student from a lone parent home, says she first tried heroin in 1984 after she had run away from home. She explained how she stayed with some older kids who were friends of her sister:

'There was one guy there who was using it [heroin] all the time and he was a real shit but everyone else in the house had sessions with it whenever he offered it around ... I hated the needle most ... that was one of the reasons I went back home.'

Mario, an articulate year 12 student ... says he cannot remember how he came to try heroin:

'One of my mates really gets into the stuff and he's always tried to get me to try some and one night I did. Problem was it didn't do anything for me ... I don't know why I tried it in the first place. It's not me, I mean I don't even smoke dope ... Drugs don't make any sense.'

Ian ... relates how one night he went with a friend to a Blacktown pub:

'There were these two guys we met there and we played pool and got pissed and one of them kept telling me I was really cute and I was going to deck him when he offered me a free taste so I thought 'what the fuck' and we went out the back and he did it for me—put the heroin into my arm and all that ... Now I think it was dumb of me. I never done that sort of thing before ... I got really sick because of it ... I got all guilty afterwards.'
(Davies, 1986, pp. 69–70)

Some proportion of those who try heroin go on to become what might be called 'recreational users'—people who use occasionally, perhaps even regularly, typically in a social setting. The transition from experimental to recreational use is determined by many factors, but the overwhelming majority do it because they enjoy one or another of the drug's effects. They are not 'hooked', nor is their use necessarily a symptom of some deep problem in their lives. The reasons they give for using are much like those given by social drinkers. Relaxation, unwinding, celebration and companionable socialising with one's friends are high on the list.

Some recreational heroin users continue at this level for many years and never progress to more intensive use. We do not know how many. They are the successes and professionals never see them. What little we do know about them suggests that among the keys to their success are pretty much what one would expect: social competence, stability and the ability to adhere to a rigid, ritualised schedule of use. In the case of alcohol, some of the rituals that help prevent misuse are defined by social custom. Most drinkers accept the convention that drinking should preferably be done with meals, that one should never drink in the morning, drink alone and so on. Perhaps if we had similar customs for heroin, if the drug were better 'domesticated', there would be more successes. We will return to this possibility again in Chapter 8.

Making addicts out of users

A certain percentage of people who experiment with heroin become recreational users, and many probably control their use quite happily for years. For some, however, use escalates further. *Intensive users* use whenever the occasion offers, although they remain largely in control of their habits. In *compulsive users* the habit dominates, and quality of life is perceived as a direct function of the level of drug intake. Both these patterns of use, and especially the latter, might qualify the user as an 'addict'. What turns use into addiction?

In 1970, Duster asked the inmates of a California rehabilitation centre whether they had consciously decided to become addicts. Most said no. But almost all knew heroin was addicting before they took it, that heroin overdose could be fatal and that the strength of any particular purchase was unknown. The overwhelming majority also knew what the legal consequences of being caught would be. So ignorance cannot possibly be used to explain the first plunge into use. For Duster, the chief ingredient that makes addiction possible is belief that the self is indestructible—'Nothing like that could happen to me'—and this is certainly very important. Another factor is the normalcy of the experience for most pre-addicts.

The popular view is that people take drugs when unhappy, to flee from anxiety or to compensate for a permanent or temporary inability to cope with the real world. In reality, the first venture is usually an unplanned affair. One happens to be in the right place at the right time. Heroin is available through a friend or a group, and on the spur of the moment an offer is accepted. As we have seen, many never take it again. For those who do, the reasons for the second time are typically as normal and social as for the first. Since the initial effects are usually so pedestrian, the development of compulsive use becomes even more of a puzzle. A common theory is that the pre-addict slips gradually into a level of use where he or she can no longer 'take it or leave it'. Physical dependence develops, and it is the threat of withdrawal that maintains the behaviour from then on. Such a drift into addiction is observed often enough, but the importance of withdrawal is arguable. Today's addicts seem to be much less committed, not only to heroin itself but also to regular use. At the same time, there are innumerable instances of physically dependent persons who do not see themselves as addicts and who do not behave like conventional addicts.

The basic requirements for the development of addiction are actually deceptively simple. First, the prospective heroin addict is one who *lacks sufficient reasons for abstaining*. As Orford (1985) points out, a better perspective on the issue might be gained by turning the question around and asking why most people are *not* heroin addicts. Becker (1966) argues that for 'normal' people things they accept as desirable— like job, family and reputation—come to seem to depend on doing certain things and avoiding certain others, including heroin use. According to this theory, when a 'normal' person experiences a deviant impulse, he or she is able to check that impulse by thinking of the negative consequences that acting on it would produce. Too much is staked on continuing to be 'normal' to allow unconventional impulses much leeway. People can avoid conventional commitments by growing up ouside conventional society. They can also do it by having nothing staked on continuing to appear conventional—that is, by having no job, reputation and so forth to lose. Or they may deliberately set out to appear unconventional. Heroin addicts of all three types exist.

The second basic requirement for the development of an addiction is that the potential addict must be able to associate certain effects with the use of a drug. And finally, these effects must be highly positive, that is, they must fill a perceived need better or more conveniently than other readily available alternatives. With all three basics in place, the stage is set for *psychological dependence*, and it is on this foundation that a full-blown addiction may eventually be built.

Psychological dependence: the basis of addiction

A full discussion of this complex phenomenon is beyond the scope of this book, and I have examined it separately elsewhere. It is a state of mind, and in *Addictions* (Krivanek 1988) I have defined it *a psychological phenomenon that can vary in intensity from a mild involvement with a behaviour to an addiction that seriously restricts the actor's other behavioural options. It can centre around any situation, person or object, although particular forms of it may be more acceptable than others. The dependent behaviour is maintained by the degree of reinforcement it provides, and this in turn depends on the actor's perception of his or her need hierarchy and the likelihood that this course of action will meet the most important needs better than other available options.* I suggest we either retain the word 'addiction' for the upper extreme of this continuum or choose another more neutral term. Since none of the alternatives seem adequate, 'addiction' has been used throughout this discussion. The intent is merely to indicate relative intensity; it is essential to avoid assigning absolute values to the phenomenon. Any attempt to do so generates enormous problems. The concept of loss of control, for example, has long dominated scientific and lay formulations of addiction, and it is usually seen as a unitary state. However, this does not actually hold in any specific way. Even people who are very involved with drugs, who would be considered addicted or dependent by almost anyone's criteria, rarely take as much drug as they could. They can say no, up to a point, or perhaps one should say beyond a point. If they doubt their own strength in this regard, they may make quite elaborate arrangements ahead of a bout of use to ensure that they will run out of drug after a certain point. In other words, the degree of dependence, even when considerable, is invariably flexible and must always be considered to be relative.

I have already suggested that a person's potential for addiction is a function of susceptibility and exposure. The behaviour initially begins for reasons that are predominantly circumstantial or social—that is, exposure factors are relatively more important. Whether the behaviour will continue, however, depends on the association of that behavior with certain effects that are personally positive in the sense that they fill or remove an existing need. Susceptibility factors are therefore relatively more important in the maintenance of the behaviour, because once the person decides that he or she wants something, exposure can usually be actively altered to make it possible. The degree of psychological dependence developed, that is, the movement toward addictive levels of the activity, depends on the status of the need being filled or removed and on the relative effectiveness of the behaviour in achieving this.

A person's perceived needs can be arranged in a general hierarchy whose order may change somewhat with circumstances. Thus, the perception of the relative importance of food will depend on whether a person is currently hungry or not. However, over a variety of situations, the ranking of an individual's needs is rather constant. It is the needs near the top of a person's hierarchy that motivate behaviour most strongly and whose fulfilment is most reinforcing. If an individual is to become addicted to an activity, it is these needs that will be involved, and the activity will be one that the individual perceives to be most relevant to their fulfilment.

In *Addictions* (Krivanek, 1988), I also concluded that while drugs have been used to meet man's bodily, mental and spiritual needs since earliest times, they seem particularly compatible with the special needs generated by modern society. The current orientation toward drug use did not simply happen, and it was not created by the pushers. The problem is the customers. Drugs are all around us because we want them to be there. Drugs can be all things to all men. Heroin can reduce a psychological or physical pain, fill a spiritual void, confer an identity or kill time—up to a point and at a price. In all cases, the addict perceives use of the drug as providing the most convenient and effective means of filling a dominant need, and has no sufficiently strong disincentives against filling it in this way.

Stereotypes of addiction

Human needs are broadly similar, but the benefits to be derived from a particular dependency must ultimately be assessed in terms of each individual's own perceptions. Almost any behaviour between total indulgence, total asceticism and total self-destruction can become a reinforcer. The mere fact that the behaviour continues means that it is benefiting the actor in some way, although it may appear totally irrational to an outside observer.

Similarly, the movement from use to addiction occurs in not one but several ways, and different forces maintain the state once it is established. Situations can maintain an addiction, addicts themselves can maintain it, more or less wilfully, and in some cases several people have a stake in the process, with the actual addict only one member of a guilty group. All these situations require different therapeutic approaches if the problem is to be managed successfully. This being the case, we might expect that the image of heroin addicts would be enormously variable, and that a variety of etiologies would be accepted as a matter of course. Quite the opposite is in fact true. Heroin addicts have acquired a rather coherent stereotype in the public mind.

A typical composite picture of addiction runs something like this. Physically, addicts are adolescent or young males, unmarried or in an unstable relationship. Their educational attainment is low and they come predominantly from lower socioeconomic clases and from minority groups. Addiction is associated with a daunting list of personality disturbance, particularly of the passive—aggressive type, and a variety of medical conditions.

Behaviourally, addicts' work history is poor and the skills they offer the job market are minimal. While they can maintain superficial relationships they have no close friends and conventional leisure activities are minimal or non-existent. Most of their time is spent in drug-related activities; any remaining time is filled with action-oriented pursuits rather than intellectual ones. Addicts live in the present, with little concern for the past or future.

With regard to their drug use, a single drug, heroin, is generally preferred. Other drugs, if used, are boosters for the opiate high, or they enable the user to cut down on the amount of heroin needed. The cycle begins with smoking marijuana and proceeds to mainlining heroin. Once heroin use begins, it becomes a daily behaviour with constant increases in the frequency of use and the amount of drug taken. And from a community point of view, once a person has begun to use only two categories exist—the active addict and the recovered addict—and there are very few of the latter.

A consistent stereotype of what an addict looks like is possible because only a certain proportion of the total population of addicts comes to public attention. The overtness of one's behaviour is determined by many factors. A number of addicts will go to considerable trouble to ensure their visibility and they will spontaneously or with varying degrees of reluctance label themselves as addicts. They may or may not be addicted, indeed they may never have used any drugs, addicting or otherwise. Thus, a client of mine, who vehemently insisted that she was a heroin addict, was finally pressured into admitting that she had not scored yet, although she was working on it. In such cases, the addiction is to the principle of addiction rather than to drugs.

Labelling oneself an addict can produce a surprising number of benefits. For some, addiction is a highly admired status symbol and my young client was by no means an isolated case. Others use drugging as a way of rebelling against the establishment. For still others, it is a way to avoid conventional demands and responsibilities. However, most addicts become visible for much more mundane reasons. In spite of their best efforts, their drug use gets them into trouble. Those who overdose or develop physical complications end up in hospitals, although we become aware only of the ones who cannot afford private, confidential care and therefore seek out or are sent to public rehabilitation facilities. We also see those who are unable to support their use in ways that avoid arrest. The reason may be socioeconomic pressure or sheer ineptitude. The physical and social characteristics of such casualties are rather predictable. We would expect them to be relatively young, lower-or working-class indigents, or persons already known to the police for theft, prostitution or drug dealing—and so they are. Our generalised picture of an addict, then, is in part a self-fulfilling prophecy. The way we cast our nets virtually ensures that we will catch a particular type of fish. Our picture of addicts is based on a fragment of the whole at best, and generalisation from such data is dangerous.

Models of addiction

Helping professionals see the same subsets of addicts as those available to the law and to the public eye. Their stereotype of addicts is therefore much the same, but their opinions about who or what is responsible for this state of affairs vary with their preferred model. There are several such models, but since there is currently no agreement on how to gather and analyse data, they can neither disprove nor validate one another. They simply coexist. Each has its loyal adherents, and each pursues its particular version of truth about addiction in its own way. It is from these models that treatment strategies emerge.

THE 'MEDICAL' MODEL

Addiction is often portrayed not merely *like* a disease but *as* disease, and one of the abiding controversies in the field revolves around the location of this entity. Is it within the individual, or within the community? Another has to do with what its symptoms are, and there is a host of arguments about both its etiology and its treatment.

The classical view of addiction as a disease has its roots in the late-eighteenth and early-nineteenth centuries, and it was worked out for alcohol, not the opiates (Levine, 1978). Until that time, the dominant theme was that humans alone in the natural world were uniquely endowed with reason. If some broke laws or accepted rules of proper conduct, they did so with full knowledge of the adverse consequences that might follow. The assumption was that people drank and got drunk because they wanted to, and not because they 'had' to. In the seventeenth century and most of the eighteenth, alcohol did not permanently disable the will, it was not addicting and habitual drunkenness was not regarded as a disease.

As society moved toward industrialisation in the early part of the nineteenth century heavy drinking increased, and with it the agitation for temperance. The American Temperance Society was formed in 1827, and the prime movers in this trend were many medical professionals. One of these, Benjamin Rush, used the reports of many drunkards that they experienced an irresistible and overpowering desire for alcohol to formulate a novel concept of addiction.

'Addiction' originally referred to a process of Roman law whereby a thing or a person was formally made over to another person. It was a way of discharging a debt, and the issue of whether addiction made one a slave was a point of controversy with ancient lawyers. This meaning generalised, certainly by the 1600s, to a 'devotion', by one's own inclination, to a person, thing or practice. No necessary pejorative sense was attached; one could be 'addicte to filthie lust', or 'sincerely addicted to Almighty God'. For a time, the term was even in common use in subscribing letters—one signed oneself as someone's 'addicted servant'. Still, a sense of intensity and permanence was always implied, and it was doubtless this that led Dr Rush to use the term in his new formulation of inebriety as a 'disease of the will' and of drunkards as 'alcohol addicts'.

Rush proposed that the chief symptom of the new disease was loss of control over drinking, that the condition was permanent, and that abstinence was the only cure. At the root of this position was the belief that alcohol was inherently addicting. The older view that drinkers were in control of their drinking had been replaced by the idea that drink took control of the drinker—an interesting reversal to the original legal meaning of addiction. In the new framework, once drink took control, drinkers were no longer responsible for their actions.

Total abstinence as a solution to inebriety was enthusiastically adopted by the majority of temperance supporters in America, and the idea spread from there to Britain and other parts of Europe. The concept was marketed vigorously throughout the 1800s and in due course led to the alcohol prohibition of the 1920s. At the same time, however, it also markedly influenced social perceptions of other drugs. As we saw Chapter 2, many early 'addiction specialists' were not only physicians but also temperance supporters. By the time strong public sentiment against the opiates began to grow, the concept of the tremendous potential power of drugs was firmly established in both Britain and America. Indeed, opiates quickly replaced alcohol as the archetypal drugs. By 1952, the WHO Expert Committee was describing drugs in its 'addiction-producing' category as causing an irresistible need 'always and in all individuals', and morphine and heroin headed the list.

In the 1920s, the disease model of opiate dependence was very much that proposed by Rush for alcohol: these drugs had an inherent property of producing uncontrollable craving and, once begun, the disease inevitably progressed. Only one element of the classic disease model as it is defined today was missing: the concept of predisposition. This emerged in response to two developments, both motivated by practical rather than theoretical considerations. The first again concerned alcohol.

Prohibition in the United States ended in the 1930s and this created a problem. The idea that alcohol was inherently addicting obviously had to be abandoned. However, since the legal code retained the classical view of human responsibility, this meant that alcohol addicts would once again be held responsible for their deviant actions. The newly formed fellowship known as Alcoholics Anonymous (AA) was concerned about this and, in collaboration with medical sympathisers, 'rediscovered' a new concept of alcoholism as a disease (Room, 1972).

The aim was to elicit a more humane response from society and to provide alcoholics with access to treatment services, sick leave, insurance benefits and the like. The essential feature of the rediscovered disease concept was that only *some* people, the 'real' alcoholics, were susceptible to alcohol addiction, and that this was so because they had a special sort of physical vulnerability. For other drinkers alcohol posed no addiction hazard, though of course it might cause other problems.

Meanwhile, experts on opiate addiction were struggling with somewhat different problems. The drugs' ability to produce craving and uncontrollable use was generally thought to reflect actual pharmacological properties, and this implied that physical dependence was the only true measure of addiction. It quickly became obvious, though, that not all people who were physically dependent on opiates were addicted in the sense that they showed craving, progression and so forth. There followed considerable confusion about definition, much of which still persists, but the majority position reached in the 1930s and 1940s was that physical dependence was necessary to addiction, but that it was not sufficient. In other words, the opiate addict, like the newly redefined alcoholic, was a specially vulnerable person. For both alcohol and the opiates, the source of addiction was no longer solely the drug. From the 1940s on, it was a function of individual bodies and minds.

The disease model of addiction, then, rested on three major assumptions: predisposition, loss of control over use, and progression. The last, in the case of the opiates, always included some statement about the development of tolerance and physical dependence. Over the years, all these assumptions have been challenged. Thus, addicts can control their intake and people insisting on the permanency of addiction—once an addict, always an addict—are forced into the uncomfortable position of having to specify how long an addict must abstain to stop being an addict and become a user. It is obviously unreasonable to hold addicts guilty until death proves them innocent, but where is the line to be drawn?

Similarly, addiction does not necessarily progress. Early studies explained the relative rarity of addicts over the age of 40 by the assumption that the addict lifestyle killed them before they reached that age. Gradually, as investigators followed addicts more carefully, it became clear that although the death rate of heroin addicts was always very high for their age group, many former addicts not only still lived but were abstinent. They had 'burned out' or 'matured out' at about that age. There was lively speculation about the process that brought this about, but no consensus was ever achieved. Those few addicts who gave up heroin before they reached the burn-out age had made such drastic changes in their lifestyle that it seemed unreasonable to expect this of more than a minority. So, while addiction could no longer be seen as permanent, it continued to be viewed as so persistent that it was for practical purposes incurable.

The problem, as usual, seems to have been sampling. Only the most intractable cases generally come for help or are forced into treatment by others. The cure rates reported by official agencies therefore tend not to include those presumably less serious cases who manage to cure themselves without coming to our attention and we now have evidence that their numbers may be substantial. A number of studies including the large-scale work carried out by Robins and her colleagues on returning Vietnam veterans (O'Donnell, 1976) suggest that 50 per cent or more of young addicts give up their addiction apparently permanently with no treatment whatsoever, and that a large majority of the remainder manage to do so with minimal help. There is even evidence that some former addicts return to regular but controlled and non-addictive use. The situation is obviously far less clear-cut than the classical disease model would predict, and there can be no doubt that some addicts remit without treatment.

As far as predisposition to addiction is concerned, research has implicated everything from biochemical abnormalities to spiritual destitution. However, in no case has it been possible to demonstrate a consistent physical or psychological factor that would distinguish the addict from the non-addict. The most effective predictor of drug use at the moment appears to be a person's familial and social context. This seems to determine the onset of use, its pattern, the problems likely to arise and the tendency to stop. A case can always be made that a personal predisposition must exist if environmental factors are to have particular effects, but this quickly becomes laboured. The fact that there is no clear dividing line between addicts and non-addicts seems inescapable.

The disease model, therefore, can neither demonstrate a clear etiology for addiction nor can it predict its course and symptoms with any accuracy. This in itself is not a problem: the same is true of a number of other conditions that are managed successfully by the medical profession. However, even if the disease model cannot be considered a scientific representation of the available evidence, we can still ask whether there is any advantage to behaving *as if* heroin addiction was a disease. Can medicine provide an effective treatment, or at least offer comfort?

The perceived effectiveness of treatment depends very much on what the goals of treatment are thought to be, and this will be taken up later. It may be said at this stage, though, that medical intervention is no more successful than other approaches. Medicine can ease the pain of withdrawal, but it is perfectly possible for addicts to withdraw without assistance and often quicker. Specialist help is needed to deal with overdose and some of the physical problems that afflict addicts, but such problems are not automatically present in all. Maintenance of heroin addicts on other, presumably safer drugs is a recognised intervention, but there are serious questions as to whether this can be considered treatment. In any case, even here the involvement of medical personnel is specifically required only for the legal formality of prescribing the drugs and monitoring the addicts' physical health.

While its record in successfully treating addicts may not be spectacular, the disease model does indeed provide comfort—but more for society than for the addicted individuals. The crux of the medical model is assignment of the 'sick role'. This legitimises people who are not bad, yet who cannot carry out their normal social responsibilities. Some addicts do respond positively to being labelled sick, and such a diagnosis may help them to recover. However, the very process of removing responsibility from them makes their deviant acts a question of abilities they *lack*, and most people do not care to have their sense of inadequacy and defectiveness increased. Moreover, a certain proportion of addicts will use the situation to provide an excuse for their drugging and to shift responsibility for their recovery upon health professionals. By doing so they in fact fulfil all their obligations within the medical model. While a sick individual cannot be blamed and as part of the sick role does have the responsibility to seek and cooperate with specific treatment, he or she does *not* have to get well. That is a function of the imposed treatment.

Throughout all this, normal people are not implicated in any way and can proceed as usual in the assurance that the problem is receiving expert attention. As Siegler and Osmond (1968) have pointed out, 'all other models require that someone be blamed for the deviant behavior: either the deviant himself, his family, or society. Only the medical model provides an explanation for a 'bad' event which does not require the detective work of finding out 'who did it'. Medicine, in this respect, is *less socially disruptive than other models which require that a wrong-doer be apprehended*' (pp. 20–1; emphasis added). The medical model precludes the need to recognise the unpalatable realities of familial, social and cultural contributions to drug use. This, together with the acknowledged prestige and authority of the medical profession, is probably the main reason for its durability.

Is the whole disease model, then, an elaborate and sinister hoax? It is very easy to see this situation as yet another example of the progressive medicalisation of society, and to some extent this is correct. But it is more realistic to say that medicine has been part of the problem—generally with full support and indeed sometimes coercion from the general public. And some of the problems that the disease model of addiction has created are major. Quite apart from the effects the concept of helplessness in the face of an external agent may have on persons actually suffering from the 'disease' of addiction, it has empowered politicians to claim that society as a whole needs to be protected from the heroin plague. The result has been a swing to eradicating the agent by increasing law enforcement and far from solving the problem, this has increased both crime and corruption. It would be ironic indeed if the application of the disease model resulted in the very thing it was designed to avoid—the culpability of the addict in the eyes of the law.

Does medicine have a role in drug addiction? Certainly, and it would continue to do so even if the disease model was completely overturned. A comprehensive response to drug addiction must include the medical profession because the phenomenon often involves some degree of physical dependence, and addicts as a group are at high risk for various kinds of physical damage. Nor is there any reason why medically-trained personnel should not take charge of behaviourally- or socially-oriented therapy. They have done so for a very long time, they do so now and their success is no worse than that of any other helping group. However, there should be no suggestion that addiction is their exclusive province, or that the treatments they offer are automatically superior.

The 'Moral' Model

Social existence as we understand it is inconceivable without some controls on human behaviour, although different aspects may be controlled at different times and in different places. Most societies have restrictions on drug use in general, and particular drugs may be singled out for special control. Most drug controls, however, are exceedingly ambiguous and ambivalent. Thus, contrary to all logic, there is no relationship between relative acceptability of a drug and its ratio of desirable and undesirable effects. Nor is there any clear relationship between the social cost of the use of various drugs and their acceptability. Even concerns about the effects of drugs on youth seem misdirected. No society has ever 'come unstuck' because its young people used drugs, despite the hysteria generated by their experimentation with coffee, tea and tobacco in the seventeenth century and with marijuana in the twentieth.

Two common themes underlie controls on drug use. One is that the drugs most rigorously controlled are typically 'alien': recent introductions or rediscoveries that have no part in routine social rituals and no system of distribution locked into the formal market economy. Such drugs can in due course be domesticated; indeed, such a process seems almost inevitable, since once a drug with desirable effects enters a society there is no historical precedent for limiting its spread let alone removing it. Alcohol, nicotine, caffeine and marijuana have all spread ubiquitously, and the opiates have been contained in the Western world only by massive efforts, the social and economic costs of which have been enormous.

The other theme is that alien drugs endanger established values, ethics and institutions. Characteristically, those seen as most at risk are ones that are already under some threat for other reasons. Most societies are concerned about containing aggressive and sexual impulses within prescribed limits most of the time. And all societies are concerned with maintaining the authority of its dominant members all of the time. Alien drugs are usually seen to threaten all these things. Beyond this, the nature of the perceived threat varies from society to society. A society that is already uneasy about its ability to maintain a particular *status quo* is going to be especially upset if the threatening behaviour threatens to occur in those subsections of itself that are already inclined to make waves: youth and the various underclasses. So it is there that trouble will be anticipated and the most comprehensive control measures taken.

Rules are not made automatically. As Becker (1966) points out, even though a practice may be harmful, the harm still needs to be discovered and pointed out. People must be made to feel that something ought to be done about it. Someone must call the public's attention to these matters, supply the push necessary to get things done and direct such energies as are aroused in the proper direction if a rule is to be created. Deviance, according to Becker, is a product of enterprise, and he calls people who exhibit such enterprise 'moral entrepreneurs'. Traditionally, they come from the healers and the spiritual or political leaders of society. In the ancient world, the roles of physician, priest and chieftain were often intertwined, and today medicine, church and state continue to collaborate in maintaining social order by regulating personal conduct. There have, however, been some important changes in emphasis.

In classical thought, man was capable of choosing between right and wrong. If he sinned, the fault was unambiguously his. In such a framework, ability to resist temptation is a measure of one's virtue in the eyes of God. The temperate person is the ideal, and the ascetic— the epitome of resistance—is a positive hero. This world-view began to dissolve during the Renaissance, and with it the concept of temptation, sacrifice and self-control. However, the position that man, knowing good and evil, must be held responsible (and must be punished, whether by God or the community) for acts performed with a guilty state of mind has persisted in the criminal laws governing major offences. This may seem like anachronistic mumbo-jumbo in our utilitarian and deterministic age. Nevertheless, as Goode (1985) points out, the position remains 'because there has simply been no system of social theory of individual responsibility which has been either acceptable or capable of replacing it and because it retains a firm hold on the concepts of moral responsibility held by our society' (p. 218).

In other areas of morality, however, emphasis has shifted from viewing man as a responsible agent acting in and on the world to the belief that man is simply a responsive organism driven by biological and social forces. Where temptation was once resisted or indulged, we now have drives and instincts that are satisfied or frustrated. Our very terminology has changed, and we have new words for temptation. For offers of legitimate goods, we speak of advertisers; when illicit substances or pleasure are offered, those who tempt us are pushers.

Szasz (1975) maintains that this precludes our seeing, much less confronting, the so-called drug problem directly. No one is compelled to take a drug by external forces. This makes the taking of illicit drugs at least partly a matter of temptation and surrender to temptation, but no modern 'scientific' approach takes any account of this. Nor can it. Man is now simply a biological organism. Drug addiction as moral insanity or a disease of the will has been transformed into underlying psychiatric disorder, personality deviancy, immaturity and inadequacy. The ostensible purpose of this view of addiction is humanitarian: drug users are sick, they need to be cared for and especially to be protected from themselves. However, all these new terms continue to contain moral assumptions about what is right and wrong, and the latent purpose of coping with individuals who offend society's idea of what is orderly and decent is at least as strong as ever.

In the scientific framework, though, it is no longer enough to say that drug use is a morally tainted behaviour; people must now be convinced that it is irrational and damaging as well and that it has such bad consequences in the real world that any reasonable person would disapprove of it.

There are several time-honoured ways to make a moral issue appear suitably scientific. First, it is important to ensure that the moral entrepreneur has scientific credentials in the public eye. Degrees, white coats and adequately high social standing all help. Second, suitably scientific evidence is needed, and there is scientific evidence in plenty, more than enough to 'prove' almost every conceivable position about drugs.

A successful case against drugs depends on four factors. The first is selection of the facts. Almost any point about the harmfulness or harmlessness of a drug can be made validly by simply attending to one segment of the drug reality and ignoring others. The relation of drug effects to dosage, chronicity of use and general status of the user can be very helpful in these selective observations.

Second, the trick is to describe bad effects profusely, but to omit discussion of their incidence relative to the total number of drug experiences.

Third, one must focus on the importance and frequency of the activity to be condemned. The idea is to assume that criminals do nothing but break the law, that prostitutes are nothing but prostitutes, and that the lives of drug users are dominated by drug use. From this, it is a simple step to the assumption that if any of these things were permitted, hordes of men and women would succumb totally to bizzare practices.

Finally, it is necessary to express a fundamental pessimism about human wisdom and judgement. If unrestricted, a significant number of individuals would destroy themselves and others as well. To be sure, such scepticism and pessimism tend to be reinforced by the entrepreneurs' daily experience. Doctors, clergy, police and similar professionals with entrepreneurial qualifications daily see those who repeat the offence and the problem may well seem intractable. Under the circumstances, it is perhaps unworthy to suppose, with Becker (1966), that at least in some cases 'one of the underlying reasons for the enforcer's pessimism about human nature and the possibilities of reform is the fact that if human nature were perfectible and people could be permanently reformed, his job would come to an end' (p. 158).

It is, then, really quite easy to represent moral and ideological judgements as science. What is particularly interesting, though, is the way in which the current sciento−moral view has reapportioned both the blame for socially disapproved activities like drug use and the responsibility for their control. How an act is judged depends critically on whether people regard the reasons for doing it as temptations or impulses. A person yielding to temptation is an actor; if the act is illegitimate, he or she is a culprit or malefactor and those injured are victims. However, if people respond to irresistible impulses, they are themselves victims and cannot be blamed. Those they injure have no real case; at best, they will be viewed and treated as victims of a natural disaster.

Today's addicts are increasingly considered to be victims—of pushers, of faulty upbringing, of their own aberrant biochemistry. Since they are not truly responsible for their actions, treatment by others is legitimised and *that* truth is rapidly becoming self-evident, rooted in the natural order and unquestionable. Thus, we debate endlessly whether this or that inpatient treatment of addicts is better than another. But any suggestion that the current view is fundamentally mistaken, that treatment attempts should be discontinued and people with bad habits left to their own devices would be dismissed as outrageous. What we seem to be saying is that the use of some drugs has consequences so serious that it must be prohibited for the public good. Moreover, people who break such prohibitions are thereby demonstrating their guilty state of mind or their sickness, and in either case they have forfeited their human freedom. They must be punished or treated, as appropriate.

Moral positions on addiction have been around for a very long time and a certain historical evolution would be expected. What is surprising, however, is the degree of confusion that actually prevails. Instead of a single model that has adapted over time to a changing society, there appear to be several, each with a considerable history. All have different definitions of addiction, different views about its etiology and very different concepts of what should be done about it and the proper way to do this. By way of illustration, consider Siegler and Osmond's (1968) analysis of the situation. They distinguished no less than five different moral models.

The retributive model defines as an addict—criminal anyone who is justly found guilty of violating drug laws. Etiologically, addicts are presumed to take drugs because of moral weakness, and the proper treatment is cold turkey withdrawal and suitable penal punishment. The idea is that if the punishment is severe enough addicts will know they have done the wrong thing and will refrain in the future. The goal, basically, is to enforce the law. This model has been in partial use in the United States since the *Harrison Act* of 1914, although punishment has been meted out differentially according to, among other things, the addict's social class.

An important variation on this theme is the *deterrent model*. Here the idea is to deter not only addicts but those who might become addicts. Punishment for addiction must be certain, severe and public, so that people will be adequately impressed by the severity of the law and will therefore not indulge. Again, this model has been in partial use in the United States since the *Harrison Act* and it continues to be recommended as an ideal by many enforcement agencies.

For the *preventive model*, drug addiction represents faulty moral education. Young people experiment with drugs because they have not been properly informed about the evils of drugs, or instructed in the seriousness and immorality of drug taking. Treatment is not an issue: emphasis is entirely on education. This is perhaps the oldest of the models, and on the whole it is effective. Most of us do not take illicit drugs presumably because such social teaching was successful. At the same time, the model does not seem helpful in the case of drug addicts. These, by definition, have already shown themselves to be impervious to the customary social indoctrination.

The *rehabilitative model* is relatively unconcerned about etiology. An addict is simply a stray sheep who needs to be restored to God and/or society. Presumably there was some kind of moral failure, but this is to be expected. The human condition is such that some people will always be in a state of sin, and the important thing is to provide the means to rehabilitate them. Appropriate 'treatment' could include confession, repentance, prayer, restitutive acts, social rehabilitation and so on. The eventual goal is abstinence, avoidance of the occasions of further sin and reinvolvement with conventional society. This model has a substantial history, and it forms the basis of self-help groups like Alcoholics Anonymous, Narcotics Anonymous and the various therapeutic communities.

The *restorative* model is basically an extension of the rehabilitative paradigm. By behaving immorally, addicts have harmed both specific victims and society in general and they must make suitable restitution. The essence of this model is to ensure that addiction does not cost society anything. In its pure form it does not seem to have been tried, although elements of it appear in several of the other models, notably the retributive and the rehabilitative.

It should be abundantly clear that while there is some overlap, the differences between these models are considerable. Yet we persist in behaving as though there is a single moral model, which is or is not appropriate for drug addiction. As Siegler and Osmond (1968) point out, 'muddlement' is sure to ensue and, 'in a general way, muddlement is unlikely to assist administrative decisions, particularly when these are enforceable by law and are expected to solve grave social problems.' Thus, there is confusion about who should be the target of our actions—addicts (retributive, rehabilitative and restorative models), the general population (preventive model) or both (deterrent model). There is also the question of who should administer the 'treatment'. The same people could hardly prove equally effective in running the several programs required.

> The inflicting of deterrence, and the exacting of retribution, call for qualities of physique and character hardly compatible with those who supervise restitutive processes, those encouraging restoration of the erring person, or those undertaking preventive programs ... If such personnel were picked indiscriminately, one could be certain that grievous consequences would arise, since there could be no conceivable agreement among those with such different preconceptions regarding what each would be bound to consider was the natural and proper goal of the enterprise. There is some evidence that many of those using moral models today are

employing internally contradictory variations on this theme, and so are wasting their zeal and energy and confusing themselves and those in their charge. (Siegler and Osmond, 1968, p. 23)

We are not even in a position to assess the relative worth of the several models by comparing the success of the treatments indicated. Faced with an apparently successful deterrence program, proponents of say the rehabilitative model will simply claim that this is not real treatment—only deep psychotherapy combined with radical and usually unspecified social changes could truly bring addicts to a point where they no longer needed drugs. All the evidence in the world could not tell us which of the two treatments is the better because the goals of the models are different.

Can anything be done to resolve this? As we have seen, attempts at 'scientific' justification of moral positions turn out to be simply more value judgements, thinly disguised. But we *could* try to be more consistent about the models we use. Many people and most programs tend to veer from one model to another. Discussions among addiction experts often have a certain Mad Hatter's tea party quality, and some of this could be avoided.

We could also admit that all moral models rely on enforcement, in one way or another, of a particular position. This may range from mandatory abstinence from particular drugs to compulsory medical treatment for those who do become users. The worth of enforcement can be measured, but only in practical terms. We need to consider whether a position is enforceable to begin with and if it is, what the costs of both the enforcement *and* of the situation that would obtain in the absence of such enforcement would be. Kaplan (1983) states this very simply:

> No one argues that just because, on principle, society has the right to prevent people from harming themselves, it should always make the attempt. We do not seriously try to prevent people from overeating, smoking, drinking, or doing many other things that we feel are not good for them—for eminently practical rather than moral reasons.
>
> In other words, to decide whether allowing heroin to be freely and legally available would be preferable to our present prohibition, we must determine the likely social cost of free availability, as compared to our present policy. To do this, we must imagine, as best we can, the hypothetical state of our society were heroin essentially freely available—and compare this with our state under the present prohibitionist heroin policy. (p. 109)

Most of our attempts to deal with the heroin problem have been so costly and so conspicuously unsuccessful that there is a temptation to jump to the conclusion that free or at least less restricted availability just has to be better. Such a step, however, cannot be taken without careful consideration of a number of exceedingly complex issues. In many cases the necessary data do not now exist, and in some they may be inherently unobtainable. In Chapter 3 we discussed some of the possible health and social consequences of unrestricted heroin availability. Some of the problems with the British system of prescribing for addicts were touched on in Chapter 2 and the whole maintenance issue will be considered further in Chapter 8. Suffice to say that loosening restrictions on heroin would not solve all our current problems and would certainly create others. The real question is whether the new costs, assuming the situation was given adequate time to stabilise, would be less than those of which we are too well aware under the present system.

RECENT ALTERNATIVES

Scientific models usually follow the *zeitgeist* rather closely. As we have seen, the public image of man has been changing from one that emphasised free will and morality to more deterministic, non-moral formulations. Freud was among the first to claim that human behaviour was more determined than humans cared to admit, and he was certainly the first to suggest that humans could experience socially disapproved wishes and feelings and yet perceive them as occurring in others. In Victorian times, the infantile urges of the *id* were reluctantly accepted, and addicts were seen as people who succumbed to them. However, the addict was always someone else. As Vaillant (1968) points out, all proper Victorians denied that they personally had such wishes to sin.

During the 1920s this projection became even more marked. Addiction became something external, something that happened *to* the addict, who thus became even more the helpless and blameless victim. Nevertheless, the blame had to be put somewhere and it came to rest in persons and circumstances. Addicts became victims of incompetent physicians, bad associates and above all seductive pushers and demoralising social conditions. The result was the creation of a variety of psychosocial models of addiction. The fundamental principle in such models is that human behaviour is dominated by predetermined social roles. If these roles cease to satisfy individual needs they will be rejected and other means of gratification will be sought. A necessary result of this process is role-strain, anomie, alienation, dissonance, conflict—or the same thing in different words—and this forms the basis of addiction.

In psychosocial theories addiction is created by the society in which it occurs on the one hand, and the laws intended to suppress it on the other. Such theories capitalise on the fact that addiction seems especially prevalent in deprived, disrupted and impoverished urban neighbourhoods. The usual claim is that families who live in such conditions necessarily instil in their children things like weak ego functioning, defective superego, inadequate masculine identification, lack of appropriate aspirations and a failure to set long-range goals, as well as a distrust of traditional social institutions. It is this 'personality', together with the ambiance of criminality and delinquency that is also typical of deprived areas, that causes young people to experiment with drugs. Drug use, therefore, is seen as part of a pattern of substitute gratification.

In general, all psychosocial models attempt to retrace what Chein and his colleagues (1964) called 'the Road to H'. There is the imagined trip through deteriorated neighbourhoods, the inside information about the addicts' disadvantaged families and finally the picture of the addicts themselves. All this is designed to explain how addicts come to have such a narrow view of the possibilities of life that even in an affluent country taking drugs constitutes their only notion of a career.

Compared with the sketchy remarks medical and moral models usually make about etiology, psychosocial models seem much more concrete, knowledgeable and promising. Yet they present very real problems. Many of the studies advanced to support psychosocial theories are fascinating. They read like novels and to some extent that is what they are: biographical and even autobiographical material, quite unsupported by any attempt at validation. For example, the often-cited work *Mainline to Nowhere* (Kron and Brown, 1965) is a biography of a single Puerto Rican heroin addict. Extrapolating from such material is simply not acceptable by the standards of today's scientific method.

More broadly based studies present difficulties too. Without exception, they centre around social groups whose lifestyles almost guarantee support for the hypotheses the studies set out to test. If one only looks at addicts from deprived areas, it should not come as a surprise that they lack access to means of achieving culturally desired goals and that they are unhappy about this. A theory of anomie might account for their addiction quite well. However, it would need quite a stretch of the imagination to extend this theory to doctor addicts who, as described, say, by Winick (1961), are often more successful than their contemporaries and who are certainly in an occupation where both culturally desired goals and culturally legitimate means of achieving them are available. And doctor addicts are by no means rare.

In any case, psychosocial theories usually tacitly assume that desired goals and legitimately available means are the same throughout society, and this is clearly incorrect. Several studies indicate that while urban addicts from depressed areas may be denied legitimate access to culturally desired goals, they are hardly retreatists. Rather, many of them are participating in an active and personally meaningful way of life. Thus, Sutter (1966) describes the world of the 'righteous dope fiend', with its own norms, values and ways of deriving status. The 'righteous' dope fiend is an addict who has successfully mastered the art of hustling. The status symbols of his world are very like those of the wider society—smart clothes, a car, money and girlfriends—and his own position in it derives from the 'style' with which he carries on his life. A similar world is described by Preble and Casey (1969). According to Sutter (1966), if street addicts retreat at all, it is when they can no longer live up to the demands of their active lives, or when they stop using drugs.

Psychosocial models, then, seem to have rather limited applicability. But even if they could explain the condition of all addicts satisfactorily, they would present serious difficulties with regard to the appropriate management of addiction. Since both addicts and the families that contributed to their unfortunate personalities are victims of forces beyond their control, neither can be held responsible for the development of the addiction. It then becomes the duty of society to try to resolve the problems. For the addicts, the goal is to bring them to a state of personal development they have never enjoyed before and which should make it possible for them to use their full human potential. For their families, the goal is to alter the physical and social living conditions so that further generations of addicts will not arise. But we do not know how to bring about such changes, nor have we reached any social consensus about the form that they should take. Since we either cannot or will not take the necessary social steps, psychosocial formulations allow us to do little except feel sad and guilty about addicts. These theories are neither truly testable nor productive and they therefore lack the two essential qualities of all good models.

We have seen public and professional opinion about addiction shift from blaming the addict in the early-1900s through blaming a disease from the 1930s on to blaming ourselves, the bad society, in more recent years. Yet blaming ourselves is also the wrong answer. To do so is to confuse the concepts of blame and responsibility. Addicts cannot be blamed for their psychosexual urges, nor can they be blamed for the psychosocial milieu of their childhood. But they can and must *own* these things, that is, acknowledge and feel that they are part of themselves, and take responsibility for them. In short, addicts have the responsibility, if not the blame, for their addiction and neither education nor medicine nor the law can change this.

A major implication of this is that addicts must also be asked to be responsible for their cure, even though much that may have happened to them was not their fault. As Vaillant (1968) puts it, 'however bad society may be, it is still the addict's responsibility that he cannot stand the sight of it' (p. 63). All the models we have discussed sidestep this issue to some degree. All spend much time on the addicts' rights; relatively few have much to say about their duties. Thus, most medical models merely require that patients cooperate by placing themselves wholly in the hands of their doctors. According to Siegler and Osmond (1968), the deterrent moral model and most psychosocial models impose no duties whatsoever. Addicts are held up as a bad example in the former, and in the latter they are held up as social victims, which is another kind of bad example. Deterrent moral models aim to produce fear and guilt in addicts and potential addicts; psychosocial models aim to make everyone except addicts anxious and guilty. In neither case is there a meaningful set of activities for the addicts themselves.

Yet the dangers of applying the medical or social sick role too rigorously are becoming very clear. The more we try to solve addicts' problems for them, and the more we sympathise with their difficulties, the less they seem to improve. Indeed, why should they? If, like guilty mothers, we blame ourselves for their plight and push treatment at them, we merely legitimate their addiction. Successful treatment depends on the degree to which addicts can be made to experience the consequences of their addiction in a meaningful way instead of projecting them on to someone or something else. The necessary step, Vaillant (1968) argues, is to place responsibility for both addiction and recovery firmly on the addict, to say 'It *is* you. It's not your fault; but what do you want to do about it? We'll offer what help we can, but it may be only to help you take responsibility'. In practice, such steps are being taken with considerable success by many helping professionals. However, they have yet to be formally incorporated into our theoretical models of addiction.

8
The war on heroin: what are our chances?

Of course, the best scheme would be to recognise people's rights to rot their minds and bodies with whatever drugs they choose, and to rely for the reduction of drug abuse on an education campaign, such as is beginning to prove effective against nicotine use.

Unfortunately this most sensible and just of suggestions is likely to be unable to be implemented because of the fanaticism of wowsers and the irrational terror of the other ill-informed opponents of drug use (B.E., Kempsey, NSW)
Australian, 3 January 1985

To say that something should be allowed is not to commend it, and the liberal individualist argument is often misrepresented. When a century ago, in the course of the temperance debate, Archbishop Magee of York said that he would rather see England free than England sober, he was not advocating mass drunkenness, he was saying just what he meant . . . Is it too much to hope that we may one day see England free, rather the England compulsorily 'drug free'?
Geoffrey Wheatcroft, *Sun—Herald*, 28 October 1984

In the course of a lecture on the diseases of civilisation, Lesley Garner showed a slide depicting two men mopping up a floor flooded by a dripping tap. 'These men are experts in floor-mopping-up,' the lecturer explained. 'They have spent ten years of their life earning degrees in floor-mopping-up. They know everything there is to be known about floor-mopping-up. Except how to turn off the tap' (Inglis, 1983, pp. 322–3). Our position with respect to the heroin problem is rather like this. We have tried a variety of strategies, some more relevant to the issue than others. For a very long time, we have mopped up—managed the addicts. This of course does little about the tap itself. Our dominant approach so far has been to tighten the tap as much as possible—to manage the drug, its availability and use—and this has not been conspicuously successful. We are only just beginning to ask why the tap leaks and, for that matter, why we need a tap in the first place. We are, in other words, beginning to look at the system itself.

Managing the addict

Traditionally, the prognosis in drug dependence of any kind has been considered poor. Once an addict, always an addict. Many professionals also came to believe that while some intervention was probably better than none, it did not much matter what the intervention was. In this we may have been unduly pessimistic.

'Addiction' is what Duster (1970) calls a 'moral category': it permeates a person's total identity. 'Prostitution' is another such category. Once a person is identified as an addict or prostitute, it is assumed that all aspects of his or her character are fixed and predictable. One of the results of this is the assumption that there must be a single, definitive treatment for addicts. In fact, addicts are as diverse as any other group of people. They may have in common only their addiction and even this may express itself in highly individual ways. The generally uninspiring results of treatment may therefore represent a simple statistical washout: clients unsuited to a particular intervention to which they are assigned 'fail', and each failure cancels a 'success' by those to whom the approach is more congenial. There is actually considerable evidence that this is the case. Unselected client groups tend to show a very high drop-out rate (Glaser, 1974). At the same time, where there is a choice, different clients tend to be assigned to different treatments, and those who achieve good results differ from program to program (Pattison et al., 1973). Most of this work has been done with alcohol-dependent persons, but some similar data also exist for opiate addicts (Sheffet et al., 1973).

In fact, it is increasingly obvious that there is an important interaction between the characteristics of the client and the characteristics of the intervention and that therapeutic success depends on matching client and therapy. An approach that will help one type of addict may be actively counterproductive for another. Discussion of addict types and the interventions most suited to them is beyond the scope of this book, and I have taken up this issue elsewhere (Krivanek, 1988). However, a few points may be made here.

It is one thing to say that different addicts need different treatments and quite another to put this into practice. One problem is assessment— the analysis of each client's needs, strengths and lifestyle. To proceed to therapy without it is effectively treatment without diagnosis but, while everyone seems to agree that assessment is a good thing, in practice it is patchy at best. The reasons are various. There is the obvious cost in both dollars and time, and the general lack of relevant training on the part of program personnel. Some workers still see all addicts and all treatment methods as essentially the same, and this of course makes assessment redundant. There is also the question of ideological bias—the feeling that one's particular treatment is the only solution for all addicts, and that all other programs are inadequate.

Probably the single most compelling reason, though, is the lack of treatment facilities to which clients may actually be directed. In some areas they simply do not exist. In others, it is more a matter of integrating and coordinating treatment resources that are already there, but this effort may be hampered by interagency competition and ideological conflict. It is not that addiction workers are generally unaware of the need for individual assessment and treatment, but what good is it, the reasoning goes, if they are all going to end up in the same treatment anyway? And even where alternative facilities exist, the data on their relative effectiveness with different sorts of clients are very incomplete. In such a climate there is no incentive for cooperation. On the contrary, there is every reason for rival programs to tout the exclusive and universal efficacy of their particular methods and to try to seize the biggest piece of the action they can.

An even more basic problem is the question of what we are actually trying to achieve. With a legal drug like alcohol, there are two options: the goal can be to help a problem drinker give up alcohol altogether, but a return to social, safe levels of drinking is also acceptable. With an illegal drug like heroin, the situation is very different. Any use is by definition misuse. Controlled use is not acceptable, even though there is evidence that some proportion of users—perhaps a substantial number—are able to manage this without particular difficulty.

Were heroin to become legally available, who would these people be? Obviously we have very little information on this. The successful heroin users do not come to our attention. Some of the factors that seem to facilitate controlled use of heroin were touched on earlier. The data seem fairly similar to what is known about resumption of controlled drinking by ex-problem drinkers, and they suggest that if heroin was as freely available as alcohol is now, a significant proportion of high-risk groups would develop serious problems with it. However, such serious problems would be by no means normative, and their incidence might well be drastically reduced by attending to factors that place these groups at high risk on the one hand, and by providing adequate help and encouraging its use on the other. On the balance, problems with heroin use under such conditions might well be less than we now experience. It is quite unlikely that they would be greater—though problems there would certainly be.

At the moment, though, abstinence is the only permissible goal for heroin addicts. Paradoxically, maintenance of the addiction is also acceptable, provided that the responsibility for this is taken out of the addict's hands. In a maintenance program, the client is obviously still addicted. Success is therefore measured by abstinence from illicit opiates and even that is sometimes assessed in a rather cavalier fashion. In practice, dirty urines and occasionally dealing in drugs are the only grounds on which a person is ever dismissed from a maintenance program. Many such programs, although by no means all, also make some effort to assess changes in criminality, employment and social functioning, but failure to improve in these areas rarely affects the client's acceptability to the program. In fact, even if abstinence is the goal, it is again remaining free of illicit opiates that is the single most important criterion of success in today's treatment programs. Yet surely we want more than that?

Ideally, abstinence from an illegal drug should be defined further in terms of *time*. The word abstinence implies permanent avoidance of the substance. The probability of eventual abstinence from heroin is actually very good. In fact, the greater the dependence, the better the clients' eventual chances—if they live. However, the recovery process is usually protracted and relapses are common. At what point should we assume that clients are securely abstinent? Clearly it is unfair to wait until they die to proclaim them successes.

No definite predictions can be made. Some people give up once and for all, and without formal treatment. The number who do so may in fact be quite large. Remember that only a very biased sample of casualties is available to researchers. Yet even in this biased sample, such an outcome is not rare. Simpson and his colleagues (1982) compared outcome in addicts receiving different forms of treatment with that in an 'intake only' group—people who completed admission procedures, but did not actually enter treatment. Six years later, 19 per cent of the 77 subjects in the latter group reported immediate and lasting abstinence, and this compares very favourably with the outcome of those entering treatment. Here, immediate abstinence rates ranged from 18 per cent to 21 per cent. The successfully abstinent intake-only clients did seem to have fewer problems than those who went into treatment. Still, the follow-up interviews suggested that they simply decided that they did not need help to quit drugs, and then just quit.

The majority of people presenting for treatment have more trouble. Vaillant and Milofsky (1982) argued that with problem drinkers six months' abstinence means nothing, and that about three abstinent years are needed before stable success can be assumed. Rather similar time frames probably apply to opiate addicts. Simpson's group found that six years after entry into treatment 61 per cent eventually remained abstinent, although this required prolonged treatment in 13 per cent of the cases. Sustained use of illicit opiates continued in 21 per cent despite treatment, and the remaining 18 per cent had other special problems such as periodic relapses, prolonged imprisonment or heavy use of other drugs. On the whole, we must assume that therapy will be a long process. There are no wonder cures.

Successful abstinence should also be defined in terms of *behaviour*. Alcoholics Anonymous has much to say about 'dry drunks': ex-problem drinkers who remain abstinent but whose behaviour is socially so dysfunctional that family and friends may long for their relapse. They may even try to enlist the therapist's help in bringing this about. 'Doctor, when can my husband drink again? I don't think I can stand it much longer.' Similar behaviour sometimes occurs in ex-heroin addicts. Technical abstinence of this sort seems hardly worth having.

There is also the question of substitute dependence. It is absolutely essential to realise that the drug is meeting real and powerful needs in the addict's life. For some people, escape from anxiety, distressing environmental conditions or social responsibility plays a role. For others, it is a matter of social interaction. For many people, too, there is a need to find a power greater than oneself, something or someone to take the responsibility and absorb the blame for one's actions. Meeting all these needs with drugs is very easy. No training and little effort is required, at least initially, and the results are gratifyingly rapid. It is not surprising, then, that ex-addicts who have given up one drug often turn to a substitute *chemical* dependency.

In Vaillant and Milofsky's (1982) study of problem drinkers, half the men who achieved more than one year of abstinence found such substitutes—chain smoking, minor tranquillisers, candy binges and marijuana, in that order. A similar pattern appears in ex-heroin addicts (Simpson et al., 1982). Here, 11 per cent of those who achieved abstinence from opiates developed what was judged to be a *dependence* on other substances. Marijuana was the most popular (81 per cent of the group), but alcohol and non-opiate drugs were also significantly represented—70 per cent and 56 per cent of the group respectively. Obviously some of these people became dependent on more than one substitute drug. *Use* of drugs was generally high in the rest of the opiate abstainers: marijuana, non-opiate drugs and alcohol were used (though not at dependence levels) by 62 per cent, 19 per cent and 29 per cent of this group respectively.

Simpson and his colleagues (1982) did not report on their ex-addicts' other activities. Vaillant and Milofsky (1982), though, found that substitute *behavioural* dependencies were also prominent in ex-problem drinkers. In order, these featured compulsive work or hobbies, religion and gambling. Most particularly, many became compulsive Alcoholics Anonymous users. Eighteen of the 49 securely abstinent men (38 per cent) each averaged 300 meetings per year, with a maximum of 1 000 meeting per year—a veritable career. All the people discussed in these two studies gave up their main problem drug, whether alcohol or heroin. The question that we must ask ourselves, though, is whether the substitute dependencies that so many of them developed represent a real improvement on their previous condition.

This of course brings us face to face with the need to provide alternatives to the primary addiction. Giving up a substance that does so many things so well and so easily means making a great sacrifice. In real life, ordinary people make great sacrifices under only two conditions: either they expect to achieve something at least as valuable as the thing being sacrificed, or they wish to avoid something extremely unpleasant. Simplistically, there is either a carrot before their eyes or a gun at their heads. Addicted people behave no differently.

Fear is a powerful motivator, but it is easy to forget that its value is limited to the continued presence of the fear-producing circumstances. In practice, addicts who improve do so not only because they fear negative consequences, but also because abstinence or control offers some latent positive reinforcements. If such positive reinforcements for abstinence cannot be found, the therapeutic outlook is bleak.

Finding alternative ways of meeting the needs currently filled by the drug can be quite difficult, particularly if the client comes from some extreme of the drug scene. The young drug user with few ties outside the street scene is a typical example. Many of these people need habilitation, not rehabilitation. They have no money, home or marketable skills, their social image is poor and they have little experience or interest in conventional living. Our available resources, even if fully engaged, may be insufficient to meet such destitution.

A far more serious problem, though, is that a large number of modern addicts actually manage rather well. The relatively small size of today's typical habit and the generosity of the welfare state mean, between them, that many addicts do not see themselves as having particular problems and have no good reasons to give up their drug. The difficulty, in other words, is to persuade heroin users to give up a life many like well enough, and which is highly rewarding for some. Just how large that difficulty is likely to be is spelled out by Kaplan (1983):

> For some, being a heroin addict is one enormous game. The addict, after all, has license to steal, in the sense that both he and

society accept as an explanation that he must do so in order to support his habit. In other words, his stealing or selling drugs is no sin over and above that of being addicted to begin with. The most common self-image of the heroin addict is that of an outlaw. (The alcoholic's, on the other hand, tends to be that of a failure). And outlaws are regarded as living exciting, romantic lives.

The addict, moreover, has no problems of existential choice. He knows who he is; he is an addict. He knows what he is going to do from the moment he gets up in the morning until the time he goes to sleep at night; he is going to try to 'score' heroin and to steal or hustle enough to do so. There are no distractions for this kind of addict. He has a far simpler life than we do. He is consumed with a single-minded and, in many ways, a very interesting and exciting game. Though we may think his situation unenviable, he may prefer it to any other he could attain. If he were not an addict, he might be unemployed—that is to say, nothing—or he might be a casual day laborer, a dishwasher, or a worker in any one of a large number of unpleasant, ill-paid, and low-status jobs. Knowing the menial alternatives available to him, the addict is hardly in a frame of mind conducive to cure. (p. 50)

Managing the drug

The prognosis for heroin addicts may be better than we would have believed 20 years ago and, as our skill in matching clients to therapies increases, we may in time be able to approach the process with considerable optimism. However, this is very different from saying either that therapy is easy or that success is assured. Here is David Bell (1974), commenting on the experience of Sydney's St Vincent's Hospital in the 1970s:

Originally we set out to manage the addict. We aimed to give every addict the opportunity of psychotherapy and to insist on it in every case where we gave a substitute drug such as methadone. And what do we do in practice? We manage the drug ... The addict must come to the hospital, where it is given to him in solution to drink in front of the nurse. At random intervals the urine is checked to see whether the addict may be taking other drugs. Even this limited approach entails a lot of extra work for the staff, but it is manageable. It suits the routine of a hospital and the way of life of the addict ... Of those who remain in treatment, some manage to return to work and avoid further criminal convictions. Our results in this respect are modest and a lot less spectacular than those of the enthusiastic advocates of methadone maintenence.

And what happens to our plans to manage the addict? Psychotherapy does not suit his way of life ... [because of] the need to attend punctually and regularly, the need to look at his failing mercilessly, the need to deliberately undertake actions that are difficult or unpleasant in order to secure a long range goal, the need to defer satisfying the appetite for pleasure when the result may be inconvenient or harmful. At the hospital level psychotherapy cannot be accomodated by the budget. We undertook our programme with the hope of being given extra staff and after two years we are still waiting. At first enthusiasm carried the staff along, but as pressure mounted fatigue and disillusionment set in. The first casualty was the time-consuming process of psychotherapy or other personal management. In many programmes the next casualty would be the time-consuming special supervision needed for methadone administration, until finally all that is left is the routine of pill pushing. Fortunately we have avoided the worst failures and we still manage some psychotherapy within the routine of the psychiatric ward and the Day Hospital at Caritas. But we feel disappointed ... (p. 39)

The St Vincent's experience is not very different from that of other institutions in Sydney, or elsewhere in the world. We profess to manage the addict, but all too often we end up by managing the drug. People pay lip service to the ideal of attending to the needs of the whole person, but the fundamental policy is still to prohibit the drug or, at most, to dole it out under specified conditions or to offer a substitute.

Maintenance approaches

As far as we can now tell, opiate addiction as such causes little permanent physical damage. Some of the potential problems of making heroin freely available have been touched on in Chapter 2 and we will return to this issue later. Whatever the logical advantages of such a system might be, though, most people would see free availability as too large a step to take, accustomed as they are to the idea that heroin is inherently evil and that the state must protect its citizens from the drug's ravages at all costs. At the same time, total prohibition is clearly not working either, and given the current emphasis on the medical model and the tendency of the media to portray heroin users as helpless victims of depraved pushers, it is easy to feel sorry for addicts. Such a sympathetic view is of course enthusiastically seconded by a majority of the visible addicts—who, as we have seen, must be regarded as the failures of the drug scene and therefore unrepresentative. So some form of maintenance is widely accepted as a compromise solution. Maintenance basically involves making a pure drug available to addicts under supervision and at minimal cost.

Maintenance can be managed in two basic ways: by prescription and by on-the-premises consumption. In a 'prescription' system, a physician prescribes an amount of drug judged adequate to each addict's needs, and the addicts then pick up their supply at a time and place to suit themselves. This, it will be recalled, was the format of the original British system. The main problem is the possibility of diversion, and this is a major and intractable disadvatage of all maintenance approaches. What a maintenance policy does is divide the drug market into two separate sections: one for addicts, the other for experimental, occasional and non-addict regular users. Price in the addict market should be as low as possible. It is not in our interest to compel addicts to pay more than necessary for something they will use anyway. At the same time, price in the non-addict market should be as high as possible. The idea is to make it prohibitively expensive to use to begin with, or at least to use sufficiently often to become addicted. And therein lies the fundamental difficulty. The greater the price difference between the two markets, the greater will be the leakage from the low-priced one to the high-priced one. Addicts receiving prescriptions for low-priced heroin or methadone will have a strong incentive to resell at least part of their supply.

There is still no easy, objective way of determining how much drug an addict actually needs. Prescribers will naturally try to keep the amount as low as possible, but addicts can always threaten to supplement the prescription with street drugs—and since the whole purpose of maintenance is to prevent illicit use, this creates an impasse. In any case, we have seen that addicts can readily do without if there is sufficient incentive, and even urinalysis cannot detect this provided they do not sell their *whole* supply—urinalysis is qualitative, not quantitative. If the market price for the prescribed drug is attractive, an addict may feel that a certain amount of sickness is worth the extra money. Even the sickness might not be too big a problem. Because of cross-tolerance and cross-dependence, a good deal of substitution is possible. Thus, if addicts are prescribed heroin, they can get by on methadone, which is likely to be available fairly cheaply on the street, and sell the more desirable heroin. If they are prescribed methadone, they might manage on street analgesics or barbiturates and sell the methadone. And so on.

Diversion would not be too worrisome if it involved only those already addicted. Unfortunately, many customers for diverted drugs are not addicts. While methadone, for instance, may not turn on an average heroin addict, it will produce a satisfactory high in a non-addict, and there is a brisk market for it among this group. The trouble is that even addicts have to start as non-addicts. The potential clientele for diverted drugs includes not only experimenters and regular non-addict users, but also those who have never used but would be willing to try if drugs were cheaper and more available. And the larger the number of addicts in maintenance, the more prescription drugs could be diverted.

These considerations, together with the practical impossibility of keeping the business practices of a large and scattered population of prescribers and dispensers under adequate surveillance, have gradually established a preference for 'on-the-premises' maintenance systems. Here, diversion is minimised by requiring the addict to obtain and consume the drug under supervision at a specified place. It will be recalled that the original British system changed over to prescription through clinics only, but addicts could still take their drug away with them—though this was often methadone and not heroin. In Australia and the United States the drug is always methadone, and worldwide there is increasing emphasis on genuine on-the-premises consumption, with take-home arrangements rare and increasingly viewed as a privilege.

There is reason to believe that much less diversion occurs with on-the-premises maintenance, but there are a number of other disadvantages. If heroin itself is to be the drug given, its short duration of action is a major drawback. Addicts would need three to four doses a day, and attending a clinic that often is a practical impossibility. Methadone, with its longer duration of action, requires only daily pickup, but the addicts' average travel time to their clinic is still 45 minutes. Moreover, their movements in general are restricted either to places where some other clinic is willing to dispense for them, or to a perimeter around their own that is not more than a day's travel away. Beside the travelling, there is the incovenience of waiting around within the clinic and the inevitable bureaucratic procedures. Addicts cannot use comfortably at home or companionably with their friends and it is unlikely that the institutional setting of the typical clinic will be particularly appealing.

The clinics, incidentally, are equally unattractive to the surrounding community and their location is a perennial source of local objection. Addicts who have nothing else to do tend to congregate in the area, so clinics can become a prolific source of both petty crime and litter. Neighbours moreover fear, not without reason, that such places may become a focus for a local drug culture, with all the problems this presents for the youth of the area. In all, it cannot be said that clinics improve the quality of life in their immediate neighbourhood, and the neighbourhoods most affected are often the ones least able to afford this.

All these problems could potentially be overcome. The real difficulties with any form of maintenance, whether heroin or methadone, are far more fundamental. The whole concept is based on some very dubious assumptions. One is that its existence would make a difference in the demand for illicit drugs. As we have seen, as long as there are two markets with a price differential between them, the only real question is how much drug will be diverted from the low-priced to the high-priced one.

Neither would the pusher disappear. The removal of a substantial number of addict customers from the illicit market would depress traffickers' profits, but there is no reason to believe that the incentive to service whatever market remained would disappear. Purveyors of illegally produced drugs would have competition from resales of prescription drugs, but from our standpoint this merely replaces one distribution system with another.

Neither does maintenance necesarily eliminate demand for illicit heroin by addicts actually in these programs. If an addict is being maintained on heroin, it is a question of dose and setting. Stimson's (1973) survey of maintained British addicts showed that many supplemented their legitimately obtained drug—to achieve a better high, to enjoy the ambiance and companionship of the drug scene and for a whole host of other reasons. Even if a maintained addict does this only occasionally, the illicit market continues to profit. In the case of methadone maintenance, it cannot be emphasised too strongly that methadone and heroin are different drugs. True, they show cross-tolerance and cross-dependence, but their effects are perceptibly different. The gentle high of oral methadone is a far cry from the rush of mainlined heroin. Neither does methadone block the euphoric effects of heroin in any absolute sense. Heroin can still produce a high in a methadone user—provided that a large amount is used. This makes methadone a very mixed blessing if it is the heroin high users are after; it raises the price they must pay for a fix. And of course methadone cannot satisfy any needs that may have been met by the heroin culture.

A second faulty assumption is that given a choice, all addicts would enter a maintenance program. As the British experience showed, this assumption is dubious at best. Several factors are involved. First, entry into any form of treatment amounts to an admission that one can no longer cope with the habit. Many attempt to quit on their own and fail, but as long as they can stay out of formal treatment they are able to persuade themselves that their next attempt will be successful. Treatment threatens the addict's perception of being in control and normal.

For others, the opposite is true—it is the self-image of the junkie, the cool cat, the standup guy, or whatever, that is threatened. The prestige of owning such a label can be a prime reason for use. If the alternative is acceptance of a 'sick' role, which the medical model of maintenance implies, many addicts would not enter willingly even if it seemed to their practical advantage to do so. In any case, addiction itself is advantageous to many. A few can only be regarded as winners.

Finally, no matter what legal arrangements we make, addicts in maintenance will be socially stigmatised—by both worlds. Straight society as a whole asserts that normal people should not need crutches (never mind the realities of wholesale alcohol, tranquilliser and other drug use for just that purpose) and maintained addicts are told so repeatedly. Moreover, their past tends to follow them. A methadone client of eleven years said 'People still make me feel I'm ripping off houses and friends.' At the same time, some former associates feel that addicts in maintenance have 'sold out', and will actively denigrate them. Others will try to engineer their relapse to illicit use. Bets are laid ostentatiously on their chances, and they may be tempted with offers or even secretly given heroin. Either way, for a substantial number of users the practical realities of life in maintenance may not seem much of an improvement over a life on illegal heroin.

A third assumption is that only addicts would seek to enter maintenance. In fact, there are considerable incentives for non-addict users and even non-users to enter. People are not always as intelligent, well-motivated, hardworking and honest as we would like. There is money to be made selling drugs and maintenance programs provide a highly marketable commodity at no or nominal cost. Provision of welfare payments is almost automatic to those enrolled in maintenance and this too can be attractive for those who do not mind the patient lifestyle (Preble and Miller, 1977). And maintenance programs provide pure drugs cheaply, reliably and for a minimal outlay of effort on the user's part. Bourne (1975) pointed out that maintenance provides a safe haven for the addict, a place to escape to when pressures of hustling become too great. He also presents evidence that there is a direct correlation between the purity of street heroin and the dropout rate from methadone maintenance: as heroin becomes more potent and more plentiful, addicts return to the street. There is no reason to believe that non-addict users would not try to take advantage of these possibilities too. In short, provision of maintenance programs may be encouraging and perhaps even enabling continued involvement with heroin.

While some programs make more effort in this direction than others, keeping non-addicts off the maintenance rolls is actually quite difficult. Addiction is extraordinarily difficult to define. It is part of a psychological continuum, and physical dependence is not always present. Physical dependence as such can be demonstrated quite readily. Injection of an opiate antagonist like naloxone will have no effect on mere users, but dependent persons will be thrown into withdrawal. However, if such a procedure is made a prerequisiste to enrolment in maintenance programs, it will make signing up considerably less attractive for those who suspect that they may be physically dependent. And it precludes those whose dependence is primarily psychological—the majority of today's addicts—from qualifying for entry.

Our only other objective recourse is to ascertain whether in fact the applicant has recently used heroin and this is not much help. Currently available assays can tell us whether a variety of drugs including heroin have been used in the last 24 hours or so, but the amount and length of use remains unknown. If heroin use were the only criterion for entry into maintenance, a person would need to buy and use only one or two doses to qualify.

A final assumption is that addicts entering maintenance want to be cured, and that maintenance can do this. Without a doubt, addicts want the maintenance drug. Whether they also want *treatment*, however, is quite another matter. The experience of an anonymous counsellor in Canberra may be taken as an example. Clients in a methadone maintenance program were individually interviewed about the possibility of encounter groups. Eighty per cent said they were interested. Only one attended the first session. The meeting between clients and staff that was then called was stormy, with strong resistance expressed toward the idea of encounter groups. The staff managed to dispel some of this, but only seven people wanted to join the group.

> They stayed together for a demonstration session and we parted in good spirit. Three clients attended the next session. They were so enthused about the group they wanted two sessions a week instead of one. I have not seen them since ... At this stage, the staff had to decide whether making counselling compulsory would be a viable treatment option. Before we took this step ... We interviewed the clients about their needs, what they considered would be helpful, and how the service could be improved ... [We] found that the word service in the clients' vocabulary meant only methadone distribution. And it was not simply a matter of linguistics. By their comments they clearly revealed that the hospital service means obtaining the drug.
>
> Most would feel quite satisfied staying on methadone for life; some prefer heroin; and others would prefer mixing the two. For most of our clients, the greatest advantage of methadone maintenance programs is that it keeps them off the streets ... The only other advantage of the program was that clients could rely on the hospital staff in difficult times. The staff pull them out of crisis situations ... Apart from these aspects, our clients apparently do not need anything else. Generally, their opinion is ... 'the less time I spend in the hospital, the better.' (*Connexions*, 1985, p. 2)

Compulsory attendance at a minimum of counselling sessions was introduced, with unknown results. Perhaps this counsellor was inexperienced. Perhaps the staff had inappropriate expectations. Whatever the case, this vignette does highlight the vast discrepancy between textbook and real-life addiction.

Experiences such as these throw considerable doubt on the idea that an offer of methadone maintenance can be used to 'hook' clients into other forms of treatment. What people keep forgetting is that 'the narcotic abuser already has a more immediate and gratifying solution to his problems than any that we can provide. His drug gives him an intense, immediate, primitive experience and is a passport to a ready made subculture. Instead, we can only offer such distant and nebulous prospects as responsibility . . .' (Wilhelm, 1975, p. 45).

Beyond this, methadone is a drug, not a treatment. In no sense can it resolve all the other things that are usually wrong with addicts beside heroin addiction. Many addicts are functionally illiterate and they have no work record or legitimate occupational skills. Others are socially incompetent. Whether or not these problems are traceable to the heroin addiction, they will remain after entry into maintenance. Even those who obey all the rules as well as they can and do not join the 'methadone, wine and welfare' subculture may never become productive citizens.

There are also those who argue that maintenance is actively counterproductive to eventual recovery. To the extent that addiction itself is a problem, the person in maintenance is of course still addicted. A very common position taken by heroin addicts is that they need their heroin to feel good, so why should they not use it? Why not indeed, but the real question surely is why they feel so bad. Whatever needs heroin was filling, methadone continues to fill to some degree.

> Since the drug is filling these emotional needs therapists cannot work with clients to achieve any emotional development whatsoever, as the emotional area is now thoroughly satiated and shielded . . . Counselling can have a definite counterproductive effect as narcotised clients learn the right words to gain approval from therapists and are able to continue in an unanxious, socially approved stone, while getting nowhere in the valuable area of therapy . . . Narcotic suppressed emotions of rage, guilt, inadequacy, frustration, and loneliness remain unreachable . . .
>
> Most clients continue to see themselves as addicts and continue their expectations of themselves as addicts. Hence, using other drugs is acceptable, selling methadone is acceptable, committing crimes and 'ripping other people off' is acceptable. There are no real expectations to get straight (drug free), either from themselves, their families, or the addiction workers, and thus no need to make any decisions. Clients can continue indefinitely the

avoiding, dependent, ambivalent lifestyle, only having to watch for the danger of losing their methadone. (Leach, 1985, p. 16)

What we are dealing with here, of course, is the issue of the goals of therapy and, as we saw earlier, there is considerable confusion about what we are trying to achieve. In an ideal world, Leach would be absolutely correct and a self-actualised, drug-free existence is always the ultimate goal. If that is the only goal we are prepared to accept, maintenance is useless in the long term, and may be counterproductive in the short term. But perhaps we should set our sights lower. Does the provision of maintenance reduce the cost of heroin addiction? For most people, this means cost to society rather than cost to addicts; bluntly, we are much more concerned with whether they steal from us than with whether they die.

To answer this, we must attempt to estimate what untreated addicts cost us (see Chapters 4 and 5) and set it against the cost of their maintenance on drugs. On-the-premises maintenance is expensive. Apart from the capital outlay needed to establish the centres, they must be staffed round the clock, and there must be adequate security. All of this amounts to a considerable financial commitment. McGlothlin and Anglin (1981) followed a group of clients in a California methadone program for a period of six years and came up with the following figures. The average annual cost of treatment per addict ranged from $US6 100 to $US9 500, depending on whether a high (up to 80 mg) or low (up to 50 mg) dose of methadone was used. However, each year each of these clients also cost the community an *additional* $US9 800 (high dose program) to $US16 000 (low dose program) on the average in welfare, court costs and similar social services.

These figures do suggest that high dose methadone seems more effective than the currently popular low doses, but this should not obscure the fact that the most successful high dose clients are still costing a staggering average of $US19 300 each per year in management alone. This does not include a number of indirect social costs like the inevitable drug diversion, not to mention the cost of prolonging each addict's addiction. If maintenance is attractive enough and easy enough to lure addicts into treatment, it is quite likely to attract them to stay—at an ongoing minimum cost of nearly $US20 000 a year, or whatever this would be for a given area at a particular time. Thus, in 1986 it was established that public methadone programs in Australia— which may involve little more than daily dispensing and occasional urinalysis—cost between $A2−3 000 per addict per annum. This does not include any setting-up costs or associated welfare costs. At the same time, a private psychiatrist counselling 120 patients on methadone (currently the maximum for a single prescriber) once a month would gross about $A101 000, with a further $A88 000 from the daily dispensing fees. (*Connexions*, 1986)

The counter-argument, that untreated addicts cost the community considerably more than this, is not particularly compelling. A causal connection between heroin and crime can be made for only some addicts (see Chapter 4), and as Leader-Elliott (1986) remarks,

> an unusual combination of cynicism and blind optimism is required before one can believe that thieves can be bought off with the offer of a substitute for heroin administered in government clinics. I doubt that we have the necessary reserves of cynicism. Experience in England, the United States and Australia has demonstrated the virtues of methadone maintenance. It is not, however, a particularly effective antidote to the theft problem. It was a mistake to suppose that heroin compels thieves to steal: it is no less mistaken to suppose that another drug will compel them to abstain from theft. (p. 147)

In any case, even if the heroin−crime connection were unassailable, maintenance could be expected to affect the crime rate only to the extent that addicts actually enrolled in the programs. The assumption that all addicts, given a choice, would choose maintenance is patently false. It may be true that existing maintenance programs turn many addicts away, but even if the total number of rejects was multiplied several times this would still account for only a tiny fraction of the estimated number of street addicts.

And there is reason to believe that those addicts who present themselves for maintenance, and especially those who stay in the programs, tend to be more stable and less criminalistic to begin with. Maddux and Bowden demonstrated this as early as 1972, less than a decade after the enthusiastic introduction of methadone maintenance in the United States. Basically, such people derive the least satisfaction from heroin, or have the most difficulty in obtaining heroin and coping with lifestyle of the drug scene, or face the most attractive prospects from a heroin-free life. They would have a high probability of success with any treatment. In their case, the relative costs of their untreated addiction and their long-term maintenance may be more nearly comparable, and the cost of either, presumably, would be significantly higher than the cost of their abstinence.

None of this should be taken to imply that maintenance approaches are worthless. Batey (1984) remarked that, in his opinion, methadone 'is bearing the brunt of much of the frustration felt by drug counsellors grappling with difficult clients and I do not believe it deserves to,' (p. 2) and there is much truth in that. Nothing is gained by making a scapegoat of methadone and the improvement in the health and social functioning of those addicts who are helped is certainly worth something. However, methadone should not be seen as 'money, mistress, magic and more' (Wilhelm, 1975, p. 46). It is dangerously naive to assume that methadone or even heroin maintenance can solve our problems with addicts, let alone addiction as a phenomenon.

Legal approaches

As we have seen in Chapter 5, 'use' of heroin is for practical purposes a crime and users are liable to prosecution. There is ample evidence that application of the usual criminal penalties like fines and prison sentences is ineffective and may actually be counterproductive. From a more practical standpoint, this process is also enormously costly. The criminal justice system therefore increasingly manages users within a coerced treatment framework. Probably the main reason for this is that there are few other options. The court and prison systems are already severely burdened, and each drug-related case is not only costly in itself but also diminishes the attention that can be given to all other crimes. We simply cannot afford to prosecute heroin users in the usual way any longer.

However, it is also increasingly recognised that heroin and other drug users may be a somewhat special problem. Many engage in no crimes other than their drug use. An analysis of 790 users and addicts who passed through Sydney's Bourke Street Drug Advisory Centre in 1981 showed that 280 (35 per cent) had no criminal record of any kind. Of the 353 who admitted to a previous record, 31 per cent had committed drug offences only (Schlosser, 1984). These figures are certainly underestimates, since some of those without criminal records had simply been lucky or clever enough to evade capture. Nevertheless, the study does suggest that perhaps as many as half of those who seek help are not criminally inclined in the usual sense, though all, of course, are criminals by virtue of their drug use. Prosecution of such people simply diverts scarce law enforcement resources from use against more serious criminals—including heroin traffickers, if that is what we are also worried about.

Coercion into treatment as an alternative to more traditional criminal penalties is very attractive. Compared with imprisonment, treatment of heroin users is both economical and cost-effective—not so much because existing treatment is so enormously successful and cheap, but because the usual process of the criminal law is singularly costly and ineffective. And while existing treatment options may not turn addicts into well-adjusted, competent and law-abiding citizens, we have reason to believe that it is probably still worthwhile trying to treat the majority. Kaplan (1983) reasons this way:

> If the addict commits six times as many property crimes when he is using heroin daily as when he is not, any means of preventing daily ... use would reduce his criminality by five-sixths. Any treatment then that costs less than five-sixths of the amount we pay for imprisonment might be, in terms of crime prevented, a better buy. Even residential treatment, the most expensive form of heroin treatment, costs considerably less than five-sixths the cost of imprisonment. (p. 225)

Note, however, that addicts and users are again being confused. We are proceeding as if all users were addicts and all addicts led irregular, non-productive, criminal lives. The reality is a spectrum that ranges from the criminal addicts who genuinely are a menace to society (never mind that society may have contributed to their becoming so), through all kinds of permutations to the controlled, socially responsible users whose only crime is their use of a prohibited substance. Both extremes raise particular problems.

In the case of the *criminal user*, that is, someone who commits other crimes as well as using heroin, should we still prefer coercion into treatment to imprisonment? Ideally, addict criminals whose crimes are unrelated to their addiction should be treated no differently than any other criminals. In most cases we cannot tell whether a given addict would still have committed crimes without the addiction, but Kaplan argues that we are probably still best off presuming that any criminal who is also an addict is likely to be criminal because of his or her addiction.

> Although we may be wasting treatment resources by coercing into treatment an addict whose criminality will not be reduced thereby, we are at least wasting a lesser sum than would be expended on unnecessary imprisonment of those addicts for whom treatment would be effective. If we are to make errors, it would seem good policy to err in the direction of the less expensive—and more humane—ones. (p. 228)

The concept of diversionary programs is still very new, and a distinction must be made between two possible types. The first is basically a suspended sentence: the offender is arrested, charged and appears in court. If the arrestee pleads or is found guilty, bail may be granted on the condition that he or she attends an assessment centre for a specified period of time. During this time, treatment options are discussed. A report with recommendations about appropriate intervention is then presented at a second court appearance and the magistrate takes this into account in determining the final sentence.

A program such as this has been operating in Sydney (after a false start in 1977) since 1980. To date, the clearest finding about the Drug and Alcohol Court Assessment Program (DACAP) is that magistrates will indeed take expert recommendations into account. Relative to those who do not comply with court referral to DACAP, those who complete the assessment have a much higher probability of receiving probation or a probation–treatment combination as a final sentence.

It has not yet been possible to validate the assessment, or its effectiveness in matching clients to treatment options. More important, the necessary follow-up studies of the effects of all this on the longer-term drug and crime careers of individual offenders have not been done (Schlosser, 1984). We know from other studies, though, that the effects of treatment on drug use and subsequent crime are not very encouraging, at least in prison samples. Thus, in their survey of NSW prison inmates, Dobinson and Ward (1985) found that a substantial number of imprisoned heroin users had in fact sought treatment. This ranged from therapeutic communities through all forms of methadone maintenance. However, most failed to complete the programs they embarked on 'because they did not like what was offered.' Predictably, previous treatment was found to have no effect at all on either drug use or subsequent crime in 51 per cent of these people and no effect in the long term in another 22 per cent. Most returned to drug use (80.5 per cent), dealing (48.8 per cent) and crime (53.7 per cent) within six months of leaving the program; indeed, the majority did so within two weeks.

Two points need to be considered before despair sets in. First, as Dobinson and Ward themselves point out, this is a very biased sample. They were interviewed in prison, and were therefore by definition treatment failures. Second, and more important, the subjects had chosen their programs themselves, and that choice doubtless depended on a host of factors that had little to do with their own suitability for the programs selected. And the majority stayed in treatment only very briefly. Perhaps the kind of in-depth assessment and matching of client to treatment that DACAP is attempting is what is really needed, and such an approach may in time yield more promising results.

The second type of program involves true diversion. An arrestee is referred to a treatment program before any adjudication is made. If he or she completes the program satisfactorily, the charges are dropped; if not, prosecution may be reinstated, a conviction obtained and the person then either imprisoned or subjected to treatment again. A few such programs have operated in the United States since the late 1970s (Weissman, 1978), but again evaluation has been very sketchy and there are as yet no studies which measure the subsequent criminality of those so diverted against those managed in more traditional ways. In fact, it may be said in summary that we have at this time no guarantee that forcing criminal users into treatment will work, or that this is the most effective way of using our treatment resources.

In practice, it is actually the *non-criminal user* who creates the greatest problems. Assuming that imprisonment is currently impractical, whatever its merits might be, should we take the plunge and repeal the use offence completely? This would mean effectively ignoring heroin use as long as it did not lead to other crimes.

As the law now stands, all use is theoretically equally culpable and no distinction is made between users and addicts. Some in both categories commit non-drug crimes in addition to their drug use, while others do not. Obviously, then, some heroin users are a greater potential threat to society than others. However, since we cannot now make a distinction between them in law, in practice the issue boils down to permitting the police and courts to select from among heroin users those most deserving of arrest and punishment. Under such circumstances, the chances are that those selected would be those most visible—the least successful users, equivalent perhaps to skid row derelicts, who are generally petty criminals at most. Such a system obviously lends itself to all sorts of corruption, not to mention all sorts of discrimination. And the non-criminal user, who would necessarily be swept into the net from time to time, could suffer considerable disruption of an otherwise law-abiding existence as a result. Social relations might be damaged, jobs lost and prospects of future employment compromised. The likelihood of committing crime might increase. And a term in prison would introduce such a person to many other heroin users, including the most criminally inclined. The experience, as well as these new friends, might make subsequent entry into the drug subculture easier.

None of this does either users or society any good. On the whole, there are excellent reasons for replacing the existing system with one in which the criminal law concerns itself with users only if they commit other crimes. It would not be too difficult to frame the law in such a way that most of the harm to society's morality and purse discussed in earlier chapters could be minimised. We might have very little to lose and perhaps much to gain from such a move. We must make some choices about our policy toward heroin and it is quite clear that our information about many aspects of its use will never be more adequate than it is now unless the drug becomes available for general use. It may well be, as Stolz (1982) has argued, that we must accept that use is a more realistic option than non-use. In accepting a policy of use, we would also have to accept that a minority will use drugs in a way that will harm individuals or the community—but this is consistent with our policies on other drugs, medicinal and recreational. In the end, it may be that the most effective way to control heroin use is to encourage the development of informal social controls—in other words, to domesticate the drug. Such a process takes time, perhaps a very long time. However, before it can begin, the criminal law must withdraw from the otherwise law-abiding heroin user.

Managing the system

Throughout this book, I have tried to embed the heroin problem within its natural setting—the moral, political and economic life of current society. Much of the time, the discussion was not about heroin at all, and that is precisely the point. The use and misuse of heroin cannot be understood in any other way. Neither will a solution to the problem be found if the natural setting is ignored.

It is abundantly clear that managing addicts is not the answer, though the needs of this subset of the community must also be met and we could do much better than we are doing.

Attempts to manage the drug, from prohibition of production to criminalisation of use, have not only failed but have been actively counterproductive, at least in some respects. Drug law enforcement does not reduce crime and the prohibition policy is itself criminogenic.

Prohibition has also seriously restricted our ability to obtain genuinely useful information. The mobilisation of hatred for traffickers and pity, mixed with condemnation and contempt, for users has required the creation of distorting myths and official dogmas. Since the activities of users and suppliers are clandestine, this has meant that the myths are reinforced by ignorance and such knowledge as we do have is partial and biased.

And because control and enforcement have traditionally been given highest priority as solutions by both politicians and the public, a pro-enforcement bias has arisen. Tinged as it is with moralistic overtones, it precludes a rational assessment of alternative approaches and perpetuates the myth that a single, simple solution must be the answer.

Should we then abandon our prohibitionist policies? Not quite, and not yet.

Before this can happen, we need to know what we are trying to do and, when it comes down to it, both politicians and the public are very confused about this. Are we trying to enforce a law simply because it is the law and certain people are flaunting it? Are we trying to eradicate heroin because this drug is inherently evil while others are not? Or is heroin simply our archetype drug and what we really want is a cessation of all drug use? Or do we just want heroin users to stop getting into trouble and harassing the rest of us?

Whatever we might like to do, the practical reality today is that if we try to get people to stop using certain drugs we will fail unless we are prepared to submit to procedures that would destroy society as we now know it. Goode (1984) summarises the situation this way:

> To be plain about it, there will always be certain forms of behavior that will produce, or will be associated with, the use of drugs. The use of mind-altering drugs is linked to broader social forces and influences that are not going to change very much, at least during this century. There will probably always be a pool of 'drug-prone' individuals. Of course, if some master visionary a hundred years ago had been able to predict future drug discoveries and use trends, it might have been possible to develop alternatives to psychoactive drugs; but history is behind us, and nothing can undo the past and present forces that have produced the existing situation . . . *the only realistic approach to the drug problem is to develop methods, not to eliminate drug use or even to drastically reduce it, but to live with it and to make sure that drug users do not seriously harm themselves and others.* Drug use is here to stay, and the only way to eliminate *illegal* drug use is to eliminate the laws outlawing the use of certain drugs. (pp. 253–4)

Wardlaw (1986) reached much the same conclusions, and he argues that instead of trying to eliminate drug use we must introduce the concept of 'management'. This management will almost certainly have to include some prohibitions. It is easy to overlook the fact that the very act of making a drug illegal conveys the cultural message that this substance is dangerous. This is, of course, a two-edged sword. Both danger and illegality can attract powerfully. However, judging by the percentage of people who actually engage in such hazardous legitimate pastimes as rock climbing or skydiving, it seems reasonable to suppose that more are deterred by danger than are attracted. Certainly, though, we do not wish to convey the message that heroin is safe. Were heroin to become generally available, restrictions at least as stringent as those now placed on alcohol use would undoubtedly have to be imposed—as a minimum. The possibility of low-cost heroin becoming freely available on supermarket shelves and at candy counters is therefore remote.

For many people, though, even the possibility of heroin—the archetype evil drug—being available in a controlled way is horrifying. Yet a brief glance at history will show that human societies have been forced into identical situations many times with other drugs. They expressed equal horror, they resisted equally strongly and they eventually capitulated. Thus, wherever coffee, nicotine or marijuana were introduced as new drugs, punitive laws were framed and authorities expressed grave concern about the continuity and safety of their communities and beliefs. As each measure and campaign failed, the initial reaction was to tighten laws further and to increase the level of punishment. In no case has one of these drugs been successfully removed, and by the twentieth century coffee and nicotine had joined alcohol as relatively unrestricted social drugs. Marijuana has been decriminalised in many places, and seems headed for legal status. It cannot be said that those societies are better off as a result of these changes. But equally, those societies (including our own) are still here and they still function.

However devoutly we may now pray that heroin will go away, history suggests that the very best we can hope to do is preserve the *status quo*, and the reality is that we cannot afford to do this, politically, economically or ideologically. So a more permissive position on heroin seems inevitable. It is too easy to interpret this as a directive to throw out all existing legislation forthwith. After all, if it is going to happen anyway, why not do it now and save a lot of people unnecessary pain? Yet such a step would be certain to fail, and for very good reasons.

First, such a tactic loses sight of political and social realities. As we saw in Chapter 6, radical solutions, whatever their theoretical worth, will not be accepted by politicians if they seem too much at odds with the prevailing moral sentiments of the electorate. As Wardlaw (1986) points out, 'the biggest challenge in any attempt to move in new directions is not in deciding which particular model to adopt, but in educating the public to accept the necessity for new perspectives on drugs and to move away from the moralistic straightjacket which so effectively stifles new initiatives at present' (p. 177). This must be done gradually. Moving too fast is certain to be counterproductive.

Second, and more important, we need to be much more hard-nosed about what goals are actually achievable. To date, most of our proposals have been strictly visionary. Goode (1984) lists some of them in a more practical perspective:

> Those who are in serious medical or psychiatric distress should be granted freedom from fear of police arrest and prosecution efforts, and they should be given medical care whenever they need it. Is this overly idealistic? Probably. After all, even those who do not use drugs, and who are poor, do not receive adequate medical care in this nation. Chronic drug users should have the option of discontinuing drug use under humane, expert, and empathetic guidance. Is this feasible? Probably not. After all, human compassion is hard to come by these days, and experts readily slip into an authoritarian role, attempting to dominate and control those who seek their help. Efforts should be made to insure that psychoactive agents do not fall into the hands of the very young. Is this realistic? No. Children obtain cigarettes and alcohol today without a great deal of effort—or heroin or barbiturates, for that matter. Realistic and factually correct education courses should be instituted in our schools and colleges. Practical? Probably not. We lie to our young about almost everything else—why not drugs? Institutions should be established for teaching people how to use drugs wisely, without

damage to themselves and to others, and to maximum advantage. Insane? No doubt. This smacks of encouraging use, regardless of how much human suffering it would eliminate. (pp. 271–2)

Some of the reasons why both politicians and the public prefer to cling to such ideals have been outlined in Chapter 6. The ideals are absolutely valid; they are also absolutely unimplementable, human beings and socioeconomic constraints being what they are. This of course seems to justify not trying to implement them at all. What has not really been considered, though, is the possibility that some of them may be *relatively* implementable, provided we are prepared to accept approximations, partial solutions and some significant and permanent costs.

This brings us to the third and most important point: every solution raises new problems and some of these will persist. What we should plan toward is not some unachievable ideal, but simply a situation which, when all the pluses and minuses have been added up, is significantly better than the one we now have. Instead of trying to halt the onslaught of change, we should actively set out to usher it in with the least pain and turmoil.

Here again, history has some valuable lessons. There is evidence that it is unwise to move directly from total prohibition, however ineffective, to free availability. When America's alcohol prohibition was lifted in 1933, an unpopular and largely unworkable legal situation was eased. Nevertheless, the fifteen-odd years of prohibition—roughly one human generation—had changed attitudes markedly. The pre-prohibition notion that alcohol was so powerful and harmful a drug that possibility of controlled use was remote was still there. Added to this was the speakeasy ambiance of prohibition itself, in which men drank either together or with prostitutes, food was replaced with alcohol and the drinking experience was coloured with illicitness and potential violence. American society had largely forgotten how to drink moderately. Repeal of prohibition left it floundering without clearcut social sanctions and rituals to control use, and at least another 30 years—two more generations—were needed to re-establish them. Today, some of the vacuum has been filled. Formal and informal alcohol education is generally available and few children grow up without some awareness of the wide range of behaviours associated with the use of this drug. The sense that it is to be used in special ways at special times and in special places is once again growing, but the process is by no means complete. And this with a drug that has a recorded history of at least 2000 years of use controlled by social ritual. Heroin has no such history within living memory and not much before that, although a number of cultures coexisted for centuries with opium and a few continue to do so.

So how should we go about loosening the prohibition? History again provides guidelines. Several problem drugs have gradually become 'safe', even non-drugs. Kalucy (1982) gives the following description of 'Drug X':

1. When first introduced, it spread rapidly throughout society to the point where its use in the adult population has approached 100%, despite powerful and punitive legislative and moral measures.
2. Drug X is known to be a cerebral stimulant; this is the primary reason for its use.
3. Drug X has important and pathological effects on the cardiovascular and gastrointestinal systems ...
4. It is known to have caused severe disease in ordinary doses in a minority of individuals.
5. It is known that high doses in animals regularly cause convulsions, self-mutilation, aggressive behavior and death due to respiratory failure.
6. One third or more of users develop clear-cut physical and psychological effects on withdrawal; craving for X is common.
7. It is known that high doses in man can cause acute delirium, insomnia and extrasystoles.
8. It is known to be widely used by children.
9. Approximately 100 billion doses are used annually in the United States. (p. 32)

Drug X is of course coffee—a substance that most people do not see as a drug at all.

What distinguishes coffee from other drugs which, if they were known to have these qualities, would be totally unacceptable in our community—as indeed coffee itself once was? Kalucy argues that the key is 'domestication'. A domesticated drug, according to him, has the following properties:

1. There is an orderly mode of production and distribution.
2. There is an orderly and enduring mode of presentation of the drug for daily usage.
3. There is widespread social conformity in terms of the way the drug is to be used, e.g., as an early morning stimulant 'to get one going', and later at *sanctified* times such as morning and afternoon tea breaks, or, taken with meals on a full stomach ...
4. The drug is generally marketed in a form which guarantees a low dose schedule.
5. Economic and legal restrictions are minor.
6. There is no public recognition of its addictive qualities, even though on reflection most people would recognise such a property about the drug (1982, pp. 32–3).

Some of these features are legal, some are economic. The most important ones, though, have to do with establishment of cultural controls. Custom is far more powerful than any law and, given the chance, all communities, both large and small, straight and deviant, will develop some sanctions about most activities. These sanctions will be symbolised and reinforced by specific social rituals. For the most part, these sanctions and rituals operate to control the activity and to protect both actor and the rest of the community.

The 1960s psychedelic drug scene provides an example from the drug subculture. Following the 'drug revolution' spearheaded by Timothy Leary in 1963, drugs like LSD were widely publicised as offering spiritual rebirth, mystical merging with the infinite and the like. They were also widely believed to cause psychosis, suicide and even murder. By the mid−1960s, psychiatric hospitals in major American cities were reporting that as many as a third of their admissions were due to these drugs. Although psychedelic drug use continued to grow rapidly well into the 1970s, the rate of such hospitalisations had declined dramatically by 1969. What seems to have happened was that the early problems came not from the action of the drugs themselves, but from the secondary anxiety generated by lack of guidelines for their proper use.

> The user of the early 1960s, with great hopes and fears and a sense of total unfamiliarity with what might happen, had a far more extreme experience than the user of the early 1970s, who had been exposed to a decade of interest in psychedelic colors, music and sensations. The later user, who might remark, 'Oh, so that is what a psychedelic color looks like', had been thoroughly prepared, albeit unconsciously, for the experience and responded accordingly, within a middle range ... (Zinberg, 1980, p. 242)

By the 1970s, the counterculture had also developed appropriate sanctions and rituals. Thus, 'Only use the first time with a guru' protected neophyte users. 'Only use at a good time, in a good place, with good people' had a similar function, and it also conveyed the message that the drug experience could be no more than a pleasant consciousness change.

In the straight culture, *the* social drug is of course alcohol and the customary sanctions about its use are legion. Zinberg (1980) has narrowed the prescriptions that define controlled, moderate use down to the following:

1. Group drinking is clearly differentiated from drunkenness and is associated with ritualistic or religious celebrations.
2. Drinking is associated with eating or ritualistic feasting.
3. Both the sexes, as well as different generations, are included in the drinking situation, whether they drink or not.

4 Drinking is divorced from the individual effort to escape personal anxiety or difficult (even intolerable) social situations. Further, alcohol is not considered medicinally valuable.
5 Inappropriate behavior when drinking (violence, aggression, overt sexuality) is absolutely disapproved, and protection against such behavior is offered by the sober or the less intoxicated. This general acceptance of the concept of restraint usually indicates that drinking is only one of many activities and thus carries a low level of emotionalism. It also shows that drinking is not associated with male or female 'rite de passage' or sense of superiority. (pp. 239–40)

Similarly, controlled use of opiates, where this has been studied, is characterised by rituals and social sanctions, many of them not unlike those in force for alcohol. Zinberg and his colleagues (1981) reported interviews with 99 controlled users of illicit drugs, 47 of them heroin users. Among the factors that seemed to contribute to controlled use was an ability to keep drugs on hand for some time without using them, to continue normal leisure activities, and to maintain ordinary social relationships with non-users, as well as a tendency to maintain regular ties to social institutions such as family, workplace or school. Virtually all controlled users at some stage also required instruction from more experienced controlled users in the social rituals which kept use within proper limits. Clearly it can be done.

Oscar Wilde wrote that 'as long as war is regarded as wicked, it will always have its fascination; when it is looked upon as vulgar, it will cease to be popular.' Perhaps making heroin 'vulgar' can come later. For the moment, we should strive to make it merely insignificant. To do this, however, we will need to relax some of our prohibitions. Social controls of a sort already exist on the use of most illicit drugs. The drug subculture sees to that. The problem is the conflict between the several sorts of sanctions—those of the law and those of group custom. Zinberg (1980) gives this illustration:

> The teenager attending a rock concert is often pressured into trying marijuana by his or her peers, who insist that smoking is acceptable at that particular time and place and will enhance the musical enjoyment . . . Nevertheless, the decision to use, so rationally presented, conflicts with the law and may make the user wonder whether the police will be benign in this instance. Such anxiety interferes with control. In order to deal with the conflict, the user will probably come forth with more bravado, exhibitionism, paranoia, or antisocial feeling than would be the case if he or she had patronised one of the little bars set up alongside the concert hall for the selling of alcohol during intermission . . . (p. 238)

We also need to recognise and accept three important points. First, the mere presence of social sanctions and rituals does not guarantee that they will be effective. Nor are all sanctions and rituals necessarily aids to controlled use. 'Booting' (drawing blood into and out of the syringe) by heroin addicts is supposed to lend enchantment to the injection procedure and therefore opposes control, even though the ritual may once have served as a protective mechanism. Some old-time users claim that the practice originated in the (erroneous) belief that a user could judge the strength and purity of the drug in this way.

Second, the existence and operation of social controls does not always produce moderate use. There is no need to condone intoxication, but we do need to appreciate that when boundary-breaking occurs, it does not automatically mean a breakdown of overall control. In practice, less-than-decorous use of drugs is sometimes culturally acceptable: at a celebration, for instance, or during an adolescent's first experiments with drunkenness. Nevertheless, moralists often present these occasions of impropriety, especially if illicit drugs are involved, as proof that there are only two ways to use drugs—abstinence or unchecked excess leading to addiction.

The persistence of this myth slows the development of strategies for rational, controlled use markedly. On the one hand, since addicts are expected to be out of control, few people recognise that even the most committed of them always exercise some degree of restraint over their use. On the other hand, since mere use can be seen as a step toward addiction, few people are prepared to show too much interest in the matter publically. Yet, as Zinberg (1980) points out, ordinary citizens, highly controlled users and even abstainers are far more preoccupied with the use of intoxicants than is generally acknowledged. Whether to use, when, with whom, how much, how to explain why one does not use—all these issues are important in the emotional life of almost everyone. Yet there is a deep-seated unwillingness to acknowledge this preoccupation throughout our culture. As a result, the importance of the many social mores that enhance our capacity to control use is played down and the whole issue becomes muddled.

> We are left with longings for that utopian society where no one would need drugs either for . . . relaxation and good fellowship or for escape or torpor. But since such idealised abstinence is socially unacceptable and impossible, the culture's reigning model of extreme decorum overemphasises the pharmaceutical powers of the drug or the personality of the user. It inculcates the view that only a disordered person would not live up to the cultural standard, or that the quantity or power of the drug is so great that the standard cannot be upheld. To think this way . . . requires considerable psychological legerdemain, for, as in most

other areas of living, people can rarely remain indefinitely on so decorous a course. (p. 239)

And finally, we need to accept that controlled use will mean different things, qualitatively and quantitatively, for different people under different circumstances. Drug use varies with age, status and even geographical location. Moreover, the same goal of controlled use may be achieved by a host of very different sanctions and rituals. Somehow, we are going to have to develop the wisdom to accept and use this diversity.

What all this means is that there will always be people who get into trouble with drugs. If that is what we mean by the drug problem, then that problem has no solution. But if we are prepared to redefine the problem as too many people getting into trouble with a particular drug, and redefine solving the problem as bringing this casualty rate down to some more acceptable level, there is every reason to believe that we can succeed.

If we are to win the war on heroin, two parallel developments will have to occur. First, we shall have to implement what the Sackville Royal Commission (1979) called an 'orderly retreat' of the criminal law from this area. Certainly there should be no tightening of current enforcement measures unless a very convincing case can be made that the change will have significant, demonstrable and long-term effects on actual drug market behaviour as opposed to such traditional but essentially meaningless indices as arrest rates. To date, there is little likelihood that such evidence will be forthcoming. This orderly retreat should be accompanied by a gradual implementation of appropriate non-criminal legal controls designed to monitor availability and discourage excessive use.

Second, we must begin to domesticate the drug, and this is probably best accomplished by domesticating drug use in general. Some of the work may already have been done for us. Most recent surveys suggest that young people seem to be less involved with drugs. A variety of factors could be responsible for this drop in demand. The novelty of drug use in general (though not necessarily of particular drugs) is beginning to wear off, and so is its shock value. Peers are no longer as impressed nor authority figures as upset as they once were.

Young people are also better able to hear us. Alienation of youth from the mainstream culture was at its peak in the early 1970s, and the use of drugs was itself an expression of sympathy with the counter-culture. The target audience for any health messages about drug use was hardly in a receptive frame of mind. Today, a number of the historical reasons for the rebellion—like the Vietnam War—have receded into the past and people over 30 are not quite such enemies. Many of them were once hippies and flower-children themselves.

We have also become more sophisticated in our communication. The early scare messages put out under the name of drug education overemphasised propaganda at the expense of accuracy and balance. The films made by the CIA to combat the 'marijuana menace' creeping up from Mexico are a case in point. In one, virginal southern belles and fine young American men are portrayed in innocent play in idyllic surroundings. A joint is passed around and the group is galvanised into sexual frenzy. In those days, of course, the orgy could merely be implied, not visualised. Adolescents may have much to learn, but they are not imbeciles. This sort of material is so absurd that it can only discredit attempts at a more rational explanation—and it did.

We are presenting facts rather better now, but the credibility of our message still leaves something to be desired. We still lack sufficient hard facts to dissuade intelligent youth from experimenting, and perhaps we always will. Therein lies part of the problem. But we also continue to place disproportionate emphasis on the harm drugs cause, and on building up a distaste and suspicion towards drugs and drug users. Zinberg (1980) put it in a nutshell: in his opinion, formal drug education will be inadequate until our culture has accepted the use not only of alcohol but of other intoxicants sufficiently to allow teachers to explain how they can be used safely and well. The primary purpose of good sex education is neither the encouragement nor discouragement of sexual behaviour, but the avoidance of unwanted pregnancy and venereal disease. Similarly, there is no need to present drug use as desirable, but we must actively give guidance about safe drug use.

A much more serious problem with our formal education strategies is that we persistently confuse what Dorn (1977) has called 'school knowledge' with 'action knowledge'. If we wish to offer the kind of information that can actually be used and acted upon, we must present facts, problems and solutions as they relate to the actual real-life situations the audience is likely to encounter. Thus, we generally emphasise that offers of drugs should be refused; we rarely provide any guidelines about how one is to do this without losing one's equanimity, friends and status. Here is one young woman's experience:

> I'd been all right when refusing drink from the age of 12 to 14—social alcohol pushers put it down to 'uninitiated youth' and didn't inquire further. But by 16 I became fed up with the common reaction which implied I was prim and so opted for wilder explanations.
> 'Why?'
> 'Hepatitis.'
> 'Oh my God how awful for you. My aunt's best friend had hepatitis and ...'
> No, this was not the solution. I'd either be regaled with catastrophically dull medical anecdotes or asked intimate details

about symptoms which I was unable to answer. At 18 I became wise to another ploy.
'*Why?*'
'A delicate question.'
Humble silence of one who is aware of having been nosey, then, 'Oh, I'm sorry.'
'No, no it's fine. I was an alcoholic when I was 15. I now only drink Perrier.'
'Of course, of course. Ice?' . . .
But it turned out to be not altogether satisfactory. It inspired a notorious reputation: I had been a child drunk. This reputation has its drawbacks. So now, at 21, I resort to the truth once more.
'*Why?*'
'I don't like it.'
'Are you sure?'
'Yes.'
'*How very odd.*'
'Yes. Very.'
That usually shuts them up . . . There are those, however . . . who resent what they think is a disciplined denial and assume I'm metaphorically spitting on them from a position high upon my moral pedestal . . . (*Connexions*, 1985–6, p. 7)

The perfect answer, of course, is another question:

'*Why?*'
'*Why should I?*'

It is this stage that we should be aiming for. The ideal attitude for the citizen is to view heroin not as a predator waiting to pounce, but as an unimportant aspect of ordinary life that is not worth a second or even a first thought.

Obviously we could do more in the area of formal drug education than we are doing. But we have generally lost sight of the fact that formal education as such is far from essential. We are dealing with the natural process of social learning and this will inevitably go on, for better or for worse, whatever we do in classrooms. It is a social fact that the perceived worth of a behaviour depends far more on the status of the models showing it and on the social rewards expected than on anything else. By and large, as a society we have hardly presented compelling models of rewarded non-use of drugs to our youth. Indeed, there is reason to believe that the opposite is true. There is, as educators are fond of saying, room for improvement here.

So what is the battle plan? Gradual relaxation of criminal sanctions, accompanied by gradual imposition of appropriate non-criminal modulators. Encouragement of domestication through development of social sanctions and rituals, with emphasis on modelling of the desired behaviours by high-status role models rather than through formal education. And a realistic acceptance of the fact that there will always be casualties, setbacks and costs.

Always means forever. Appropriate use and non-use of heroin, and of every other drug, will need to be taught afresh to every generation for the foreseeable future. The least costly way to manage this training in the long term is to ensure that, like 'manners' or personal hygiene, it becomes so basic that most young people will be adequately educated in these matters by the community, with minimal state intervention.

Even so, it is impossible to predict whether increased permissiveness about drug use generally, and heroin use in particular, will produce a more or less rewarding society. Certainly it will produce change, but we may take some comfort in the thought that this change is likely to be much smaller and more diffuse than the present level of concern about drugs seems to foreshadow. Societies have an enormous capacity for absorbing and transforming all manner of seemingly radical behaviours and beliefs into prosaic and unremarkable patterns. As Goode (1984) remarks, 'Drug ideologues who once claimed that psychedelic drug use was inherently revolutionary were as mistaken as traditionalists who believed that psychedelic drugs would destroy society as we know it' (p. 276). The reality was much less dramatic—indeed, psychedelics today seem rather *passé*. Perhaps some day it may be possible to say the same thing about heroin.

References

Arboleda-Florez, J., reported in *The Journal*, 1984, 13:11, p. 2
Ashton, M., 'What's happening with heroin?' *Druglink*, 1982, 17, pp. 1–5
Asiaweek, 'A tidal wave of heroin', 5 August 1983, pp. 20–8
Ausubel, D., *Drug Addiction*, New York: Random House, 1968
Batey, R., 'Methadone doesn't mean a "lifetime of ingestion"', *Connexions*, 1984, 4:12, p. 2
Baume, P., *Drug Problems in Australia: An Intoxicated Society?*, Report from the Senate Standing Committee on Social Welfare, Canberra: AGPS, 1977
Baumrind, D., 'Familial antecedents of drug use: a developmental perspective' *NIDA Research Monographs*, 1985, No. 56, , pp. 13–44
Bean, P., *The Social Control of Drugs*, Oxford: Martin Robertson, 1974
Beaumont, A. and Hughes, J., 'Biology of opioid peptides', *Annual Review of Pharmacology Toxicology*, 1979, 19, pp. 245–67
Becker, H.S., *Outsiders*, New York: The Free Press, 1966
Beecher, H., *Measurement of Subjective Responses*, New York: Oxford University Press, 1959
Bejerot, C. and Bejerot, M., 'Exposure factors in drug use, abuse and addiction', in Fishman, J., *Bases of Addiction*, Berlin: Dahlem Konferenzen, 1978
Bell, D.S., 'Whether to manage the drug or the addict—that is the question', *Australian Journal of Alcohol and Drug Dependance*, 1974, 1:2, pp. 37–9
Bell, P., 'Drugs and the media' *Australian Drug and Alcohol Review*, 1985, 4:2, pp. 235–42
Berridge, V. and Edwards, G., *Opium and the People*, Allen Lane: St Martin's Press, 1981
Bewley, T., Ben-Arie, O. and Marks, V., 'Morbidity, mortality from heroin dependence. 3: Relation of hepatitis to self-injection techniques', *British Medical Journal*, 23, 1968, pp. 730–2
Black, J.R., 'Advantages of substituting the Morphia habit for the incurably alcoholic', *The Cincinnati Lancet—Clinic*, 1889, 22, pp. 538–41
Bourne, P., *Methadone: Benefits and Shortcomings*, Washington: Drug Abuse Council, 1975
Brain Committee, *Drug Addiction*, Report of the Interdepartmental Committee, London: HMSO, 1961
Brain Committee, *Drug Addiction*, Second Report of the Interdepartmental Committee, London: HMSO, 1965
Brecher, A.D., *Licit and Illicit Drugs*, Boston: Little, Brown & Co., 1972
Brown, G.F. and Silverman, L.P., 'The retail price of heroin: estimation and applications', *Journal American Statistics Association*, 1974, 69, pp. 595–606
Brown, V.A., Manderson, D., O'Callaghan, M. and Thompson, R., *Our Daily Fix*, Canberra: ANU Press, 1986
Burroughs, W., *Junkie*, New York: Ace Books, 1953

REFERENCES

Caplovitz, D., *The Working Addict*, New York: M.E. Sharpe, 1976
Chambers, C.D., 'Narcotic addiction and crime: an empirical review', in Inciardi, J. and Chambers, C., *Drugs and the Criminal Justice System*, Beverly Hills: Sage, 1974
Chein, I., Gerard, D.C., Lee, R.S. and Rosenfeld, E., *The Road to H*, New York: Basic Books, 1964
Committee on Foreign Affairs, *The world heroin problem*, 92nd Congress, 1st Session, Washington: USGPO, 1971
Commonwealth Department of Health, *Statistics on Drug Abuse in Australia*, Canberra: AGPS, 1985
—— *Statistics on Drug Abuse in Australia*, Canberra: AGPS, 1986
—— *Technical Information Bulletin*, No. 3, Canberra: AGPS, 1971, pp. 12–4
—— *Technical Information Bulletin*, No. 68, 1981, pp. 23–34
Commonwealth of Australia: Baume, P., see Baume, P.
Commonwealth of Australia: Williams, R.S., see Williams, R.S.
Connexions, 'Drug reports in the Sydney media', 1985a, 5:2, pp. 1–12
—— 'Letters', 1985b, 5:4, p. 2
—— 'The methadone controversy', 1986, 6:7, p. 1
—— 'When drinking is just a matter of bad taste', 1985–6, 5, p. 7
Cook, G.A. and Flaherty, B., *Analysis of Street Drugs*, Sydney: NSW Drug and Alcohol Authority, 1978
Cowling, J., 'Press treatment of the drug issues in WA media', *Media Information Australia*, August, 1981
Davies, S., *Shooting Up*, Sydney: Hale and Iremonger, 1986
Dobinson, I., and Ward, P., *Drugs and Crime*, Sydney: NSW Bureau of Crime Statistics and Research, 1985
Dole, V.P., 'A clinician's view of addiction', in Fishman, J., *Bases of Addiction*, Berlin: Dahlem Konferenzen, 1978
Dorn, N., *Teaching Decision-making Skills with Legal and Illegal Drugs*, London: ISDD, 1977
Drew, L.R.H., 'Commonwealth policy on drugs and drug-related problems', in *Proceedings of the Drug Trade and Drug Use Conference, ANU, 1980*, AFADD: Canberra Publishing and Printing Co., 1982
Drew, L.R.H., 'The disease concept', *Connexions*, 1985, 5:4, p. 8
Durkheim, E., 'Address to the Sociological Society of London', quoted by Edwards, G., in Fishman, J., *Bases of Addiction*, Berlin: Dahlem Konferenzen, 1978, pp. 15–36
Duster, T., *The Legislation of Morality*, New York: The Free Press, 1970
Eckermann, W., Bates, J., Rachel, J. and Poole, W., *Drug Usage and Arrest Charges*, Final Report, BNDD Contract No. J–70–35, Washington, 1971
Edwards, G., Orford, J., Egert, S., Guthrie, S., Hawker, A., Hensman, C., Mitechson, M., Oppenheimer, E. and Taylor, C., 'Alcoholism: a controlled trial of "treatment" and "advice"', *Journal of Studies in Alcoholism*, 1977, 38, pp. 1004–31
Fellows of the Drug Abuse Council, 'Disabusing drug abuse', *Social Policy*, 1974, 4:5, pp. 43–5
Field, T., *Escaping the Dragon*, London: George Allen & Unwin, 1985
Frank, B. and Lipton, D., 'Epidemiology of the current heroin crisis', in

Serban, G., *Social and Medical Aspects of Drug Abuse*, New York: Spectrum Publications, 1984, pp. 93–9

Garfield, S., 'Multiphasic health testing and medical care as a right', *New England Journal of Medicine*, 1976, 294, p. 925

Gilbert, P. and Martin, W., 'The effect of morphine- and nalorphine-like drugs in the non-dependent, morphine-dependent and cyclazocine-dependent and cyclazocinal dog', *Journal of Pharmacology and Experimental Therapy*, 1976, 198, pp. 66–83

Glaser, F.B., 'Splitting: attrition from a drug-free therapeutic community', *American Journal of Drug and Alcohol Abuse*, 1974, 1, pp. 329–48

Gold, M., Redmond, D. and Kleber, H., 'Clonidine blocks acute opiate withdrawal symptoms', *Lancet*, 1978, 2, pp. 599–602

Goldman, F., 'Drugs, crime and economics', in Inciardi, J., *The Drugs–Crime Connection*, Beverly Hills: Sage, 1981, pp. 67–84

Goldstein, P.J., 'Getting over: economic alternatives to predatory crime among street drug users', in Inciardi, J., *The Drugs–Crime Connection*, Beverly Hills: Sage, 1981, pp. 67–84

Goode, E., *Drugs in American Society*, 2nd edn, New York: Alfred Knopf, 1984

Goode, M., 'Drugs, alcohol and the law', *Australian Drug and Alcohol Review*, 1985, 4:2, pp. 217–24

Gould, L.C., 'Crime and the addict: beyond common sense', in Inciardi, J. and Chambers, C., *Drugs and the Criminal Justice System*, Beverly Hills: Sage, 1974, pp. 57–75

Greene, M.H., 'Estimating the prevalence of heroin use in a community', *Special Action Office Monographs*, Series A, No. 4, Washington: USGP, 1975

Guillemin, R., 'Peptides in the brain: the new endocrinology of the neuron', *Science*, 1978, 202, pp. 390–402

Gusfield, J., 'Moral passage', in Bersani, C.A., *Crime and Delinquency*, London: Macmillan, 1970

Hackett, E., 'Postcript', in Brown, V.A. et al., *Our Daily Fix*, Canberra: ANU Press 1986, pp. 270–2

Halper, S.C., *The heroin trade: from Poppies to Peoria*, Washington: Drug Abuse Council, 1975

Hartnoll, R., Lewis, R. and Bryer, S., 'Recent trends in drug use in Britain'. *Druglink*, 1984, 19, pp. 22–4

Hawks, D.V., 'An analysis of the conspiracy: media, industry, health and welfare workers and government', *Australian Drug and Alcohol Review*, 1985, 4, pp. 211–15

Heine, W. and Mant, A., *Drug use in Adelaide*, Research Paper No. 4, Royal Commission into Non-medical use of Drugs, South Australia, Adelaide: South Aust. Govt., 1978

Himmelsbach, C., 'Clinical studies of drug addiction: physical dependence, withdrawal and recovery', *Archives of Internal Medicine*, 1942, 69, pp. 776–82

Ho, W., Wen, H. and Ling, N., 'Beta-endorphin-like immunoreactivity in the plasma of heroin addicts and normal subjects', *Neuropharmacy*, 1980, 19, pp. 117–20

Homel, P., Flaherty, B., Trebilco, P. and Dunoon, D., *1983 Survey of Drug Use by School Students in NSW*, Sydney: NSW Drug and Alcohol Authority, 1984

Hughes, H.M., *The Fantastic Lodge: Autobiography of a Girl Addict*, Boston: Houghton Mifflin, 1961

Hughes, J., Smith, T.W., Kosterlitz, H., Fothergill, L.A., Morgan, B.A. and Morris, H.R., 'Identification of two related pentapeptides from the brain with potent opiate agonist activity', *Nature*, 1975, 258, pp. 577–9

Hughes, P., Crawford, G., Barker, N., Schumann, S. and Jaffee, J., 'The social structure of a heroin-copping community', *American Journal of Psychiatry*, 1971, 128:5, pp. 551–8

Iiyama, P., Nishi, S.M. and Johnson, B.D., *'Drug Use and Abuse among US Minorities*, New York: Praeger, 1976

Inciardi, J., 'Heroin use and street crime', *Crime and Delinquency*, 1979, 25:3, pp. 551–8

Inglis, B., *The Diseases of Civilisation*, London: Granada Publishing Ltd, 1983

Jaffe, J., 'Drug abuse: strategies, terminology and the role of the medical professions', *Australian Drug and Alcohol Review*, 1984, 3:4, pp. 9–14

—— and Martin, W., 'Opioid analgesics and antagonists', in Goodman, L. and Gilman, A., *The Pharmacological Basis of Therapeutics*, 6th edn, London: Macmillan, 1980, pp. 494–534

Johnson, B.D., 'Once an addict, seldom an addict', *Contemporary Drug Problems*, 1978, 7:1, pp. 48–9

Johnston, L.D., 'The etiology and prevention of substance use: what can we learn from recent historical changes?' *NIDA Research Monographs*, 1985, No.56, pp. 155–77

Judson, B., Himmelberger, M. and Goldstein, A., 'The naloxone test for opiate dependence', *Clinical Pharmacology & Therapy*, 1980, 22, pp. 492–501

Julien, R., *A Primer of Drug Action*, San Francisoco: Freeman Press, 1981

Kalucy, R.S., 'Sources of ambivalence in drug-related problems—problems for policy-makers', *Australian Alcohol and Drug Review*, 1982, 1:1, pp. 31–5

Kaplan, J., *The Hardest Drug*, Chicago: The University of Chicago Press, 1983

Krivanek, J., *Drug Problems, People Problems*, Sydney: George Allen & Unwin, 1982

—— *Addictions*, Sydney: George Allen & Unwin, 1988

Kron, Y.J. and Brown, D.B., *Mainline to Nowhere*, New York: Pantheon Books, 1965

Krupinski, J. and Stoller, A., *Drug Use by the Young Population of Melbourne*, Melbourne: Mental Health Authority, Victoria, 1973

Lamour, C. and Lamberti, M.R., *The Second Opium War*, London: Allen Lane, 1974

Laurie, P., *Drugs*, Penguin, 1971

Leach, A., 'Trouble with methadone', *Connexions*, 1985, 5:1, p. 16

Leader-Elliott, I.D., 'Heroin in Australia: the costs and consequences of prohibition', *Journal of Drug Issues*, 1986, 1, pp. 131–49

Leech, K., *Keep the Faith, Baby*, London: SPCK, 1973

LeFevre, C.G., 'A factual study of drug dependence and drug abuse during 1965–1969 in NSW: a summary', *Medical Journal of Australia*, 1971, February 13, pp. 395–7

Lehmann, H.E., 'The impact of scientific models on clinical psychopharmacology: a psychiatrist's view', *Seminar in Psychiatry*, 1972, 4:3, pp. 255–64

Levi-Strauss, C., *Totem and Taboo*, Harmondsworth: Penguin Books, 1981

Levine, D., '"Needle Freaks": compulsive self-injection by drug users', *Archives of General Psychiatry*, 1974, 131:3, pp. 297–300

Levine, H.G., 'The discovery of addiction: changing concepts of habitual drunkenness in America', *Journal of Alcohol Studies*, 1978, 39, pp. 143–74

Lewis, R., Hartnoll, R., Bryer, S., Daviaud, E. and Mitcheson, M., 'Scoring smack: the illicit heroin market in London, 1980–83', *British Journal of Addictions*, 1985, 80, pp. 281–90

Lewis, R., 'The illicit traffic in heroin: Introduction and Part I, cultivation and production', *Druglink*, 1984, Spring, pp. 7–14

Lindesmith, A., *Addiction and Opiates*, Chicago: Aldine, 1968

Maddux, J.F. and Bowden, C.L., 'Critique of success with methadone maintenance', *American Journal of Psychiatry*, 1972, 129, pp. 440–6

Mant, A. and Thomas, B., Estimating prevalence of opiate use in South Australia', Research Paper No. 5, *Royal Commission into Non-medical Use of Drugs, South Australia*, Adelaide: South Aust. Govt., 1978

Martin, W., 'Relationship of biological influences on the subjective states of addicts', in Serban, G., *Social and Medical Aspects of Drug Abuse*, New York: Spectrum Publications, 1984, pp. 1–8

—— and Fraser, H., 'A comparative study of physiological and subjective effects of heroin and morphine administered intravenously in post-addicts', *Journal of Pharmacology and Experimental Therapy*, 1961, 133, p. 388

McCoy, A.W., *Drug Traffic*, Sydney: Harper and Row, 1980

McGlothlin, W.H. and Anglin, M.D., 'Long-term follow-up of clients of high-and low-dose methadone programs, *Archives of General Psychiatry*, 1981, 38:9, pp. 1055–62

McLellan, A.T., MacGahan, J.A. and Druley, K.A., 'Changes in drug abuse clients, 1972–1978: implications for treatment', *American Journal of Drug and Alcohol Abuse*, 1979, 6, pp. 151–62

Merton, R.K., *Social Theory and Social Structure*, Illinois: Free Press, 1957

Meyer, R. and Mirin, S.M., *The Heroin Stimulus: Implications for a Theory of Addiction*, New York: Plenum Medical Book Co., 1979

Moore, M.H., 'Economics of heroin distribution', *Teaching and Research Paper* No. 4, Harvard University: Public Policy program, March, 1971

Mugford, S., 'Some political and economic features of the drug trade: historical perspectives and policy implications', in *Proceedings of the Drug Trade and Drug Use Conference, ANU, 1980*, AFADD: Canberra Publishing and Printing Co., 1982, pp. 59–68

Negrete, J.C., *The Sociocultural Dimensions of Drug Use*, paper prepared for the Advisory Group meeting of WHO Project on Development of Strategies and Guidelines for the Prevention of Drug Dependence, London, 1982

New Republic, 'A little less illegal', 1969, 161, p. 11

Newmeyer, J., '*The Junkie Thief*, San Francisco: Haight–Ashbury Free Medical Clinic, 1972

REFERENCES

Nixon, R.M., 'Message to Congress on the drug problem', *US News and World Report*, 28 July 1969, p. 60
—— *Time*, 28 June 1971, p. 20
NSW Drug and Alcohol Authority, *Report for the Year Ended June 30, 1984*, Sydney: NSW Govt., 1984
—— *Report for the Year Ended June 30, 1985*, Sydney: NSW Govt., 1985
NSW Drug and Alcohol Services, 'Media study nearing completion', *Connexions*, 1982, 3:1, p. 8
NSW Government, *NSW Joint Parliamentary Committee upon Drugs*, Sydney: NSW Govt, 1978
—— Woodward, P.M., see Woodward, P.M.
NSW Health Commission, *Psychosocial Problems of Sydney Adults*, Sydney: NSWGP, 1979
O'Donnell, J.A., 'Young men and drugs—a nationwide survey', *NIDA Research Monographs*, 1976, No. 5
O'Neill, P., 'The patient—where should I go for help?' *Australian Alcohol and Drug Review*, 1985, 4:1, p. 103
Orford, J., *Excessive Appetites*, London: John Wiley and Sons, 1985
Pattison, E.M., Bishop, L.A. and Linsky, A.S., 'Changes in public attitudes on narcotic addiction', *American Journal of Psychiatry*, 1968, 125:2, pp. 56–63
Pattison, E.M., Coe, R. and Rhodes, R.J., 'Population variation among alcoholism treatment facilities', *International Journal of Addictions*, 1973, 8, pp. 199–229
Pileggi, N., 'There's no business like drug business', *The New Yorker*, 13 December 1982, pp. 38–43
Plant, M., 'Let's come out of the closet', *British Journal of Addictions*, 1986, 81:4, pp. 447–9
Pomeranz, B. and Chiu, D., 'Naloxone blockade of acupuncture analgesia: endorphin implicated', *Life Sciences*, 1976, 19, pp. 1757–62
Powell, D., 'A pilot study of occasional heroin users', *Archives of General Psychiatry.*, 1973, 28, pp. 586–94
Preble, E. and Casey, J., 'Taking care of business—the heroin user's life on the street', *International Journal of Addictions*, 1969, 4:1, pp. 1–24
Preble, E. and Miller, T., 'Methadone, wine and welfare', in Weppner, R.S., *Street Ethnography: Selected Studies of Crime and Drug Use in Natural Settings*, California: Sage Publications, 1977
Raab, S., 'Stiff antidrug laws hold no deterrent', *New York Times*, 2 January 1977, p. 1
Rajah, K.S., 'Singapore Country Report', *Report of the 3rd International Conference on NGOs on Dadah Prevention*, Kuala Lumpur: Colombo Plan and ICAA, 1981, pp. 102–7
Ray, O.S., *Drugs, Society and Human Behavior*, 2nd edn, St Louis: The C.V. Mosby Co., 1978
Reilly, D., Twyman, D. and Williams, R., 'Assessment of opioid dependence', *Australian Alcohol and Drug Review*, 1985, 4:1, pp. 43–7
Rexed, B., 'The making of national drug abuse control policy', *The Journal*, May 1986, pp. M1–M4
Robins, L., Helzer, J. and Davis, D., 'Narcotics use in SEA and afterwards',

Archives of General Psychiatry, 1975, p. 32

Rolleston Committee, *Departmental Committee on Morphine and Heroin*, London: HMSO, 1926

Room, R., 'Comments on Robinson, D., "The alcohologist's addiction"', *Quarterly Journal of Studies in Alcohol*, 1972, 33, pp. 1049–59

Rosenthal, E., 'Addiction: is it a disease?' in *Drugs, Society and Behavior 86/87*. Connecticut: Dushkin Publishing Group,, 1986, pp. 168–70

Sackville, R., *Royal Commission into Non-medical Use of Drugs, South Australia*, Adelaide: SA Govt Printer, 1978

Sandland, R.L., *Methods of Estimating the Number of Heroin Users in NSW*, Sydney: NSW Drug and Alcohol Authority, 1984

Sapira, J. and Cherubin, C., *Drug Abuse*, Amsterdam: Excerpta Medica, 1975

Saunders, J., 'Editorial. The Year of the Summit', *Australian Alcohol and Drug Review*, 1985, 4:2, pp. 155–6

Schlosser, D., 'An investigation of court referrals and voluntary referrals at Bourke Street Drug Advisory Service, *Research Grant Report Series*, B84/2, Sydney: NSW Drug and Alcohol Authority, 1984

Schut, J., Wohlmuth, TR. and File, K., 'Low dosage methadone maintenance', quoted in Warlaw, G.R., 'Drug use and crime: how real is the connection?' *Proceedings of the Drug Trade and Drug Use Conference, ANU, 1980*, AFADD: Canberra Publishing and Printing Co., 1982

Science, 'The Mexican heroin flow continues unabated', 1977, 196, pp. 509–10

Senate Report No. 1440, *The Illicit Narcotics Traffic*, 77th Congress, 2nd Session, Washington: USGPO, 1956

Senate Standing Committee on Social Welfare, *Another Side to the Drug Debate ... a Medicated Society*, Canberra: AGPS, 1981

Senay, E., quoted in *Drugs, Society and Behavior 1986/87*, Connecticut: Dushkin Publishing Group, 1986

Shafer, J., 'Designer drugs', in *Drugs, Society and Behavior 1986/87*, Connecticut: Dushkin Publishing Group, 1986, pp. 67–73

Sheffet, A., Hickey, R.F., Lavenhar, M., Wolfson, E., Duval, H., Millman, D. and Louria, D.B., 'A model for drug abuse treatment program evaluation', *Preventive Medicine*, 1973, 2, pp. 510–23

Shore, M.F., 'Correlates and concepts: are we chasing our tails?' *NIDA Research Monographs*, 1985, No. 56, pp. 127–35

Siegler, M. and Osmond, H., 'Models of drug addiction', *International Journal of Addictions*, 1968, 3:1, pp. 3–24

Simpson, D.D., Joe, G.W. and Bracy, S.A., '6-year follow-up of opioid addicts after admission to treatment', *Archives of General Psychiatry*, 1982, 39:11, pp. 1318–23

Singer, M., 'The vitality of mythical numbers', *Public Interest*, 1971, 23, pp. 3–9

Smart, R.G., *Forbidden Highs*, Toronto: ARF, 1983

—— Murray, G. and Archibald, H.D., *Psychotropic substances and their International Control*, Toronto: ARF, 1981

Smith, G.M., 'Perceived effects of substance use: a general theory', *NIDA Research Monographs*, 1980, No. 30, pp. 50–8

Smith, R., 'The world of the Haight–Ashbury speed freak', *Journal of*

REFERENCES

Psychedelic Drugs, 1969, 2, pp. 77–83
Sobell, M.B. and Sobell, L.C., 'Under the microscope yet again', *British Journal of Addictions*, 1984a, 79, pp. 157–68
—— 'The aftermath of heresy', *Behavioural Research Therapy*, 1984b, 22, pp. 413–40
Sonnenreich, R., quoted in Szasz, T., *Ceremonial Chemistry*, London: Routledge & Kegan Paul, 1975
South Australia Government: Sackville, R. *see* Sackville, R.
Spear, H., 'British experience in the management of opiate dependence', in Glatt, M.M. and Marks, J., *The Dependence Phenomenon*, London: MTP Press, 1982, pp. 51–80
Stimson, G.V., *Heroin and Behavior*, New York: John Wiley and Sons, 1973
Stolz, P., 'In search of a national policy on drug use', in *Proceedings of the Drug Trade and Drug Use Conference, ANU 1980*, AFADD: Canberra Publishing and Printing Co., 1982 pp. 15–28
Straton, J., 'Evidence before the Senate Standing Committee on Social Welfare', Canberra: AGPS, 1981, pp. 328–9
Su, C., Lin, S.H., Wang, Y., Li, C., Hung, L., Lin, C.S. and Lin, B.C., 'Effects of beta-endorphin on narcotic abstinence syndrome in man', *Journal of Formosan Medical Association*, 1978, 77, pp. 133–41
Sutter, A.G., 'The world of the righteous dope fiend', *Issues in Criminology*, 1966, 2, pp. 177–222
Suwanwela, C. and Poshyachinda, V., 'Thailand: traditional patterns of opium use', in Edwards, G. and Arif, A., *Drug Problems in the Sociocultural Context*, WHO Public Health Paper No. 73, 1980, pp. 32–8
Swank, I.C., 'North American heroin', *Drug Enforcement*, 1977, 4:1, pp. 8–9
Szasz, T., *Ceremonial Chemistry*, London: Routledge & Kegan Paul, 1975
Taylor, R., *Medicine out of Control*, Melbourne: Sun Books, 1979
Terry, C. and Pellens, M., *The Opium Problem*, New York: Bureau of Social Hygiene, 1928
Thomas, L., 'The health care system', *New England Journal of Medicine*, 1975, 293, p. 1245
Trebach, A., 'Heroin and pain relief', *The Journal*, 1984, 13:5, pp. 5–6
U.N. Secretariat, 'The drug abuse problem: international policy', *International Review of Criminal Policy*, 1978, 34, pp. 43–51
United Press International, 20 May 1974, quoted in *New York Times*, 21 May 1974
US News and World Report, 1956, 41, p. 22
US Revenue Act, May 1928, quoted in Ray, O.S., *Drugs, Society and Human Behavior*, 2nd edn, St Louis: The C.V. Mosby Co., 1978
US Supreme Court, *Robinson vs California*. US 370, 1962
Vaillant, G.E., 'Discussion', *American Journal of Psychiatry*, 1968, 125:2, pp. 56–63
—— and Milofsky, E.S., 'Natural history of male alcoholism. IV. Paths to recovery', *Archives of General Psychiatry*, 1982, 39:2, pp. 127–33
Wardlaw, G.R., *Drug Use and Crime*, Canberra: Australian Institute of Criminology, 1978
—— 'Drug use and crime: how real is the connection?' *Proceedings of the Drug*

Trade and Drug Use Conference, ANU, 1980, AFADD: Canberra Publishing and Printing Co., 1982
—— 'Evaluating drug enforcement strategies'. *Reporter*, 1985, 6:4, pp. 1–2
—— 'The realities of drug enforcement', *Journal of Drug Issues*, 1986, 16:2, pp. 171–82
Weissman, J.C., 'Survey of State Drug Offender Diversion Authorities', *Contemporary Drug Problems*, 1978, 7, p. 533
Wender, P., 'Vicious and virtuous circles: the role of deviance-amplifying feedback in the origin and perpetuation of behaviour', *Psychiatry*, 1968, 31:4, pp. 309–24
Wexler, D.B., 'Therapeutic justice', in *Drug Use in America: Problem in Perspective*. Washington: USGPO, 1973, pp. 435–9
White, P., *Alcohol and Drug Issues in the Sydney Media—1984*, Sydney: CEIDA, 1985
Whitlock, A.F., 'Evidence before the Senate Standing committee on Social Welfare', *Official Hansard*, 1976–77, Vol. 2
Whitlock, F.A., 'Terminology and concepts of addiction and their effect on management', *Australian Alcohol and Drug Review*, 1982, 1, pp. 28–30
Wilhelm, K.A., 'The magic of methadone', *Australian Journal of Alcohol and Drug Dependance*, 1975, 2:2, pp. 45–6
Williams, R.S., *Royal Commission of Inquiry into Drugs*, Canberra: AGPS, 1980
Windshuttle, K., 'Drugs and the press', in Sackville, R., *Royal Commission into the Non-medical Use of Drugs, South Australia*, Adelaide: South Australian Govt, 1978
Winick, C., 'Physician narcotics addicts', *Social Problems*, 1961, 9, pp. 174–81
Woodward, P.M., *Royal Commission into Drug Trafficking*, Sydney: NSWGP, 1980
World Health Organisation Memorandum, 'Nomenclature and classification of drug-and alcohol-related problems', Bulletin of WHO, 1981, reprinted in *Australian Alcohol and Drug Review*, 1984, 3:2, pp. 76–85
Zinberg, N., 'Rehabilitation of heroin users in Vietnam', *Contemporary Drug Problems*, 1972, 1:2, p. 290
—— 'The social setting as a control mechanism in intoxicant use', *NIDA Research Monographs*, 1980, No. 30, pp. 236–44
—— Harding, W. and Winkeler, M., 'A study of social regulatory mechanisms in controlled illicit drug users', in Shaffer, M. and Burglass, M., *Classic Contributions in the Addictions*, New York: Brunner/Mazel, 1981

Index

abstinence, as a goal, 218−21; conditioned, 89−93; primary, 84−9; protracted, 90; *see also* withdrawal

addict, and labelling, 199; as a casualty, 167, 199; changing character of (UK), 41−2; changing character of (US), 53−9, 61; management of, 217−36; stereotype of, 183−4, 198−9

addiction, alternatives to, 221; as a disease, 200−5; as a medical issue, 34−51 *passim*; criminal penalties for, 232−6; definitions of, 200−15 *passim*; models of, 200−15; potential for, 190, 197; process of, 74; reasons for, 74−6, 90−3, 195−9; social costs of, 94−9, 120−9, 230−1; *see also* psychological dependence

addiction specialists, 34−5, 201

addiction treatment, assessment in, 217−18; coerced, 232−6; goals of, 218−22, 230; legal approaches, 232−6; maintenance approaches, 223−32

alcohol, 83, 200−2; addiction (alcoholism), 200−1; controlled use of, 171; prohibition, 201, 239

Alcoholics Anonymous (AA), 171, 201, 210, 220−1

amphetamines, 45

anti-opium movements, 33−4

assessment, 217−18

barbiturates, 46, 58, 83

black market, development of (UK), 43−51 *passim*; development of (US), 60−7; *see also* drug trafficking

Brain Committees, 42−4

British System, 32, 37−51 *passim*

caffeine, 240

Chinese immigrants, in US, 54

clinics, development of (UK), 43−8; development of (US), 57; maintenance, 225−32 *passim*

clonidine, 89−90

cocaine, 26, 35, 41−50 *passim*

conditioning, 91−3

controlled use, drug subcultures and, 241−2; of alcohol, 171, 241−2; of heroin, 194−5, 218−19, 242−7

Convention on Psychotropic Substances, 133

designer drugs, 145−6

dipipanone (Diconal), 46−7, 70

disease model, *see* medical model

diversionary programs, 232−6; effectiveness of, 234−6; types of, 233−6

'domestication' of drug use, 240−7

drug education, 209−10, 244−7

drug related crime, 63−4, 102; and means of support, 123−4; cost of, 120−9, 231; definition, 120; rate of use and, 121; sampling problems in, 122−3; varieties of, 120, 125−6; *see also* drug trafficking, drug use offences, legal control

drug subculture, and controlled use, 241−2; psychedelic, 241; role of, 92−3

drug trafficking, domestic, 142−7; freelance operators, 111, 119; in Asia, 107−14; international, 137−8, 147−8; on the streets, 114−19; risks in, 117−19, 143; *see also* drug related crime, legal control

drug use, adolescence and, 191−5; barriers to, 192, 196;

'domestication' of, 240–7; medicine and, 185–90; mythology of, 181–4; prevalence of, 184, 188–90; reasons for, 181–95

drug use indicators, 159–63 *passim*; drug related morbidity, 161–2; drug overdose, 112; enforcement-related records, 163–5; indicator-dilution method, 166–7; overdose multiplier formula, 162–3; serum hepatitis, 160–1; types of records, 159–63; *see also* statistics on drug addiction

drug use offences, and coerced treatment, 232–6; definition, 139–40; rationale for, 140–2; *see also* drug related crime, drug trafficking, legal control

drugs, action of, 76–86 *passim*; as scapegoats, 177–8; definition of, 181–2; 'domestication' of, 240–7; experimentation with, 191–5; mythology of, 181–4

endogenous opiates, 78–80; role in withdrawal, 85
endorphins, *see* endogenous opiates
enkephalins, *see* endogenous opiates

Hague Convention, 35, 56
Harrison Act, 35, 56–60
heroin, as an analgesic, 71–4; controlled use of, 103–4, 218–19; effects of, 74–6, 81–2, 94–9, 101–2; experimentation with, 191–5; harm caused by, 95–9; intravenous use, 96, 99–100; legalisation of, 94–5, 218, 236–47 *passim*; medical use of, 71–4; methods of use, 99–101; pharmacology, 69–71, 81–7; recreational use of, 194–5; rush, 70–1, 91; signs of use, 99–102; sniffing, 50, 64, 67, 99; social consequences of, 94–6; types of, 99, 106; *see also* opiates

indicator-dilution method, 166–7

legal control, and cost of drugs, 120–9, 146, 230–1; and management of addiction, 232–6; effectiveness of, 65, 103, 135–48, 232–6; goals of, 107–47 *passim*, 236–7; in Britain, 35–51; in United States, 57–67; international, 41, 130–4; of domestic trafficking, 142–7; of international smuggling, 137–8; of opiate production, 41, 130–7; of use, 138–42; *see also* drug related crime, drug trafficking, drug use offences

legalising heroin, and 'domestication', 240–7; goals of, 238–9; potential problems, 94–5, 218

maintenance approaches, 223–32; heroin, 224–5; methadone, 225–32; on-the-premises system, 225; prescription system, 224; problems with, 225–32; *see also* British System
maturing-out, 202
media, 1–29; and creation of drug problems, 25–9; and drug advertising, 184–5, 188; and drug statistics, 149–50; moral content of stories, 27–8; selective coverage by, 26; structure of stories, 27–8
medical model, 200–5; critique of, 203–5
medicalisation, 188–90
medicine, and medicalisation, 188–90; and patientisation, 187–8; historical developments in, 185–90; relevance to recreational drug use, 190
methadone, clinic attendance, 159–60; cost of, 230–1; effects of, 87, 226, 229; heroin use with, 236; maintenance, 225–42; maintenance dose of, 230; policies on, 178; substitution equivalent, 88; use in British clinics, 46–7; withdrawal from, 87–8

INDEX

moral categories, 217
moral crusaders (entrepreneurs), activities of, 206; institutionalisation and, 171–2
moral models, 205–12; critique of, 211–12
morality, 205–12 passim; drug use and, 239–47; science and, 207–8
morphine, and analgesia, 71–3, 81; conversion to heroin, 106; pharmacology of, 69–71, 81–7; see also opiates

naloxone (Narcan), 77, 80; precipitated withdrawal, 87–8; see also opiate antagonists, withdrawal
narcotic, definition of, 69

opiate antagonists, 69, 77; 'pure' and 'partial', 78
opiates, controlled use of, 242; definition of, 69; early use (in Australia), 32–3, (in Britain), 33–51, (in China), 33–4, (in United States), 51–60; medical uses of, 71–4; pharmacology of, 69–71; current statistics on use of, 150–68
opium, eating, 31; early history of, 30; medical use of, 31–2, 51–3; pharmacology of, 69, 106; popular use (in Britain), 39, (in United States), 51–5; production of, 105–13, 135–7; smoking, 31, 54–5; Wars, 31, 33
overdose multiplier formula, 162–3
overprescribing, in Britain, 39–40, 43–7

pain, endogenous opiates in, 79; opiates in 71–4; 'psychic', 74–5
patent medicines, 52
patientisation, 187–8
physical dependence, and addiction, 195–6; cross-dependence, 87, 224; determining extent of, 86–9, 224, 227–8; development of, 86–90; endogenous opiates in, 85; mechanisms of, 84–90; see also withdrawal
physician addicts, 95–6, 213
placebo effects, 80
politics, and drug policy, 169–71; corruption in, 168–9
psychedelic drugs, 241
psychological dependence, definition of, 182–3, 196; relation to addiction, 196–8; see also addiction
psychosocial models, 212–15

receptors, 76; opiate, 77–9
Rolleston Committee, 35–8

serum hepatitis, 160–1
sick role, 204; see also medical model
Single Convention, 131–3
social control, of drug use, 205, 239–47
statistics on drug addiction, and research, 172–3; and treatment success, 217; in Australia, 149–78; in Britain, 38–42; in United States, 53, 60, 65, 67; reasons for paucity of, 168–79; types of, 151–2; validity of, 150–68; see also drug use indicators, surveys of drug use
street drugs, purity of, 86, 96, 116–19, 163–4
substitute dependence, 220–1
surveys of drug use, problems with, 152–6; results of, 156–9

temperance movements, 34, 53–4, 175, 201
tolerance, cross-tolerance, 83, 224; mechanisms of, 82–4; psychological factors in, 83
transmitters, and endogenous opiates, 79; role of, 76–7

vested interests, anatomy of, 168–73; and control of drug use, 168–79

Vietnam, drug use by troops in, 64–5; trafficking in, 107–8

withdrawal, medical supervision in, 88–9; mental state in, 85; opiate antagonists in, 77; symptoms of, 85–90; *see also* physical dependence

world views, as shaping drug policy, 174–9; nature of, 174–6, 181

youth culture, in Britain, 40, 50